MODELING MADE SIMPLE

With Embarcadero ER/Studio® Data Architect

Adapting to Agile Data Modeling in a Big Data World

second edition

Steve Hoberman

Published by:
Technics Publications, LLC
2 Lindsley Road, Basking Ridge, NJ 07920 U.S.A.
www.technicspub.com

Cover design by Mark Brye
Edited by Erin Elizabeth Long
Cartoons by Abby Denson, www.abbycomix.com

ISBN, print ed.	9781634620925
ISBN, PDF	9781634620956
ISBN, Kindle	9781634620932
ISBN, ePub	9781634620949

First Printing 2011
Second Printing 2015 completely revised

Library of Congress Control Number: 2015910686

Embarcadero Technologies, Inc. is a leading provider of award-winning tools for application developers and database professionals so they can design systems right, build them faster and run them better, regardless of their platform or programming language. Ninety of the Fortune 100 and an active community of more than three million users worldwide rely on Embarcadero products to increase productivity, reduce costs, simplify change management and compliance and accelerate innovation. The company's flagship tools include: Embarcadero® DBArtisan®, Delphi®, ER/Studio®, Rapid SQL®, and RAD Studio. Founded in 1993, Embarcadero is headquartered in Austin, Texas, with offices located around the world. Embarcadero is online at www.embarcadero.com.

Contents at a Glance

Contents

Data Modeling Made Simple with Embarcadero ER/Studio Data Architect will provide the business or IT professional with a practical working knowledge of data modeling concepts and best practices, along with how to apply these principles with ER/Studio. You'll build many ER/Studio data models along the way, applying best practices to master these ten objectives:

1. You will know why a data model is needed and which ER/Studio models are the most appropriate for each situation.
2. You will be able to read a data model of any size and complexity with the same confidence as reading a book.
3. You will know how to apply all of the key features of ER/Studio.
4. You will be able to build relational and dimensional conceptual, logical, and physical data models in ER/Studio.
5. You will know how to create an efficient physical data model both by forward engineering a logical data model and by reverse engineering a database.
6. You will improve data model quality and impact analysis results by leveraging ER/Studio's compare/merge utility.
7. You will achieve enterprise architecture through ER/Studio's data lineage functionality.
8. You will be able to apply ER/Studio's data dictionary features.
9. You will learn ways of importing and exporting the data model as well as how to print and report from ER/Studio.
10. You will leverage ER/Studio's naming standards functionality to improve naming consistency.

This book contains four sections. Section I introduces data modeling along with ER/Studio functionality and landscape. You will learn why data modeling is so critical to software development, and even more importantly, why data modeling is so critical to **understanding the business**. You will also learn about the ER/Studio environment. Chapter 1 explains the data model and why it is an invaluable wayfinding tool in eliciting requirements and capturing a precise representation of the business. This chapter also introduces the publisher case study, which we will use throughout the text to explain data model concepts and ER/Studio functionality. Chapter 2 introduces you to ER/Studio Data Architect (the data modeling software and the main component in the ER/Studio suite). Learn what ER/Studio can do and how to install and start the software. Chapter 3 covers at a broad level what features are within each ER/Studio tab, window, menu, and toolbar. By the end of this section, you will have created and saved your first data model in ER/Studio and be ready to start modeling in Section II!

Section II explains all of the symbols and text on a data model. Chapter 4 defines a submodel and how to work with one. Chapter 5 defines an entity and instances and discusses the different categories of entities. The three different levels at which entities may exist—conceptual, logical, and physical—are also explained. Chapter 6 defines an attribute and key, distinguishing the terms *candidate*, *primary*, *surrogate*, *foreign*, and *alternate key*. Domains are also introduced in this chapter. Chapter 7 defines rules and relationships. Cardinality and labels are explained so that the reader can read any data model as easily as reading a book. Other types of relationships, such as recursive relationships and subtyping, are also discussed. By the end of this section, you will be able to "read" a data model of any size or complexity as well as create and modify entities, attributes, and relationships in ER/Studio.

Section III explores the three different levels of models: conceptual, logical, and physical. A conceptual data model (CDM) represents the business need within a defined scope, a logical data model (LDM) the detailed business solution, and a physical data model (PDM) the detailed technical solution. Chapter 8 focuses on the CDM, Chapter 9 the LDM, and Chapter 10 the PDM. By the end of this section, you will be able to create conceptual, logical, and physical data models in ER/Studio.

Section IV discusses additional features of ER/Studio: Chapter 11 covers the data dictionary; Chapter 12 data lineage; Chapter 13 import, export, printing, and reporting; Chapter 14 naming standards; Chapter 15 the compare and merge functionality; and Chapter 16 iterative development practices including agile, macros, reusable procedure logic, change management, and model validation.

To connect the book's content with the key objectives stated on the previous page, the following table shows the primary sections that support each objective.

	Objective									
Section	1	2	3	4	5	6	7	8	9	10
I	✓	✓	✓							
II	✓	✓	✓							
III	✓	✓	✓	✓	✓					
IV						✓	✓	✓	✓	✓

Key points are included at the end of each chapter as a way to reinforce concepts. Every chapter starts with a poem in the form of a haiku, which is a three-line poem containing five syllables in the first line, seven in the second, and five in the third. After all, there is a lot of creativity in data modeling!

The book is loaded with hands-on exercises along with their answers provided in Appendix B. Appendix A contains all of the book's references, Appendix C a glossary of the terms used throughout the text, and Appendix D a quick reference sheet of ER/Studio commands. There is also a comprehensive index.

Conventions Used in This Book

You will see the term *object* used frequently throughout the text. Object includes any data model component such as entities, attributes, and relationships. As you work through the book, you will see references to objects in data models, keys on the keyboard, and sections of the ER/Studio environment such as options on ER/Studio menus, tools on the palette, and dialog buttons. We make use of the following simple conventions:

Object names	e.g., **Customer Last Name** is an attribute within the **Customer** entity.
`menu options`	e.g., `Insert > Entity` refers to the "Entity" option on the "Insert" menu.
Tool, tab, screen, or window name	e.g., *Datatype Mapping Editor, Data Model Explorer*
<keyboard keys>	e.g., <ALT + I>, then <E> (Means press and hold the <ALT> key and then press the <I> key, then release both and press the <E> key.)
<dialog buttons>	e.g., <OK> <Cancel> <Help>

In addition to the above conventions, there are two types of spreadsheets you will see frequently throughout the text, one describing different ways to invoke the same command, and one describing tabs available on a screen. Here is an example of the spreadsheet showing different ways to invoke the same command, in this case creating an entity:

Menu	Toolbar	Explorer	Shortcut Key	Shortcut Menu
`Insert > Entity`	Modeling toolbar:	Right-click on `Entities, New Entity...`	<ALT + I>, then <E>	Right-click on white space, `Insert Entity`

Become an ER/Studio Hotshot:

- Choose `View > Diagram And Object Display Options`, or click on the icon, and then experiment with the display level settings. The three settings that are relevant in this chapter are `Definition`, `Note`, and `Entity`. `Definition` displays the definition of each entity in the entity box, `Note` displays the note, and `Entity` just displays the entity name in the box. Choose `Entity` for the following example.

This spreadsheet describes five ways to create an entity such as selecting the `Insert` menu and then selecting `Entity` or right-clicking on any white space around the data model and then selecting `Insert Entity`. In the same spreadsheet, there are often tips related to these commands such as choosing different ways to view the entities on the diagram. These tips will help you quickly become an ER/Studio Hotshot! The second spreadsheet describes each tab on a screen as in this example from Chapter 5 on submodels:

Tab	Here's what you need to know:
Attributes	Choose which attributes of the entities selected to include in the submodel. If you deselect an attribute, ER/Studio can display an ellipsis to indicate that not all attributes are displayed.
Definition	Enter a definition for the submodel.
Attribute Bindings	Bind an external piece of information, such as a Microsoft Word document or PDF file, to the submodel. Very useful for requirements documents, user stories, etc.
Security Information	Change or view the current security information as defined in the Data Dictionary. (Data Dictionary will be discussed in Chapter 11.)

To keep this book simple, instead of going into detail on each tab, we'll briefly describe each tab as shown in the above spreadsheet including covering which settings are most important to know.

WHAT'S DIFFERENT IN THE 2ND EDITION?

ER/Studio has been updated with many powerful features that are described in this text including support for NoSQL and for agile development. In addition, a number of corrections from the first edition were applied as well as updates based on my evolving perspective on data modeling and updates on how to use ER/Studio based on my continued experience using the tool on many data modeling assignments.

HOW TO GET THE MOST OUT OF THIS BOOK

Here is a suggested approach to leveraging this book based upon your data modeling and ER/Studio experience:

Data Modeling Experience	ER/Studio Experience	Suggested Approach
Little or None	Little or None	Start at the beginning of the text and read through Chapter 10 on Physical Data Models (Sections I through III). Make sure you do all of the data modeling and ER/Studio exercises, and save Section IV for after you get comfortable with basic ER/Studio functionality.
Good or Great	Little or None	You can skip Chapter 1 and go straight to Chapters 2 and 3 to get comfortable with the ER/Studio landscape. Then, in each of the chapters in Sections II and III, briefly scan the data modeling sections and focus on the ER/Studio-specific sections. Save Section IV for after you get comfortable with the basic ER/Studio features.
Good or Great	Good or Great	You can treat this book as a reference, and whenever you need a refresher in a certain topic, you can use the table of contents and index to find that topic. Make sure you read about the latest features of ER/Studio in Chapter 2 and read the feature chapters from Section IV.

This book will explain data modeling and how to use ER/Studio while still maintaining the spirit of keeping it simple. Keeping it simple required resisting the temptation to go into more detail than necessary and saving the more advanced stuff for the ER/Studio User Guide that comes with the product.

I am a firm believer in the 80/20 rule; you can learn 80 percent of data modeling and ER/Studio functionality in 20 percent of the time, and then learn the remaining 20 percent you need to know over time by practicing with the tool and by taking on more and more challenging data modeling assignments.

I am also a firm believer in playing. We might as well have fun learning, so throughout the book, feel free to play with the buttons and menus and see what happens. You can always hit the undo button or close your data model without saving it.

Data modeling is more than a job or a career—it is a mindset, an invaluable process, a healthy addiction, a way of life. Remember to Keep It Simple and enjoy the ride!

Steve

SECTION I
Foundation

This section introduces data modeling and the ER/Studio landscape. Learn why data modeling is so critical to software development and, even more importantly, why data modeling is so critical to **understanding the business**. You will also learn about the ER/Studio environment.

Chapter 1 explains the data model and why it is an invaluable wayfinding tool in eliciting requirements and capturing a precise representation of the business. This chapter also introduces the publisher case study we will use throughout the text. Chapter 2 introduces you to ER/Studio Data Architect (ER/Studio). Learn what ER/Studio can do and how to install and start the software. Chapter 3 covers at a broad level what features are within each ER/Studio tab, window, menu, and toolbar. By the end of this section, you will have created and saved your first data model in ER/Studio and be ready to starting modeling in Section II!

CHAPTER 1
Data Model Overview

How do I get there?
Maps, blueprints, data models
Please show me the way

I gave the steering wheel a heavy tap with my hands as I realized that, once again, I was completely lost. It was about an hour before dawn, I was driving in France, and an important business meeting awaited me. I spotted a gas station up ahead that appeared to be open. I parked, went inside, and showed the attendant the address of my destination.

I don't speak French and the attendant didn't speak English. The attendant did, however, recognize the name of the company I needed to visit. Wanting to help and unable to communicate verbally, the attendant took out a pen and paper. He drew lines for streets, circles for roundabouts along with numbers for exit paths, and rectangles for his gas station and my destination, MFoods. The picture he drew resembled Figure 1.1.

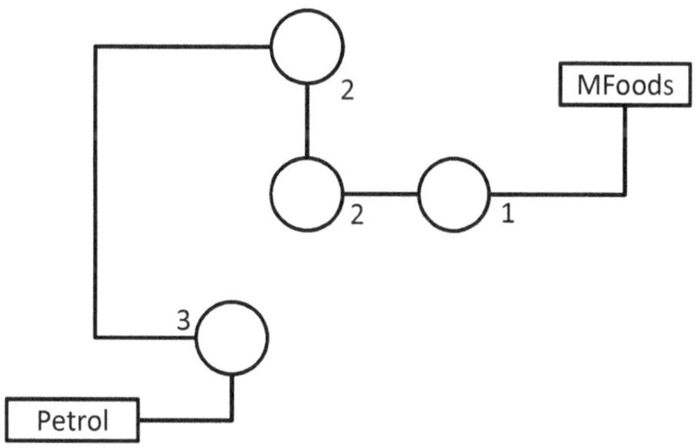

Figure 1.1 Simplification of geographic landscape

With this custom-made map, which contained only the information that was relevant to me, I arrived at my address without making a single wrong turn. This map was a model of the actual roads I needed to travel.

A map simplifies a complex *geographic* landscape in the same way that a data model simplifies a complex *information* landscape. In many cases, the complexities in the actual data can make those roundabouts in France look ridiculously simple.

This chapter explains the data model and introduces the publishing case study that appears in each chapter, allowing you to build on prior work.

FINDING YOUR WAY

If the term *data model* does not excite you or your business users, try the term *wayfinding tool* instead. Wayfinding encompasses all of the techniques and tools used by people (and animals) to find their way from one site to another. If travelers navigate by the stars, for example, the stars are their wayfinding tools. Maps and compasses are also wayfinding tools.

All models are wayfinding tools. A model is a set of symbols and text used to make a complex concept easier to grasp. The world around us is full of obstacles that can overwhelm our senses and make it very challenging to focus only on the relevant information needed to make intelligent decisions. A map helps a visitor navigate a city. An organization chart helps an employee understand reporting relationships. A blueprint helps an architect communicate building plans. The map, organization chart, and blueprint are all types of models that represent a filtered, simplified view of something complex, with the goal of improving a wayfinding experience by helping people understand part of the real world.

It would probably have taken me hours of trial and error to reach my destination in France, whereas that simple map the gas station attendant drew provided me with an almost instantaneous broad understanding of how to reach my destination. A model makes use of standard symbols that allow one to grasp the content quickly. In the map he drew for me, the attendant used lines to symbolize streets and circles to symbolize roundabouts. His skillful use of those symbols helped me visualize the streets and roundabouts.

REPRESENTING AN INFORMATION LANDSCAPE

A data model is a wayfinding tool for both business and data professionals that uses a set of symbols and text to precisely explain a subset of real information to improve communication within the organization and thereby lead to a more flexible and stable application environment. A line represents a motorway on a map of France. A box with the word "Customer" within it represents the concept of a real Customer, such as `Bob`, `IBM`, or `Walmart`, on a data model.

Our broad definition of a data model as "a set of symbols and text that precisely explain a subset of real information" encompasses models in many different forms. Data models can look like the box and line drawings that are the subject of this book, or they can take other forms such as Unified Modeling Language (UML) Class Diagrams, spreadsheets, or State Transition Diagrams. All of these models are wayfinding tools designed with the single purpose of simplifying complex information to facilitate communication in our real world.

LEVERAGING THE DATA MODEL

Precision, with respect to data modeling, means there is a clear, unambiguous way of reading every symbol and term on the model. You might argue with others about whether the rule is accurate, but that is a different argument. In other words, it is not possible for you to view a symbol on a model and say "I see A here" and for someone else to view the same symbol and respond "I see B here." In a data model, precision is primarily the result of applying a standard set of symbols. The traffic circles the gas station attendant drew for me were standard symbols we both understood. There are also standard symbols used in data models, as we will discover shortly.

Traditionally, data models have been built during the analysis and design phases of a project to ensure the requirements for a new application are fully understood and correctly captured before the actual database is created. Due to being precise, the data model has additional uses as well:

- **To understand an existing application.** The data model provides a simple and precise picture of the concepts within an application. We can derive a data model from an existing application by examining the application's database and building a data model of its structures. The technical term for the process of building data models from existing applications is *reverse engineering*. Recently, a manufacturing organization needed to move a 25-year-old application to a new database platform. This was a very large application, so to understand its structures, we reverse engineered the database into a data model.

- **To manage risk.** A data model can capture the concepts and interactions that are impacted by a development project or program. What is the impact of adding or modifying structures for an application already in production? How many of an application's structures are needed for archival purposes? Many organizations today purchase software and then customize it. One example of managing risk through impact analysis would be to use data modeling to determine what impact modifying its structures would have on the purchased software.

- **To learn about the business.** As a prerequisite to a large development effort, it usually is necessary to understand how the business works before you can understand how the applications that support the business will work. Before building an order entry system, for example, you need to understand the order entry business process. One of my favorite sentences in the classic 1978 text *Data and Reality* by William Kent occurs during a section where Kent is discussing the steps required to build a database to store book information: *So, once again, if we are going to have a database about books, before we can know what one representative stands for, we had better have a consensus among all users as to what "one book" is.*

- **To educate team members.** When new team members need to come up to speed or developers need to understand requirements, a data model is an effective explanatory medium. A picture is worth a thousand words, and a data model is a picture that can convey information at different levels of detail. Whenever a new person joined our department, I spent some time walking through a series of data models to educate the person on concepts and rules as quickly as possible.

EMBARKING ON OUR PUBLISHING ADVENTURE

In addition to being a data modeler, I am also the CEO of a large publishing empire called *Technics Publications, LLC.* “Empire” might be a slight exaggeration, as I am also the only employee. Being a one-person company has a very large advantage however, in that I know the publishing business inside and out. I can describe every step necessary to produce a book. Publishing is a great example to use in this book because I can be your business expert, and together we will build the data models from idea through design.

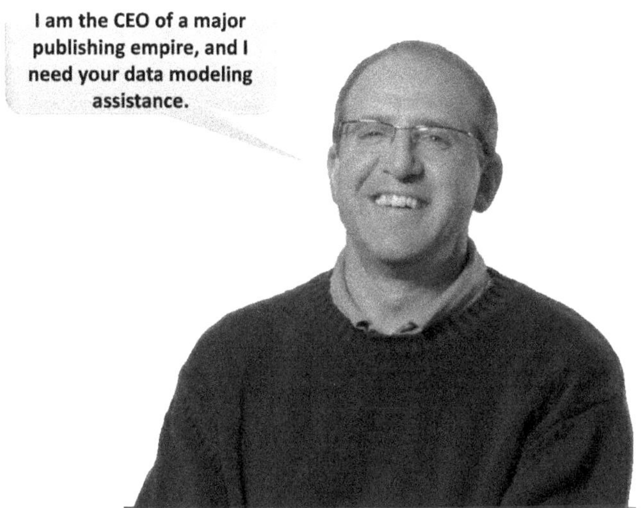

In fact, let’s build our first publishing data model right now! However, instead of the typical boxes and lines we associate with a data model, let’s start with a data model in the form of a spreadsheet. Data models come in many forms, and perhaps the most common form of data model we work with on a daily basis is the spreadsheet. A spreadsheet is a representation of a paper worksheet containing a grid defined by rows and columns where each cell in the grid can contain text or numbers. The columns often contain different types of information.

As a publisher, I need to submit information about each new title to many stores and distributors. Businesses such as Amazon.com® and Barnes & Noble® need to know information about an upcoming title so they can sell the title on their Websites and in their stores.

Take a moment and look at the front and back covers of this book. What information do you see? Table 1.1 contains a subset of the information I saw when doing this exercise.

```
Data Modeling Made Simple with Embarcadero ER/Studio Data Architect
Steve Hoberman
$59.95
DATA MODELING / DATABASE DESIGN
Build a working knowledge of data modeling concepts and best
    practices, along with how to apply these principles with
    ER/Studio...
```

Table 1.1 Information on the front and back cover of *Data Modeling Made Simple with Embarcadero ER/Studio Data Architect*

We can also list the graphics, barcode, etc., but this is enough to get us started.

We can now take this information and list it in the form of a spreadsheet, as you see in Table 1.2.

Title Name	Author Name	Title Retail Price	Category Name	Title Description
Data Modeling Made Simple with Embarcadero ER/Studio Data Architect	Steve Hoberman	$59.95	DATA MODELING / DATABASE DESIGN	*Build a working knowledge of data modeling concepts and best practices, along with how to apply these principles with ER/Studio...*

Table 1.2 Spreadsheet of front and back cover of *Data Modeling Made Simple with Embarcadero ER/Studio Data Architect*

In the first row we listed the type of information and in the second row, the values from Table 1.1. This is a data model because it is representing data using a set of symbols and text—in this case, in the common form of a spreadsheet. Of course, there is quite a bit more information we can model in this spreadsheet, but in order to keep things readable in the layout on this page, we can stop here for now and confidently conclude that we have completed our first data model.

There are three very important similarities between the exercise we just completed on modeling the information on this title and any modeling assignment we do for real:

1. **Process.** The process we went through, where we looked at something ambiguous (such as a book cover) and brought precision to it, is what the data modeler spends at least half their time working on. Data modelers are fantastic organizers. We can take complete chaos and bring clarity by organizing and sorting "things"—in this case, descriptive information about a title becomes neatly organized into a spreadsheet.

2. **Creativity.** There are many ways we can communicate information via a data model. You can choose Information Engineering (IE, for short), which is the notation used in this book; Integration Definition for Information Modeling (IDEF1X); Object Role Modeling (ORM); the Unified Modeling Language (UML) Class Diagram; spreadsheets—the list goes on. It comes down to knowing which notation the audience for the data model would best understand. After all, a data model is a communication tool, and therefore we should choose the visual that is easiest to communicate. So we can be very creative on which formatting to use in a given situation. In this first publishing example, we have chosen to use the easy-to-understand spreadsheet format.

3. **80/20 rule.** Every modeling assignment I have ever worked on has been constrained by time. I always wish I had more time to complete the data model: "If only I had one more week, I could really make this perfect." In reality, we never reach perfection, and I have learned over the years to follow the 80/20 rule of data modeling: in 20 percent of the time we can get the data model 80 percent complete. Questions and issues are raised during the data modeling process, and to go from 80 to 100 percent complete requires answering these questions and resolving these issues. In this book example, you were given just a few moments to think about the information on this cover—that's not a lot of time!

However, there is one very important difference between the model you just completed and the ones we do for real: There is no one around to argue our solution with us! That is, should we call it a "Title" or a "Book"? What's a good definition for "Title" anyway? These types of discussions are often where the data modeler spends quite a bit of time.

If the data modeler spends about 50 percent of their time organizing information, the other 50 percent can be spent working with different groups to come to consensus on terminology and definitions. So half the time we are Organizers and the other half we are Diplomats—pretty important roles!

EXERCISE 1.1: EDUCATING YOUR NEIGHBOR

Reinforce your own understanding of what a data model is by explaining the concept of a data model to someone completely outside the world of IT such as a neighbor, family member, or friend. Did they get it?

Key Points

- A data model is a wayfinding tool for both business and data professionals that uses a set of symbols and text to precisely explain a subset of real information. The goal is to improve communication within the organization and thereby lead to a more flexible and stable application environment.

- In addition to using data models to build new applications, data models can also be leveraged in understanding existing applications and business areas, performing impact analysis, and educating team members.

- Practice the 80/20 rule when it comes to data modeling:20 percent of the time, we can get it at least 80 percent right—and that last 20 percent takes a lot more time to complete and may not be worth the effort anyway.

CHAPTER 2
ER/Studio Functionality

Go – Give it a Try
Install ER/Studio
A powerful tool

In this chapter, we introduce you to ER/Studio Data Architect (often shortened to "ER/Studio," which is the term we will use in this book). You will learn what ER/Studio can do and how to install and start the software. ER/Studio is a data modeling tool for eliciting, representing, and reporting on data requirements and for designing and describing databases. We will learn how to leverage ER/Studio functionality, which will allow you to build applications with greater accuracy and success, increase the use of data standards, and enhance collaboration within your organization. ER/Studio Data Architect offers:

Model-driven design environment
Complete database life cycle support
Enterprise model management
Data lineage documentation
Enterprise communication capabilities
Data warehouse and integration support
Quality database designs

ER/Studio Enterprise Team Edition contains a number of software development productivity tools including ER/Studio Data Architect. ER/Studio Enterprise Team Edition is a powerful business-driven data architecture solution that combines multi-platform data modeling, design, and reporting with cross-organizational team collaboration. Data, business process, and software modeling interfaces allow business analysts and data architects to understand, design, and communicate about data architectures across the organization for improved alignment between business and IT. In addition to ER/Studio Data Architect, ER/Studio Enterprise Team Edition includes:

- **Business Architect**. This process modeling tool enables architects to create conceptual and business process models for data context.

Business Architect enables companies to visualize, understand and refine the relationships between business processes and data as part of their enterprise architecture. Business Architect makes it easy to model how data is incorporated into business processes by allowing users to both model and analyze the relationships between business processes and data. With this capability, data architects and business users can come to a common understanding of the business. A shared repository between Data Architect and Business Architect means users can seamlessly model systems conceptually, logically, and physically in a collaborative and integrated environment.

- **Repository**. The server-side model management system solves the day-to-day challenges of modeling in a team environment, where model collaboration, versioning, security, and object reuse are vital. The Repository allows multiple users to collaborate on data and business process modeling projects with real-time concurrent access that allows team members to share and re-use assets across projects. This collaborative working environment allows organizations to maintain compliance with business standards and mandatory regulations while more effectively leveraging enterprise data as a corporate asset. The Repository also provides support for model version management, designed to allow data professionals to easily manage all successive states of models and model metadata and track changes made to the models.

- **Software Architect**. An object-oriented modeling tool for application architects to visually analyze and design complex software applications. Software Architect simplifies the design stage of a project by organizing and visualizing the requirements, subsystems, logical and physical elements, and structural and behavioral patterns of intensive software systems. It provides developers with powerful productivity facilities through pre-defined patterns, model audits and metrics for quality assurance, and project report documentation. Software Architect supports popular industry standards like OMG's Unified Modeling Language (UML) 2.0 and Object Constraint Language (OCL) as well as providing XMI import/export options and exports to many other common formats.

- **MetaWizard**. These bridges help data professionals integrate metadata from multiple data sources, including modeling tools, business intelligence, ETL platforms, and industry-standard exchange formats (XMI, XML, and XSD). This tool enables ER/Studio to integrate with more than seventy other applications by sharing metadata through an import-export capability.

- **Team Server**. This server-side component serves as the central hub for business glossaries and metadata for the business-driven data architecture. It provides a web user interface that provides the right level of access to both business and data stakeholders. This data model and metadata collaboration platform for data professionals, developers, and business analysts provides greater meaning and value to enterprise data, helping companies find, know, and protect their valuable assets. Employees across the organization have the ability to use and improve metadata, adding context, consistency, and compliance, and enabling faster and more effective decision-making using more accurate data.

EXERCISE 2.1: Learning More About the ER/Studio Family

You can learn more about each of the ER/Studio components and editions and download trial versions at http://www.embarcadero.com/products/er-studio.

New Features in ER/Studio

This book is based on ER/Studio Data Architect release 11, which is a major release with a number of new features including numerous database-specific enhancements. The key features for release 11 are:

- **Change Management.** Allowing you to collaborate in an Agile environment, the *Change Management Center* manages multiple modelers working in the same model as well as providing the ability to track and manage the changes made to the model. Model changes can be associated with agile development workflow stories and tasks. More on this in Chapter 16.

- **Welcome Page.** The *Welcome Page* is the opening window that opens when you start ER/Studio. It contains links to your recent files, plus the ability to create new models, open the reverse engineer, or import wizards in a single click. The *Welcome Page* also includes a number of helpful videos to guide you through some of the more important features and, for new users, a simple getting started video. More on the *Welcome Page* later in this chapter.

- **Automated Naming Standards.** Naming Standards have been an effective method of keeping your models in line with any organizational naming conventions and compliance that is in place; however, now the *Automated Naming Standards* feature allows you to create and modify while automatically applying your naming standard templates. More on this in Chapter 14.

- **New Installer.** Streamlining the install process, the new WiX installer means you have more power with fewer keystrokes. More on this later in this chapter.

- **Enhanced Platform Support.** While release 11 did not introduce additional platform support, it does include the new platform support added to recent releases, including native round-trip support for Hadoop Hive tables and MongoDB databases. ER/Studio also keeps current on the latest releases of popular platforms including Oracle and Teradata. More on this in Chapter 10.

- **Glossary Integration.** The business glossary is an extremely important source of information for collaboration between all stakeholders including data modelers, business analysts, developers, and subject matter experts. More on this in Chapter 11.

- **User Interface Enhancements.** To ease keyboard navigation, the tab order has been improved on the dialog boxes. To learn about all of the new features, or for more details on these features, please refer to the ER/Studio User Guide.

My "Top 10" Favorite Features of ER/Studio

1. **Intuitive**. ER/Studio is very easy to learn. The commands I was looking for seemed to be where I expected to find them. This is due in part to being very comfortable with the Microsoft Windows environment and ER/Studio having been built with a high degree of consistency with products like Microsoft Word® and navigation like Microsoft Explorer®. I also like that the list of possible commands from the menus changes based on what I am working on. For example, highlighting an entity would bring up entity-specific commands under the menus.

2. **Cannot start with physical**. To promote sound software development practices, ER/Studio does not permit creating a physical data model from scratch. Instead the physical data model must be based upon an existing logical data model or reverse engineered from an existing database (such as the actual database or data definition language like SQL). More on this in Chapter 10, Physical Data Models.

3. ***Modeler Explorer***. The *Modeler Explorer* window is extremely useful and intuitive. In most modeling tools, I close all of the windows except for my diagram window to maximize real estate for the diagram. In ER/Studio I can keep *Modeler Explorer* open during my modeling and it is an extremely quick and user-friendly way to navigate or modify a data model.

4. **Level of customization**. The level of customization with ER/Studio is extremely impressive. For example, `Tools > Options` brings up an incredible number of settings that can be changed to personalize the display, enforce rules on the model, facilitate SQL generation, etc. You will learn more about this powerful feature throughout the book.

5. **Lineage**. You can document and view mappings right in ER/Studio as well as use ER/Studio Data Lineage, which is a separate tool in the ER/Studio XE family that allows you to explore existing or proposed Extraction, Transformation, and Load (ETL) mappings to quickly and accurately perform impact analysis. As a data modeler, we are responsible for not just the models, but also the mappings. ER/Studio

allows you to capture the mappings. Chapter 12 is completely dedicated to lineage.

6. ***Universal Naming Utility***. Using the *Universal Naming Utility*, you can globally search for, and replace if desired, names, strings, and attachment value overrides for bound attachments. You define your search and then confine the search to specific objects within your models. More on this in Chapter 4 on finding entities, and Chapter 6 on finding attributes.

7. **Help!** The User Guide in ER/Studio is extremely comprehensive. In addition, hitting <F1> or selecting help from the *Help* menu or on any of the screens brings up detailed and hyperlinked information straight from the User Guide. The documentation is informative and explains many of the more advanced features of ER/Studio. If you would like more details on any ER/Studio feature as you go through this text, just hit <F1>.

8. **Version compatibility**. ER/Studio can load models from earlier versions into newer versions, bringing the models up to the latest release.

9. **Macros**. ER/Studio comes shipped with over 70 macros and also provides you with the functionality to edit these existing macros or create your own. These macros can save you lots of time and improve data consistency within your organization.

10. **Data Dictionary**. Even without using the Repository, you can share domains, rules, reference values, and other valuable types of metadata across models using the Data Dictionary.

EXERCISE 2.2: INSTALLING AND STARTING ER/STUDIO

If you do not yet own a license of ER/Studio Data Architect, you can download a 14-day trial at http://www.embarcadero.com/downloads.

Double click on the downloaded file and follow the wizard to install the software. Accept the licensing terms, click <Next>, and then select the destination folder where the application should be stored. I chose the default location and hit <Next>.

The next screen in the installation wizard will let you choose the Repository Server you would like to connect with. Choose your server from the drop-down list or keep the default of `None` if you do not have a server or do not want to decide on one at this point. You can always select the server later. Click <Next>.

The next screen will let you set how you would like the application to appear in the *Start* menu. I kept the default and hit <Next>. Then click <Install> and ER/Studio will be installed. After installation, you are given the option of displaying the Readme file or just clicking <Finish>.

You can now launch ER/Studio from the *Start* menu and enter the provided license details. For the default notation, choose `IE (Crow's Feet)`. This is the notation we will be using throughout the book. You can always change the notation later under `Tools > Options` and then click the *Logical* or *Physical* tab where you can choose the notation type.

After completing registration, the first screen you will see is the *Embarcadero Product Registration* screen. If you downloaded a trial version, enter the temporary serial number on the product registration screen. If you have an account for the Embarcadero Developer Network (EDN), enter your EDN login name or email and password information on this screen as well. (Contact http://www.embarcadero.com/support if you have issues registering.)

If you are using the ER/Studio Repository, make sure you have compatible versions of the Repository and Data Architect. That is, if you upgrade one, upgrade the other to ensure compatibility. Also, multiple versions of ER/Studio can be run on the same machine, but it is not advisable to share models between versions. Once you have upgraded your models, you may want to remove the older versions.

Along with the installation of the software comes a number of sample models you can play with. We will be opening one of these sample models in the next chapter.

The *Welcome Page* shown in Figure 2.1 is the first screen we encounter after starting ER/Studio.

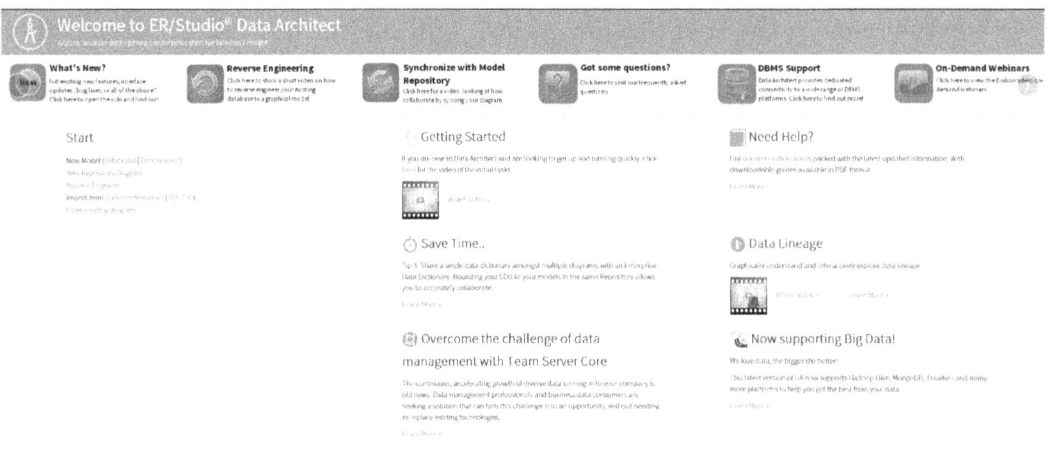

Figure 2.1 Welcome Page

This is a great starting point for both new and experienced users. There are shortcut links to your most recently opened files plus links to creating new models, reverse engineering, and importing external metadata. The *Welcome Page* also includes a number of helpful videos to guide you through some of the more important features and, for new users, a simple getting started video.

The *Welcome Page* acts as both a window and a toolbar. It acts as a window because it can stay active while other windows are opened during the course of your modeling activities and can also be closed similar to any window by clicking the 'x' in the upper right hand corner. It acts a toolbar because there are many functions that can be invoked from this window, and it can be made to appear or disappear as with any toolbar through these commands:

Menu	Toolbar	Explorer	Shortcut Key	Shortcut Menu
`View`, followed by the toolbar name	n/a	n/a	<ALT + V>, followed by the letter for the appropriate toolbar name	n/a

Key Points

- ER/Studio is a data modeling tool for eliciting, representing, and reporting on data requirements and for designing and describing databases.
- ER/Studio Enterprise Team Edition contains a number of software development productivity tools along with ER/Studio Data Architect. ER/Studio Enterprise Team Edition is a powerful data architecture solution that combines business, data, and application modeling in a multi-platform environment.
- There are a number of new features in ER/Studio Data Architect including Auto Naming Standards and enhanced database platform support.
- You can learn more about each of the ER/Studio Enterprise Team Edition products and download trial versions at http://www.embarcadero.com/products/er-studio.

CHAPTER 3
ER/Studio Landscape

Get the big picture
Windows, menus, shortcut keys,
Time to get feet wet

In this chapter, learn at a broad level what features are within each ER/Studio window, menu, and toolbar. By the end of this chapter, you will have opened an existing data model as well as created and saved your first data model in ER/Studio. Are you ready?

The application interface shown in Figure 3.1 has a standard Microsoft® Windows® look and feel and is divided into several tabbed windows that let you navigate and customize your workspace. We will briefly describe each of the different sections of this workspace including all of the callouts in Figure 3.1.

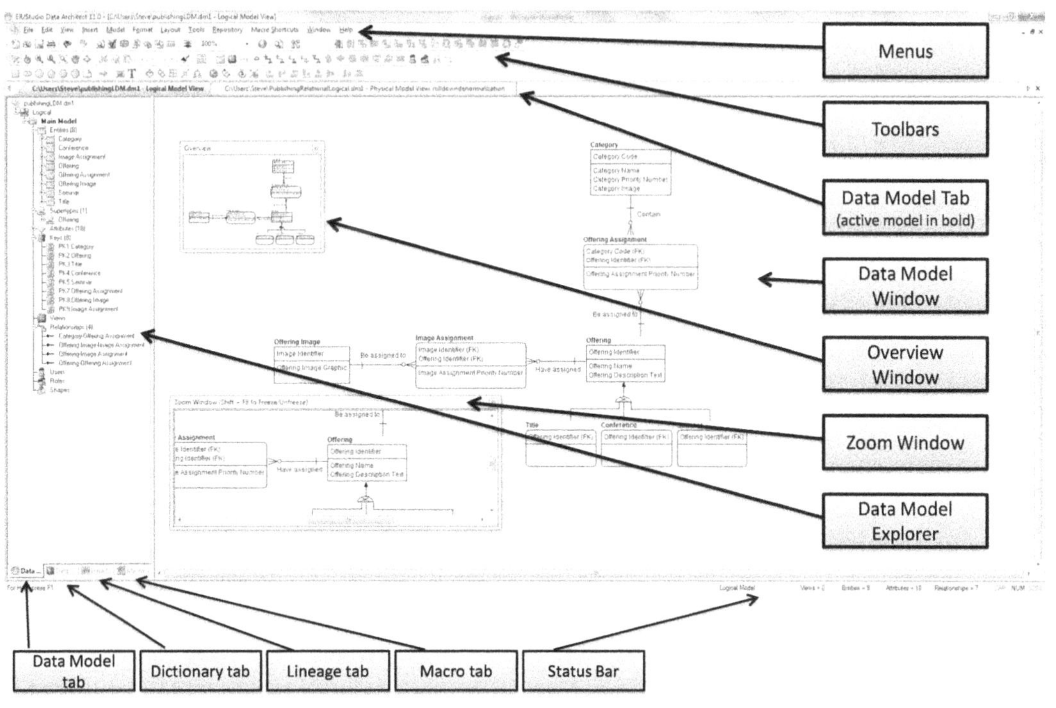

Figure 3.1 ER/Studio Landscape

USING THE WINDOWS

In addition to the *Welcome Page*, there are four windows in ER/Studio: *Data Model Explorer*, *Data Model*, *Overview*, and *Zoom*. We'll describe each in this section.

DATA MODEL EXPLORER

The *Data Model Explorer* helps you navigate data models and their objects, reuse design elements, and create new objects. The *Data Model Explorer* has four tabs that offer access to important functionality, enabling you to efficiently manage your data models:

- **Data Model**. Uses a Windows-like file structure to navigate and modify a data model. This containment-type structure works very well for data models as you can navigate from a data model to a submodel (submodels discussed in Chapter 5) to the entities within this submodel (entities discussed in Chapter 4) and then to the attributes within each entity (attributes discussed in Chapter 6).

- **Data Dictionary**. Helps you manage data dictionary objects including attachments, defaults, rules, reference values, user-defined datatypes, domains, reusable procedural logic, reusable procedures, and libraries.

- **Data Lineage**. Provides a visual, drag-and-drop interface to enable you to document how data moves between the target and source systems along with why and when the data is moved. Data lineage documents the Extraction, Transformation, and Load (ETL) of data movement and the relevant computations required when moving data between disparate systems. You can create data movement rules that can dictate, for example, when the data should be archived or a specific value range the data must fall within in order to be moved.

- **Macros**. Allows you to add, edit, rename, delete, and run macros. You can also create folders in which to store macros for easier reference. ER/Studio comes with many useful macros installed right out of the box.

DATA MODEL WINDOW

The *Data Model Window* is the palette where we do the data modeling and display the data models. We can move diagram objects, copy and paste them into a new location, resize the diagram objects, and change their colors.

OVERVIEW WINDOW

The *Overview Window* allows you to navigate large data models by providing a thumbnail view of the entire model. It is a good idea to hide the *Overview Window* when working in small diagrams. You can open and close the *Overview Window* as needed using the *View* menu or by pressing <F9>. When you zoom in or out, the *Overview Window* places a border around the portion of the model displayed in the *Data Model Window*. In the *Overview Window*, click on the section of the model you would like to see displayed in greater detail.

ZOOM WINDOW

The *Zoom Window* is useful when working on a large diagram as it shows the area that your cursor passes over in larger scale—very similar to how a magnifying glass works. It is a good idea to hide the *Zoom Window* when working in small diagrams. You can open and close the *Zoom Window* as needed using the *View* menu or by pressing <F8>. You can also move the window by dragging it by its title bar.

USING THE MENUS

There are both application and shortcut menus that can be used in ER/Studio. You can access the entire ER/Studio feature set from the application menus. You can also access selected features from shortcut menus. ER/Studio application menus are across the top of the user interface, and shortcut menus are available when you right-click on an object or on the white space in a diagram. All menus are context-sensitive and therefore change depending on what is selected in the *Data Model Window*. Note that functionality available in application menus or shortcut menus is also available through the toolbars.

APPLICATION MENUS

ER/Studio application menus provide access to all functionality. The menus are context-sensitive and change depending on what is selected in the *Data Model Window*. The application menu differs for logical and physical data models. Here is a brief description on each of the menus:

- **File**. Use this menu for model level operations such as to create, open, close, and save data models. You can also import, export, and print models under this menu. Under `Diagram Properties...`, you can capture descriptive information about the model including model name, modeler, and attachments.

- **Edit**. Use this menu for object level operations such as undo and redo, copy and paste, and to find and edit objects. You can also select all of the objects on the model or select all of a given object type (such as selecting all entities).

- **View**. Use this menu for determining what should be displayed on the screen such as which toolbars and what to display when hovering your mouse over objects. You can also zoom in and out using this menu or enter the `Diagram and Object Display Options...` feature, which allows you to decide what will display on the model.

- **Insert**. Use this menu for creating new model objects such as entities and relationships. You can also pan around the model with the relationship navigation feature, which is a wonderful way to walk through the model by highlighting each relationship on a selected entity.

- **Model**. Use this menu for model level operations such as invoking the data dictionary, capturing lineage, and generating physical data models. You can change the model notation here between relational and dimensional, perform data model validation functions, and create and edit submodels. You can also set model options, such as the maximum length of an entity name, under this menu.

- **Format**. Use this menu for object colors, fonts, and alignment. Alignment includes arranging entities consistently, such as left-justified, as well as selecting whether straight or elbowed relationship lines are preferred.

- **Layout**. Use this menu for deciding which layout theme works best such as circular and tree layout. These settings can be applied to the entire model or to just a selected subset.

- **Tools**. Use this menu for accessing various ER/Studio tools such as the *Universal Naming Utility* and the *Datatype Mapping Editor*. You can also invoke the `Options` function from the `Tools` menu, which contains many tabs on model preferences such as defining naming rules, model notation, default datatype, datatype mappings, rolename prefixes, and attribute order. Throughout this book, we will return to the `Options` function to set model defaults.

- **Repository**. Use this menu for interacting with the Repository and models that have been saved there. You can also login to establish a Team Server connection in order to activate business glossary integration with ER/Studio Data Architect.

- **Macro Shortcuts**. Use this menu for adding up to ten pre-defined macros or your own macros to the menu for easy access.

- **Window**. Use this menu for arranging the open windows or for minimizing, closing, or restoring them.

- **Help**. Use this menu for accessing the *User Guide* as well as other useful references such as the *Online Community*. This menu also includes licensing and version information.

SHORTCUT MENUS

ER/Studio shortcut menus offer an easy method of accessing object functionality. Shortcut menus offer a subset of the functionality you can access from the toolbars or menus, specific to the object of interest. To access a shortcut menu, right-click on an object or on any white space in the *Data Model Window*.

USING THE TOOLBARS

Toolbar buttons offer quick access to common features of ER/Studio. All functionality accessible from toolbar buttons are also accessible from the menus (and shortcut menus). ER/Studio toolbars are context-sensitive and therefore become active or inactive (grayed out) according to what you are doing.

There are six toolbars in ER/Studio: *Application*, *Diagram*, *Modeling*, *Layout & Alignment*, *Drawing Shapes*, and *Repository*. We'll describe each in this section, with the exception of the *Repository* toolbar because the Repository is a separate tool. The toolbars can be displayed or hidden through these commands:

Menu	Toolbar	Explorer	Shortcut Key	Shortcut Menu
`View`, followed by the toolbar name	n/a	n/a	<ALT + V>, followed by the letter for the appropriate toolbar name	n/a

Become an ER/Studio Hotshot:
ER/Studio allows you to move toolbars anywhere on the ER/Studio workspace. You can also dock toolbars anywhere on the perimeter of the workspace. To undock a toolbar, click and hold the toolbar handle (the four vertical dots to the left of the toolbar) and drag it to a new location. To dock a toolbar, double-click the title bar of the toolbar.

The *Application* toolbar contains icons for creating, opening, and saving models as well as icons for some handy tools such as the naming standard utility. Figure 3.2 shows each of the icons on this toolbar along with its name.

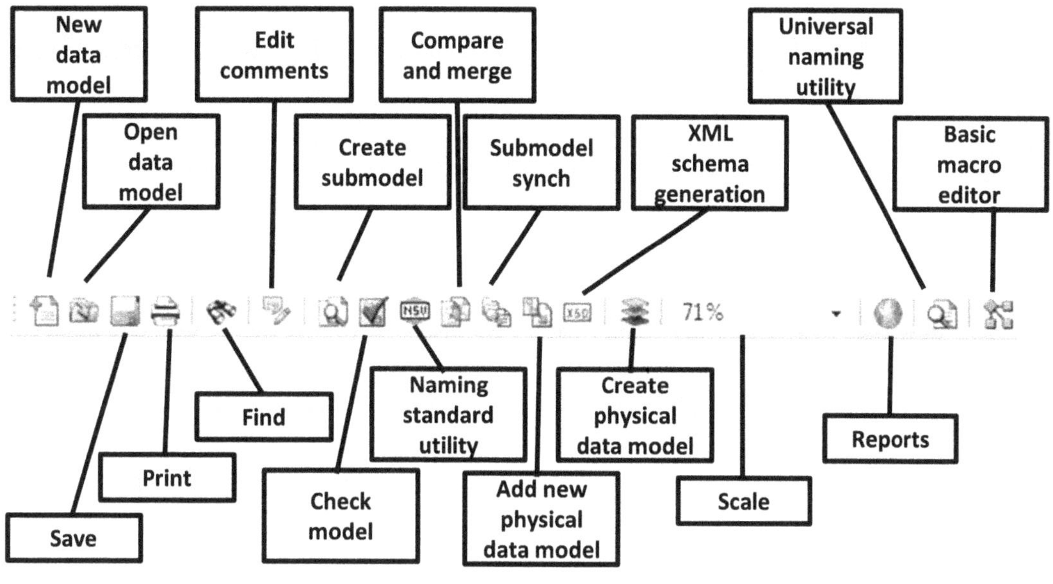

Figure 3.2 Application toolbar

The *Diagram* toolbar contains icons for selecting and viewing objects. Figure 3.3 shows each of the icons on this toolbar along with its name.

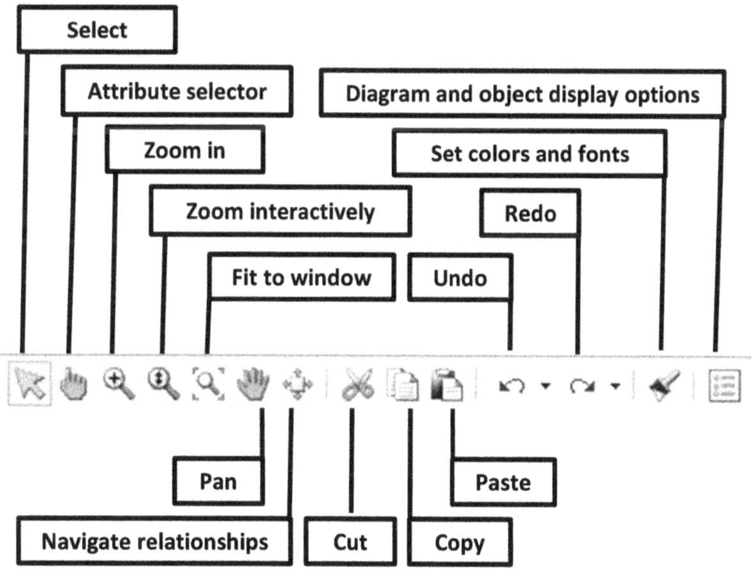

Figure 3.3 Diagram toolbar

The *Modeling* toolbar contains icons for creating objects. The tools available on the *Modeling* toolbar depend on whether your data model is logical or physical, relational or dimensional, and the designated platform for the physical data model. More on these types of models in Section III. Figure 3.4 shows each of the icons on this toolbar along with its name.

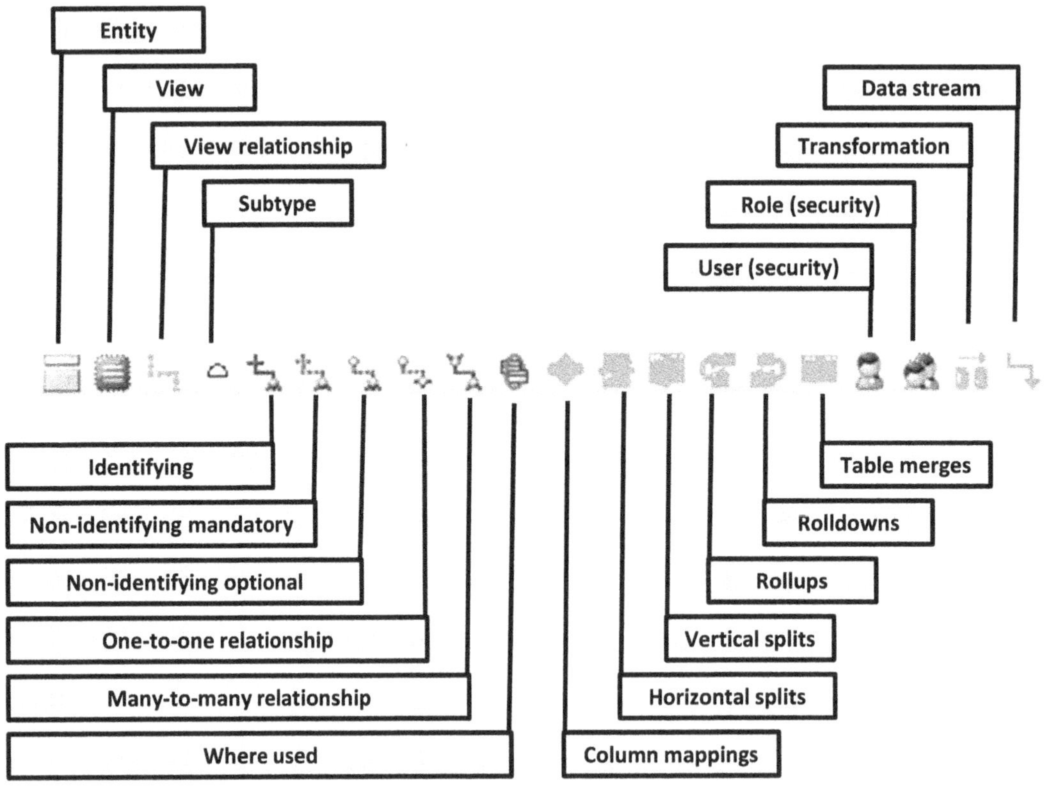

Figure 3.4 Modeling toolbar

The *Layout & Alignment* toolbar contains icons to quickly and accurately arrange your entire diagram or a subset of entities. More on this toolbar in Chapter 4, Entities. Figure 3.5 shows each of the icons on this toolbar along with its name.

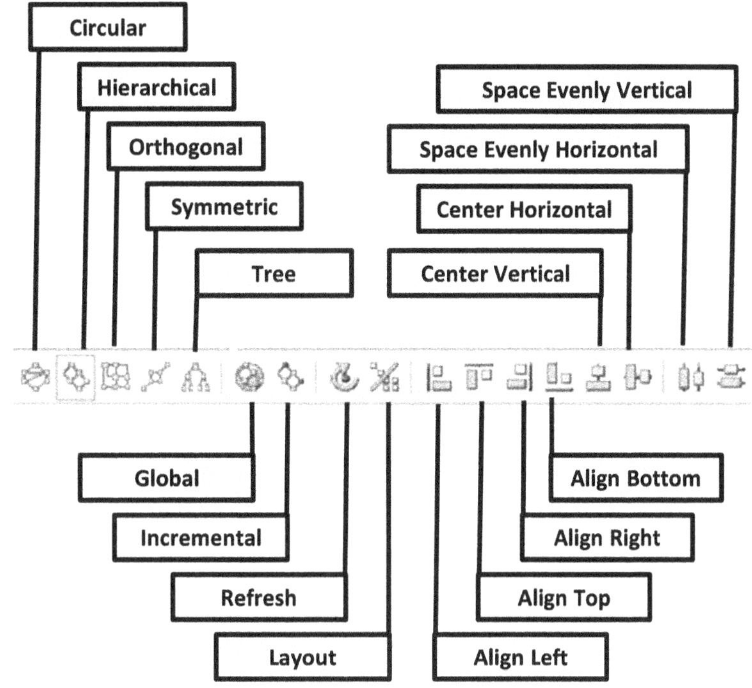

Figure 3.5 Layout & Alignment toolbar

The *Drawing Shapes* toolbar contains icons for different shapes such as rectangles and lines. Figure 3.6 shows each of the icons on this toolbar along with its name.

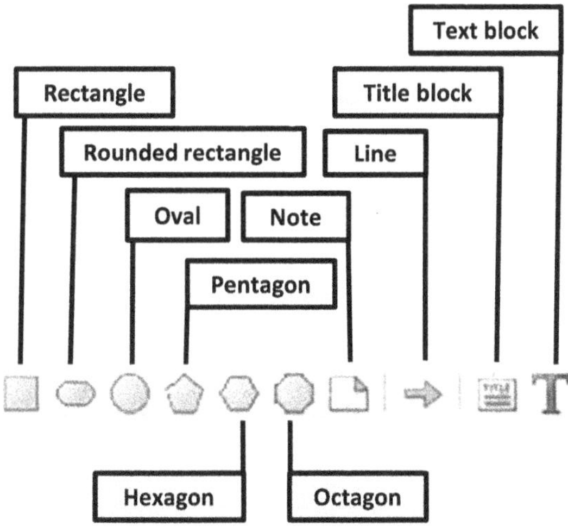

Figure 3.6 Drawing Shapes toolbar

Drawing shapes have no fixed meaning in your diagrams, so you can determine how they are used and interpreted. They can represent objects in your model that are not commonly represented by data modeling syntax as well as communicate the concept of containment such as grouping objects by subject area or status (e.g., "The box around these five entities indicates they will be implemented in Phase II.").

USING KEYBOARD COMMANDS

Keyboard commands, function keys, and shortcuts offer alternative ways to access ER/Studio functionality without using the mouse. Below are the most common commands; we will cover additional commands throughout the book.

Here are the most common keyboard commands:

- Page Up: Scrolls up the *Data Model Window*.
- Page Down: Scrolls down the *Data Model Window*.
- Up Arrow: Scrolls up one line.
- Down Arrow: Scrolls down one line.
- Right Arrow: Scrolls over one position to the right.
- Left Arrow: Scrolls over one position to the left.
- <->: Decreases zoom level by one step (first click on model white space).
- <SHIFT + F8>: Allows you to freeze the Zoom window so that you can pan around the diagram and still maintain focus on a specific diagram object. The same command unfreezes the Zoom window.
- <CTRL + Home>: Scrolls to the upper left hand page of the model.

Here are the function keys:

- <F1>: Opens the online *Help*.
- <F4>: Opens the *Find Entity/View* dialog.
- <F7>: Activates or deactivates shadowing.
- <F8>: Opens or closes a zoom window.
- <F9>: Opens or closes the overview window.

Here are the most common shortcuts:

- Double-click: Allows you to edit the object you double-clicked on.
- <CTRL + A>: Selects all entities in the *Data Model Window*.

- <CTRL + C>: Copies the selected structures.
- <CTRL + V>: Pastes what has been copied into the active window.
- <CTRL + Z>: Restores your model to the last stage of edit (the invaluable "undo" command).
- <CTRL + Y>: Redoes the last undo command (the "redo" command).
- <Delete>: Removes what is highlighted from the data model.

Using the Status Bar

ER/Studio provides statistics pertaining to your data model in the status bar at the bottom of the application. Table 3.1 describes the statistics available on the status bar.

Diagram Mode	Statistic	Definition
Logical	Entities	Total number of entities in the current model or submodel
	Views	Total number of views in the current model or submodel
	Attributes	Total number of attributes in the current model or submodel
	Relationships	Total number of relationships in the current model or submodel
Physical	Tables	Total number of tables in the current model or submodel
	Views	Total number of views in the current model or submodel
	Columns	Total number of columns in the current model or submodel
	Foreign Keys	Total number of foreign keys in the current model or submodel

Table 3.1 What appears on the status bar

Note that in the physical diagram model, what is displayed is specific for that type of database. For example, the number of tables would display for an

Oracle database and the number of collections would display for a MongoDB database. You can display or hide the *Status Bar* under Options:

Menu	Toolbar	Explorer	Shortcut Key	Shortcut Menu
`Tools > Options…`	n/a	n/a	<ALT + T>, then <P>	n/a

Once the *Options* window appears, go to the *Application* tab and change the setting shown circled in Figure 3.7.

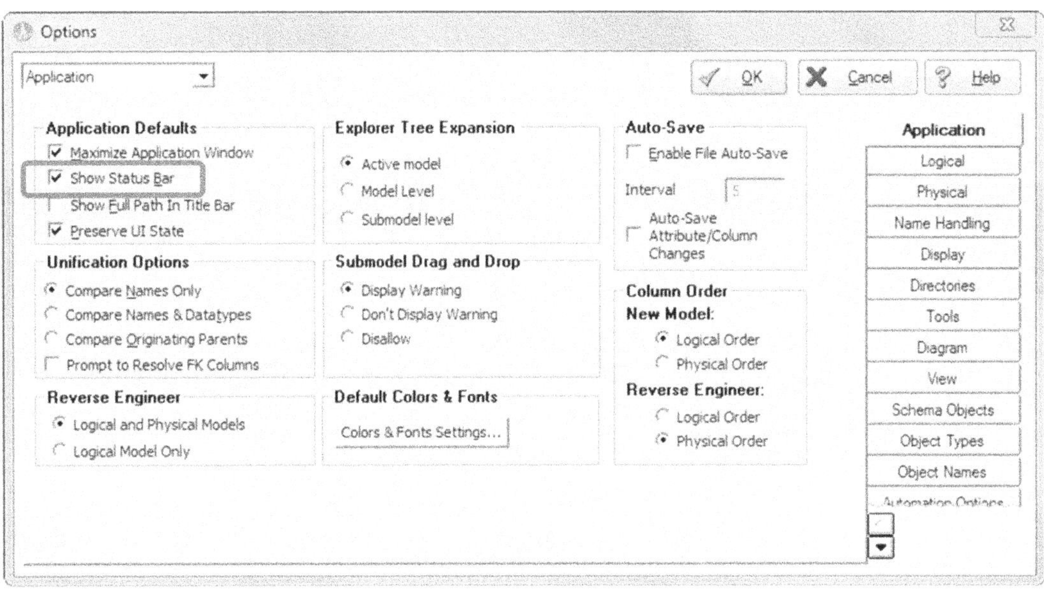

Figure 3.7 Where to turn the *Status Bar* on and off

Turning the status bar on and off using *Options* will determine whether this bar will appear when you create a new model. To hide or show the status bar in your currently open model, use `View > Status Bar`.

EXERCISE 3.1: CREATING A NEW DATA MODEL

If ER/Studio is not open, click `Windows Start > Embarcadero > ERStudio Data Architect`. If you are using the All-Access Toolbox, open the Toolbox and click on `ER/Studio Data Architect`. The version you are using, such as 11.0, will appear as the suffix in the names of the product. This book is based on version 11.0.

Create a new data model using one of the following commands:

Menu	Toolbar	Explorer	Shortcut Key	Shortcut Menu
`File > New`	`Application toolbar:`	`n/a`	`<CTRL + N>` or `<ALT + F>`, then `<N>`	`n/a`

Become an ER/Studio Hotshot:

- You can change the look and feel of the screens by right-clicking in the gray space near the menus and toolbars and selecting `Customize`. You can experiment with the different styles and choose your favorite. I am partial to the Microsoft® Office 2003 style.
- `Model > Model Options` will allow you to set some important data modeling parameters including model notation and text case.

The screen in Figure 3.8 appears.

Figure 3.8 New Model screen

This screen defaults to creating a new data model, and from the drop-down you can select either `Relational` or `Dimensional`, which will both be discussed in Section III starting in Chapter 8. You can also reverse-engineer an existing database. Reverse-engineering means taking an actual database structure and importing it into ER/Studio to create a picture of what the database looks like. Reverse-engineering is a great first step in understanding how an existing application works (especially when that existing application may not have been properly data modeled to begin with). You will learn how to reverse-engineer in Chapter 10. The third option on this submenu is to import a data model from different formats such as CA ERwin® Data Modeler® (discussed in Chapter 13) or SQL files (discussed in Chapter 10). For the publishing data model, which we will use and modify throughout the text, go with the default and click <OK> to create a new relational data model.

CREATING TITLE BLOCKS

The first object we are going to create in this new model is a *Title Block*, which provides important identification information such as the project name and modeler. It is always a good idea to start with a *Title Block* before modeling so printouts of our model will never get mixed up with other printouts.

Menu	Toolbar	Explorer	Shortcut Key	Shortcut Menu
`Insert > Title Block`	Drawing Shapes toolbar:	n/a	<ALT + I>, then <B>	Right-click on white space, `Insert Title Block`

Become an ER/Studio Hotshot:

- ER/Studio supports "sticky buttons," meaning you can create many occurrences of an object and then, when you are done, right-click on any white space to return the cursor to the default selector symbol.

EDITING TITLE BLOCKS

Once you have created a title block, you can edit it to modify its contents by selecting it and choosing one of these commands:

Menu	Toolbar	Explorer	Shortcut Key	Shortcut Menu
`Edit > Edit Title Block…`	n/a	n/a	<ALT + E>, then <E> Or Double-click on the title block	Right-click on Title Block, `Edit Title Block…`

Fill in the options. I filled this out for me, as shown in Figure 3.9. You should fill it out for yourself and click <OK>. Note that the `File Name` and `Submodel` are read-only, as are the creation and modification dates. Note, too, that the blank box to the right of the copyright year contains the copyright holder information.

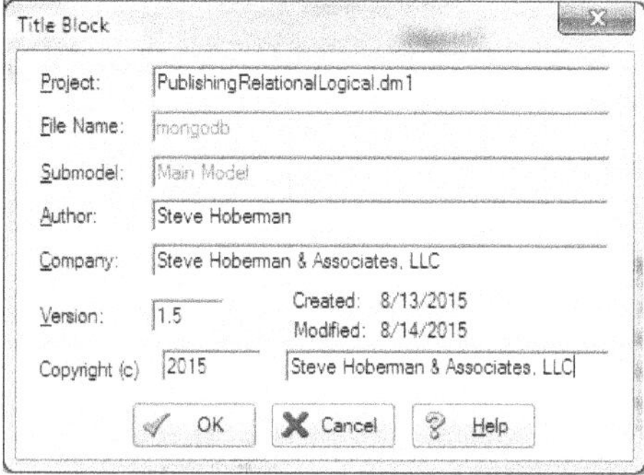

Figure 3.9 Title Block screen

After clicking OK, the object in Figure 3.10 appears (with the information you entered in it).

Project	: PublishingRelationalLogical.dm1
File Name	: mongodb
SubModel	: Main Model
Author	: Steve Hoberman
Company	: Steve Hoberman & Associates, LLC
Version	: 1.5 | Modified: 8/14/2015
Copyright (c)	2015 Steve Hoberman & Associates, LLC

Figure 3.10 Title Block object

DELETING TITLE BLOCKS

Create a few title blocks, highlight them, and use one of the following options to remove them:

Menu	Toolbar	Explorer	Shortcut Key	Shortcut Menu
`Edit > Delete Title Block`	n/a	n/a	<DELETE> or <ALT + E>, then <D>	Right-click on Title Block, `Delete Title Block`

EXERCISE 3.2: SAVING YOUR DATA MODEL

Menu	Toolbar	Explorer	Shortcut Key	Shortcut Menu
`File > Save` or `File > Save As`	Application toolbar:	n/a	<CTRL + S> or for Save: <ALT + F>, then <S> or for Save As: <ALT + F>, then <A>	n/a

Find a good file location to store your model, type `Publishing`, and click <Save>. We will be working on this publishing data model throughout the text. Note that ER/Studio files have the .dm1 file type.

Congratulations! You have just created and saved your first data model in ER/Studio. Now let's start filling it in with data modeling objects in the next section!

EXERCISE 3.3: CLOSING AND OPENING EXISTING DATA MODELS

Close the model that you have just created:

Menu	Toolbar	Explorer	Shortcut Key	Shortcut Menu
`File > Close`	n/a	n/a	<ALT + F>, then <C>	n/a

Note that if you didn't already save your model, you will be prompted to save it before it is closed. Now open one of the sample models that comes installed with the tool:

Menu	Toolbar	Explorer	Shortcut Key	Shortcut Menu
`File > Open`	Application toolbar:	n/a	<CTRL + O> or <ALT + F>, then <O>	n/a

Let's open *Adventure Works*, which is in the *Sample Models* folder. In the *Diagram Properties* dialog, you can document basic information about your data model. Data entered on this dialog is used when generating reports about the model and is also used to populate the *Title Block*. Choose `File > Diagram Properties`, then make yourself the author in the *Information* tab. Impress everyone because you created this model even though you are only up to Chapter 3 in this book!

There are three tabs on this screen:

Tab	Here's what you need to know:
Information	Capture basic information about the model that will appear in the *Title Block* object by default including **Name**, **Author**, **Company**, **Version**, and **Copyright**.
Description	Enter a definition for the model.
Attribute Bindings	Bind an external piece of information, such as a Microsoft Word document or PDF file, to the model. Very useful for requirements documents, user stories, etc. Attachments are created in the Attachments folder of the Data Dictionary (discussed in Chapter 11) and must be added to the model before they will display on this tab.

EXERCISE 3.4: GETTING COMFORTABLE WITH ER/STUDIO

Before you close the *Adventure Works* model, let's change some options for future models. ER/Studio has an incredible number of customizations we can choose from under *Options*:

Menu	Toolbar	Explorer	Shortcut Key	Shortcut Menu
`Tools > Options`	n/a	n/a	<ALT + T>, then <P>	n/a

We will play with different tabs under *Options* throughout the book, but for this exercise let's look at three tabs: *Application, Directories*, and *Logical*.

Under the *Applications* tab, there is a section for *Application Defaults*. If the checkbox `Show Status Bar` is checked, the status bar will appear at the bottom of the ER/Studio Landscape. Check `Show Full Path In Title Bar`, click <OK>, and see what happens. You will notice that in the tab that previously just contained the name of the model, we now have the full path name. If you like this setting, you can keep it; otherwise, go back into *Options* and turn it off.

Let's go back into *Options*, and this time to the *Directories* tab. This tab allows you to define the default directories for models and model-related artifacts such as macros. Choose where you would like your models to be stored or just keep the default path.

The *Logical* tab has some neat features we'll cover shortly, but for now click the `Background Color` button and choose your favorite color for the background. Note that my personal preference is a light gray background, but choose what suits you!

Click <OK> and notice that the background color did not change to your selection. This is because you changed the background color for all models going forward. Some of the settings under *Options*, such as displaying the path name, apply directly to the model you are working in and all subsequent models. Some settings, such as the background color, apply only to models going forward.

Here's how you can change the background color of the currently open model:

Menu	Toolbar	Explorer	Shortcut Key	Shortcut Menu
`Format > Colors & Fonts…`	Diagram toolbar:	n/a	<ALT + O>, then <C>	Right-click on white space, `Colors & Fonts…`

Click on <Set Color> to select a color for the open model and click <OK> to apply this color to the background of your open model. Note that if you close the model and create a new one, you will see the background color you selected from the *Options* menu.

As an aside, if you click on any of the objects (e.g. Entity, View, Key) that appear in the *Colors & Fonts* window, the object clicked on will appear in the drop-down menu and you can set the color for this object.

For the remainder of this exercise, continue playing with the tools in the new model you created. Just spend some time clicking around and getting yourself into trouble. It's the best way to learn. We'll formally go through ER/Studio functionality, but it doesn't hurt to give yourself a preview by just clicking on things and seeing what happens. Your data model is already saved, and you can always exit the model without saving or create a new data model and play there.

Key Points

- There are four windows in ER/Studio: *Data Model Explorer, Data Model, Overview*, and *Zoom*.
- Menu and toolbar selections are context-sensitive and change depending on the type of data model or what is currently selected.
- Shortcut menus offer an easy method of accessing object functionality. Shortcut menus offer the same functionality you can access from the toolbars or menus.
- There are six toolbars in ER/Studio: *Application*, *Diagram*, *Modeling*, *Layout & Alignment*, *Drawing Shapes,* and *Repository.*
- ER/Studio provides statistics pertaining to your data model in the status bar at the bottom of the application.
- A *Title Block* provides important identification information such as the project name and modeler.
- The *Options* window contains an extremely comprehensive set of customizations.

SECTION II
Data Model Objects

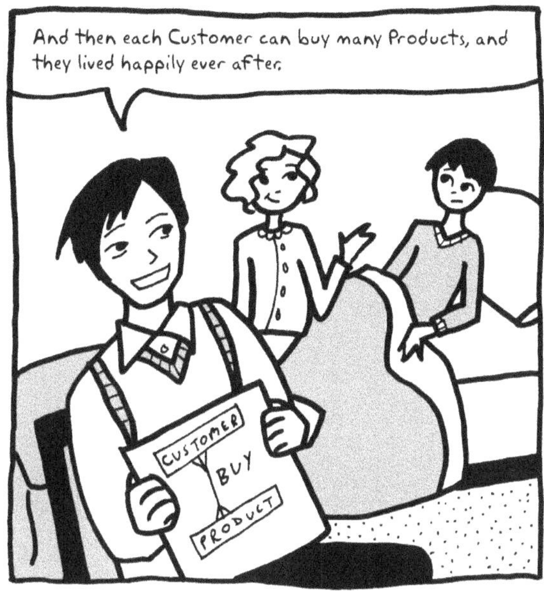

This section explains all of the objects on a data model. By the end of this section, you will be able to "read" a data model of any size or complexity as well as create and modify entities, attributes, and relationships in ER/Studio.

Chapter 4 defines an entity and instances and discusses the different categories of entities. The three different levels at which entities may exist—conceptual, logical, and physical—are also explained. Chapter 5 defines a submodel and how to work with one. Chapter 6 defines an attribute and key, distinguishing the terms *candidate*, *primary*, *surrogate*, *foreign key*, and *alternate key*. Domains are also introduced in this chapter. Chapter 7 defines a rule and relationship. Cardinality and labels are explained so that the reader can read any data model as easily as reading a book. Other types of relationships, such as recursive relationships and subtyping, are also discussed.

CHAPTER 4
Entities

Concepts of interest
Who, What, When, Where, Why, and How
Entities abound

This chapter defines an entity and instances and discusses the different categories of entities. The three different levels at which entities may exist—conceptual, logical, and physical—are also explained. We will practice creating entities in ER/Studio.

ENTITY EXPLANATION

An entity represents a collection of information about something that the business deems important and worthy of capture. A noun or noun phrase identifies a specific entity. An entity fits into one of six categories: who, what, when, where, why, or how. Table 4.1 contains a definition of each of these entity categories along with examples.

Category	Definition	Examples
Who	Person or organization of interest to the enterprise. That is, "*Who* is important to the business?" Often a "who" is associated with a role such as Customer or Vendor.	Employee, Patient, Player, Suspect, Customer, Vendor, Student, Passenger, Competitor, Author
What	Product or service of interest to the enterprise. It often refers to what the organization makes that keeps it in business. That is, "*What* is important to the business?"	Product, Service, Raw Material, Finished Good, Course, Song, Photograph, Title
When	Calendar or time interval of interest to the enterprise. That is, "*When* is the business in operation?"	Time, Date, Month, Quarter, Year, Calendar, Semester, Fiscal Period, Minute

Category	Definition	Examples
Where	Location of interest to the enterprise. Location can refer to actual places as well as electronic places. That is, "*Where* is business conducted?"	Mailing Address, Distribution Point, Website URL, IP Address
Why	Event or transaction of interest to the enterprise. These events keep the business afloat. That is, "*Why* is the business in business?"	Order, Return, Complaint, Withdrawal, Deposit, Compliment, Inquiry, Trade, Claim
How	Documentation of the event of interest to the enterprise. Documents record the events such as a Purchase Order recording an Order event. That is, "*How* does the business keep track of events?"	Invoice, Contract, Agreement, Account, Purchase Order, Speeding Ticket, Packing Slip, Trade Confirmation

Table 4.1 Definitions and examples of entity categories

Entity instances are the occurrences or values of a particular entity. Think of a spreadsheet as being an entity with the column headings representing the pieces of information (or properties) about the entity. Each spreadsheet row containing the actual values represents an entity instance. The entity **Customer** may have multiple customer instances with names `Bob`, `Joe`, `Jane`, and so forth. The entity **Account** can have instances of `Bob's checking account`, `Bob's savings account`, `Joe's brokerage account`, and so on.

ENTITY TYPES

The beauty of data modeling is that you can take the same information and show it at different levels of detail depending on the audience. In this book we discuss three levels of detail: conceptual, logical, and physical. Entities exist at all three levels.

For an entity to exist at a conceptual level, it must be both basic and critical to the business. What is basic and critical depends very much on the concept of scope. At a universal level, there are certain concepts common to all companies such as **Customer**, **Product**, and **Employee**. Making the scope slightly narrower, a given industry may have certain unique concepts. **Campaign**, for example, will be a valid concept for an advertising company, but perhaps not for other industries like healthcare. In the publishing data model, **Author**, **Title**, and **Order** are conceptual entities, shown as names within rectangles (see Figure 4.1). ER/Studio Business Architect can be used to create conceptual models that can then be exported to Data Architect.

Author	Title	Order

Figure 4.1 Sample conceptual entities

Entities at a logical level represent the business at a more detailed level than at the conceptual level. Frequently, a conceptual entity represents many logical data model entities. Logical entities contain properties called "attributes," which we will discuss in Chapter 6. Figure 4.2 shows the three corresponding logical entities based upon the conceptual entities from Figure 4.1.

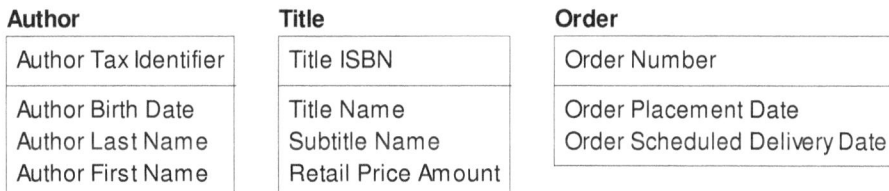

Author	Title	Order
Author Tax Identifier	Title ISBN	Order Number
Author Birth Date	Title Name	Order Placement Date
Author Last Name	Subtitle Name	Order Scheduled Delivery Date
Author First Name	Retail Price Amount	

Figure 4.2 Sample logical entities

At a physical level, the entities correspond to technology-specific objects such as database tables in a relational database management systems (RDBMS) or collections in the NoSQL database MongoDB. The physical level is the same as the logical level with the exception of compromises that were needed to make up for deficiencies in technology (often related to performance or storage).

Figure 4.3 shows the three corresponding physical entities based upon the logical entities from Figure 4.2. The physical entities also contain database-specific information such as the format and length of an attribute (**Author Last Name** is 50 characters) and whether the attribute is required to have a value (**Author Tax Identifier** is not null and therefore required to have a value, but **Author Birth Date** is null and therefore not required to have a value).

Author

Author Tax Identifier (PK)	CHAR(9)	NOT NULL
Author Birth Date	DATETIME	NULL
Author Last Name	CHAR(50)	NULL
Author First Name	CHAR(30)	NULL

Title

Title ISBN (PK)	CHAR(13)	NOT NULL
Title Name	CHAR(100)	NULL
Subtitle Name	CHAR(100)	NULL
Retail Price Amount	DECIMAL(5,2)	NULL

Order

Order Number (PK)	CHAR(5)	NOT NULL
Order Placement Date	DATE	NULL
Order Scheduled Delivery Date	DATE	NULL

Figure 4.3 Sample physical entities

In an RDBMS, these physical entities become database tables or views. In NoSQL databases, these physical entities become transformed into how the underlying technology views the entity. For example, in MongoDB (a document-based database) these entities become collections. The general term "structure" will be used to refer to the underlying database components independent of whether the database is a RDBMS or NoSQL solution.

ENTITIES IN ER/STUDIO

In this section we will practice creating and editing entities for the publishing data model.

CREATING ENTITIES

Menu	Toolbar	Explorer	Shortcut Key	Shortcut Menu
`Insert > Entity`	Modeling toolbar:	Right-click on `Entities`, `New Entity...`	<ALT + I>, then <E>	Right-click on white space, `Insert Entity`

Become an ER/Studio Hotshot:

- Choose `View > Diagram And Object Display Options`, or click on the icon, and then experiment with the display level settings. (If a warning message appears that the current undo history will be cleared, this means that the buffer holding the list of changes you made up to this point will be emptied. So, for example, if you created an entity before clicking on, you will not be able to undo creating this entity. You can still delete the entity; you just can't remove it by hitting <CTRL-Z>. If you don't want to see this warning again, click `Do not display this dialog again.`) The three settings under the *Entity* tab that are relevant in this chapter are `Definition`, `Note`, and `Entity`. `Definition` displays the definition of each entity in the entity box, `Note` displays a place for text other than the definition (such as questions and issues), and `Entity` just displays the entity name in the box. Choose `Entity` for our example.
- The status bar at the bottom of the screen shows the number of entities in the model or submodel. You can hide or show this status bar using `View > Status Bar` or <ALT + V>, then <S>.
- You can customize the information that pops up when you hover the mouse over an entity under `View > Cursor Popup Help Options > Entity Help`.

Create the entities **Author, Title, Electronic Title,** and **Print Title** using a variety of the options above. (Electronic titles are ebooks such as those in Kindle or Adobe PDF format.)

You may have a model that looks similar to Figure 4.4.

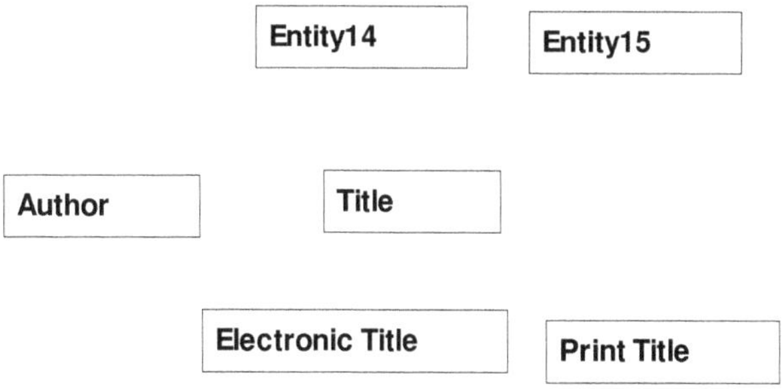

Entity14
Entity15
Author
Title
Electronic Title
Print Title

Figure 4.4 First entities

Notice that I accidently created the extra entities **Entity14** and **Entity15.** Did you do something similar? This might have happened because the cursor remained in the entity symbol so that when we clicked, an entity appeared. Notice that having these "sticky buttons" is a great feature because we can create a lot of entities in very little time just by clicking.

When you want to turn the sticky buttons feature off, just right-click on any white space and the cursor returns to its default selector symbol. Now how do we get rid of these extra entities that we created? Stay tuned for the Deleting Entities section later in this chapter. (You can play though and experiment with how to delete them—playing is always strongly encouraged!)

Creating Text Blocks

Use text blocks to insert useful information into the diagram such as examples of an entity. You can add multiple text blocks at specific points throughout the diagram to add clarity and help with organization. When you no longer need to use a text block in your diagram, you can delete the text block.

Menu	Toolbar	Explorer	Shortcut Key	Shortcut Menu
`Insert > Text Block`	Drawing Shapes toolbar: T	n/a	<ALT + I>, then <X>	Right-click on white space, `Insert > Text Block`

In the *Data Model Window*, click and drag where you want to place the text block, enter the text you want to display, and then right-click to deselect the *Text Block* creator. Double-click on the text block to enter or change text at a later time. To resize the text box, select the text box, grab a sizing handle and drag to the desired position. Change the font attributes by right-clicking the text block and then clicking `Colors & Fonts`.

EDITING ENTITIES

Highlight the entity and use one of these techniques:

Menu	Toolbar	Explorer	Shortcut Key	Shortcut Menu
`Edit > Edit Entity…`	n/a	Right-click on entity, `Entities, Edit Entity…`	<ALT + E>, then <E> Or Double-click on the entity	Right-click on entity, `Edit Entity…`

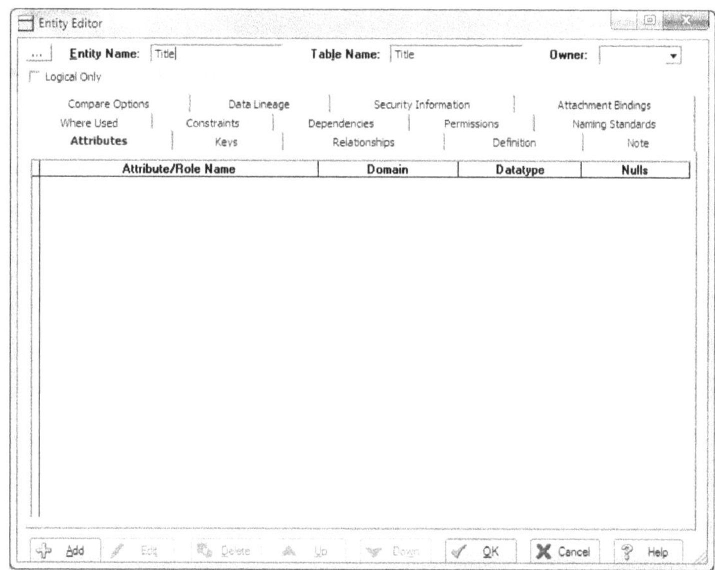

Figure 4.5 Entity Editor screen

The screen in Figure 4.5 can be resized by clicking and dragging the lower right corner. This screen can also become maximized by clicking the square symbol in the upper right corner (to the left of the "x" that closes the window) and then returned back to its original size by clicking the two square symbols in the upper right corner. There are 14 tabs on this screen:

Tab	Here's what you need to know:
Attributes	Create, edit, and arrange attributes. We'll cover this tab in Chapter 6, Attributes and Domains.
Keys	Define primary, alternate, and inversion entry keys on the attributes. We'll cover this tab in Chapter 6, Attributes and Domains.
Relationships	View and edit relationships between entities. We'll cover this tab in Chapter 7, Relationships.

Tab	Here's what you need to know:
Definition	Define the entity. If the target database supports it, ER/Studio adds this definition as a table comment when generating SQL code. The macro **Definition Editor** allows for easily entering definitions for multiple objects. More on macros in Chapter 16.
Note	Capture any other text outside the definition such as questions to ask business experts, known issues, or action items. HTML tags used in *Notes* will be applied as formatting in the HTML reports. The macro **Notes Editor** allows for easily entering notes for multiple objects. More on macros in Chapter 16.
Where Used	See which logical and physical data models and submodels contain the entity. From this tab you can edit mappings and user-defined mappings.
Constraints	Display, create, and edit constraints. A constraint is a rule that is checked before data is allowed in the database. For a table instance (also called a record), these are rules that can be created and edited to determine what can be added to the database table. These constraints become part of the SQL used to build the table. This is a tab that would be used in the physical data model but not the logical data model.
Dependencies	Display the views that depend on this entity. This is a tab that would be used in the physical data model but not the logical data model.
Permissions	Select detailed permissions (e.g., insert, select, update, and delete) for users and roles for this entity. This is a tab that would be used in the physical data model but not the logical data model.
Naming Standards	Apply different naming standards to different objects when portions of a model require different versions of a standard. For example, some objects already exist in the database and you may not want to apply a newer naming standard to them. When selected, the `Freeze Names` option prevents changes to the name of the selected attribute when naming standards are applied. We'll cover this tab in Chapter 14, Naming Standards.
Compare Options	Select which, if any, properties (e.g., entity name, definition, notes) of the entity to ignore when comparing this entity to another using the *Compare and Merge Utility*, which will be discussed in Chapter 15.
Data Lineage	Map the rules from source to target entities in the model. We'll cover this tab in Chapter 12, Data Lineage.

Tab	Here's what you need to know:
Security Information	Assign security settings that are defined in the Data Dictionary to this entity. The Data Dictionary will be discussed in Chapter 11.
Attachment Bindings	Bind an external piece of information, such as a Microsoft Word document or PDF file, to the entity. Very useful for requirements documents, user stories, etc. Attachments are created in the Attachments folder of the Data Dictionary (discussed in Chapter 11) and must be added to the model before they will display on this tab.

Changing the Name of an Entity

Highlight the entity and use one of these techniques:

Menu	Toolbar	Explorer	Shortcut Key	Shortcut Menu
`Edit > Edit Entity` (in the upper left corner you can rename the entity)	n/a	`Modify Name`	<ALT + E>, then <E> (in the upper left corner you can rename the entity)	Right-click on entity, `Edit Entity...` (in the upper left corner you can rename the entity)

MOVING ENTITIES

To move entities, make sure the cursor is in the selection shape (the arrow button from the **Diagram Toolbar**). Then click and drag the entities to their desired spots. You can move multiple entities at the same time by clicking and dragging over them to select them or by pressing and holding <CTRL> while you click each entity.

Once the entities are selected, the cursor changes to ✥ and then you can drag the entities to a new location. A very quick and accurate way of aligning entities with each other, such as left justified or spaced evenly, is to use the *Layout and Alignment* toolbar. Recall Figure 3.5 repeated here as Figure 4.6.

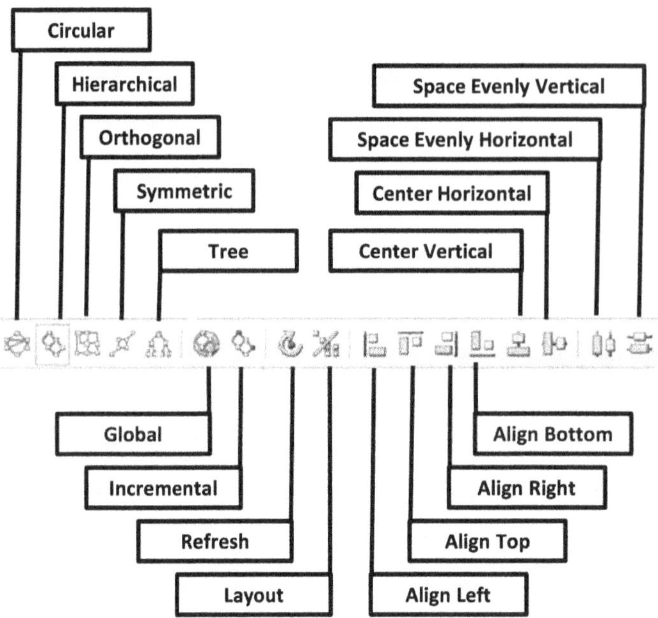

Figure 4.6 Layout & Alignment toolbar

Highlight the entities you would like to align and then click on one of these icons.

The *Layout & Alignment* toolbar contains icons to quickly and accurately arrange your entire diagram or a subset of entities. There are five types of layouts that will arrange the entire diagram or a subset of highlighted entities:

- **Circular layout**. Reveals the dependencies and relationships between the data model objects, emphasizing group structure by rearranging the data model into one or more circular patterns. This layout can be used for an initial star schema design as discussed in Chapter 10, Physical Data Models. It is also useful when you have a very large data model and want to show "clumps" of related entities for easier communication. For example, if each clump is a subject area, you could apply a circular pattern to just the order-related entities, another circular pattern to just the customer-related entities, and so on for each subject area to make the model easier to read.

- **Hierarchical layout**. Organizes entities in a hierarchical pattern based on the direction of the relationship between the entities. You can use this layout for arranging logical dimensions, which will be discussed in Chapter 9, Logical Data Models. It can also be easier to read a data model from the top of the page down, making this a useful arrangement pattern.

- **Orthogonal layout**. Rearranges the data model into square-line, rectangular patterns that use only horizontal and vertical line routing. Orthogonal layouts have few crossings and allow minimal stretching of entities that have a high number of relationships. This layout is very useful for highly normalized data models. Normalization will be discussed in Chapter 9, Logical Data Models.

- **Symmetric layout**. Provides a symmetrical pattern centered on a single entity where peripheral entities move to the edge of the diagram. This is great for a star schema design (similar to the circular layout).

- **Tree layout**. Rearranges your diagram into a tree pattern with parent and child entities, producing a data model that contains a root entity and only one unique path from the root entity to any other entity. Tree layouts can have branches and siblings where parent to child relationships are inherent. This can be ideal for explaining complex hierarchies, taxonomies, and subtyping structures (subtyping discussed in Chapter 7).

The `Global` icon on this toolbar makes the arrangement all at once. `Incremental` performs the arrangement in stages. `Layout` allows you to set parameters for each of the five types of layouts, and `Refresh` applies these changes to the diagram. The remaining buttons on the toolbar allow you to align selected entities different ways.

RESIZING ENTITIES

ER/Studio automatically determines the proper dimensions of the entity to fit the text that it displays. However, you can still resize the entity by selecting it and using one of these commands:

Menu	Toolbar	Explorer	Shortcut Key	Shortcut Menu
`Format > Resize Entity/View`	n/a	n/a	<ALT + O>, then <R>	n/a

Become an ER/Studio Hotshot:

- The simplest way to resize an entity is by selecting the entity and then dragging the size handles. ER/Studio can automatically resize entities, tables, and views.
- You can highlight multiple entities by using the <SHIFT> or <CTRL> keys (or by clicking and dragging over multiple entities) and resize all of the selected entities at once.
- You can restore the entity to its original size by right-clicking on the entity and choosing `Resize` or by clicking <CTRL + R>.

CHANGING THE APPEARANCE OF ENTITIES

There are a number of settings for changing the way entities appear on the screen and when printed. One such setting is the shadow feature, which makes the entities appear three-dimensional. This shadow feature is turned on by default but can be turned on and off under *Options*:

Menu	Toolbar	Explorer	Shortcut Key	Shortcut Menu
`Tools > Options`	n/a	n/a	<ALT + T>, then <P>	n/a

Select the *Display* tab and then click or unclick the `Shadow` checkbox under *Model Display*. As with a number of other settings under options, turning on and off shadows impacts future models but not the one currently open. To turn on and off shadowing in your current model, simply hit <F7>. Using certain colors and fonts can help highlight portions of the model and distinguish sections of the model from other sections:

Menu	Toolbar	Explorer	Shortcut Key	Shortcut Menu
`Format > Entity Color and Font Settings`	n/a	Right-click on entity, `Entity Color and Font Settings`	<ALT + O>, click on `Entity Color and Font Settings`	Right-click on entity, `Entity Color and Font Settings`

> **Become an ER/Studio Hotshot:**
> - You can highlight multiple entities by using the <SHIFT> or <CTRL> keys (or by clicking and dragging over multiple entities) and then change their fonts and colors all at once.

After applying one of the commands above, you are given three options:

1. `Entity/Attributes Colors and Fonts`. This option provides the most functionality in adjusting colors and fonts.
2. `Entity Background/Outline Color`. This is the simplest way just to change the entity background or outline color.
3. `Set Entity to Use Submodel Defaults`. This will reset the colors and fonts to the submodel defaults.

If you choose the first option, the screen in Figure 4.7 appears.

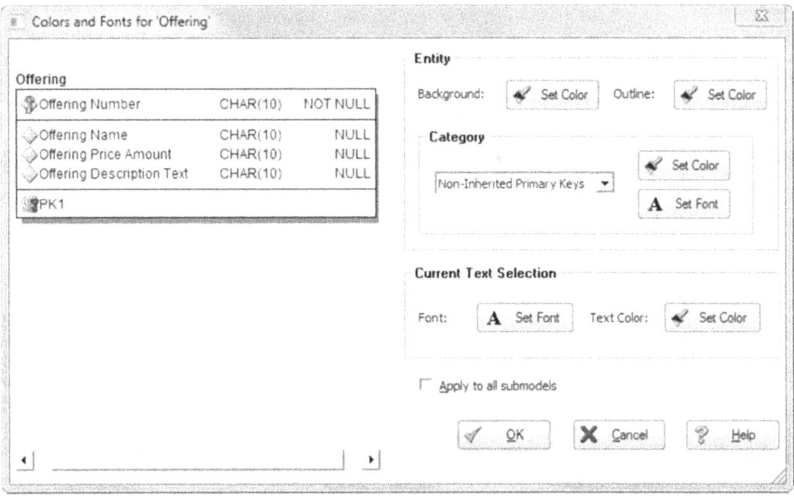

Figure 4.7 Colors and Fonts screen

From this screen you can change the colors and fonts of entities and also attributes. To change the color or fonts of attributes, make a selection from the drop-down menu and click <Set Color> and <Set Font>. If you click the checkbox `Apply to all submodels`, the color and font changes you make here will apply to this same object in every submodel in which it appears. (Submodels are the subject of the next chapter.) Click <OK> to exit the screen and have your changes applied.

There is a very quick way to change the color of all of a particular object such as for all entities:

Menu	Toolbar	Explorer	Shortcut Key	Shortcut Menu
`Format > Colors & Fonts`	Diagram toolbar:	n/a	<ALT + O>, then <C>	Right-click on white space, `Colors & Fonts`

Click on the entity symbol or text or choose the appropriate entity property from the drop–down, and click <Set Color> to select the color you would like. Click <OK> to exit this screen and apply your changes.

COPYING ENTITIES

Highlight the entity or entities you would like to copy and then choose one of these commands:

Menu	Toolbar	Explorer	Shortcut Key	Shortcut Menu
`Edit > Copy`, then `Edit > Paste`	Diagram toolbar: (copy), then (paste)	Drag entities to the *Data Model Window*	<CTRL + C> then <CTRL + V> or <ALT + E>, then <C> for copy, <ALT + E>, then <P> for paste	Right-click entity, `Copy`, then right-click on white space, `Paste`

Become an ER/Studio Hotshot:

- You can highlight multiple entities by using the <SHIFT> or <CTRL> keys (or by clicking and dragging over multiple entities) and copy all of the selected entities at once.
- You can also cut and paste by using the icon on the Diagram toolbar.

The name of the new object will be the name of the original object appended by _1 such as Entity_1. If you create another copy of the object, the new object would be named Entity_2. The copied object can be pasted into another model or submodel in the same file or in another open diagram.

FINDING ENTITIES

There are two techniques for finding entities: *Find Entity/View* and the powerful *Universal Naming Utility*.

Find Entity/View

Find Entity/View is very useful for locating a single entity by the first few letters of the entity's name.

Menu	Toolbar	Explorer	Shortcut Key	Shortcut Menu
`Edit > Find Entity/View...`	Application toolbar:	n/a	<F4> or <ALT + E>, then <F>	Right-click on white space, `Find Entity`

Universal Naming Utility

If you need a more powerful search, such as locating several entities or attributes or even searching by any part of the entity's name, use the *Universal Naming Utility*. Using the *Universal Naming Utility*, you can globally search, and replace if desired, names, strings, and attachment value overrides for bound attachments. You define your search and then confine the search to specific objects within your models.

Menu	Toolbar	Explorer	Shortcut Key	Shortcut Menu
`Tools > Universal Naming Utility`	Application toolbar:	n/a	<CTRL + F>	n/a

Become an ER/Studio Hotshot:
Once your results come back from a search, you can highlight all or a subset of the returned entities and click `Create Submodel` to create a new submodel that contains just the highlighted entities. This is a great feature for quickly creating a submodel of just the area you are interested in, which is very useful for impact analysis.

The screen in Figure 4.8 appears. Let's replace any *Title* term on our model with the word *Book*. I will ignore whether it is upper or lower case (☑ Ignore Case) and I want to replace it everywhere the term appears, regardless of whether the entity is named *Title* or *Title Category*, so I make sure Whole Word is not checked.

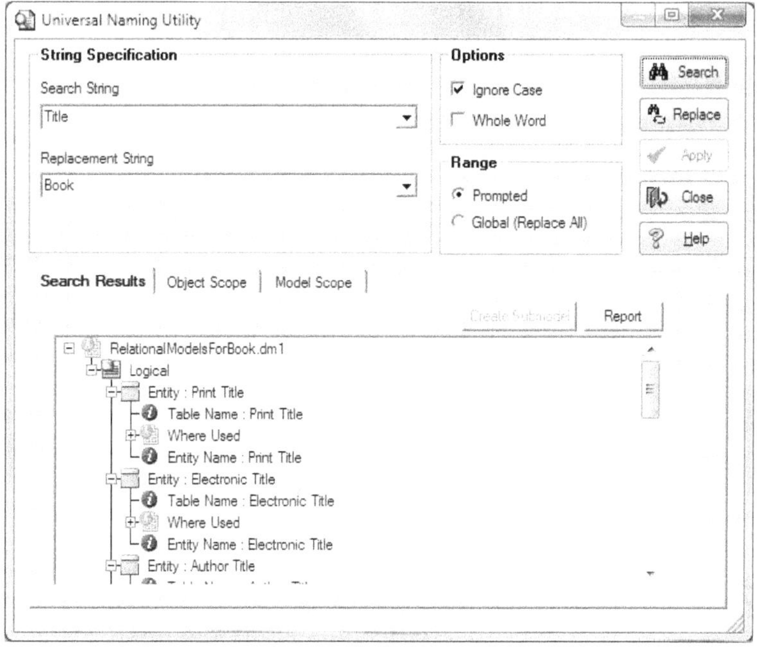

Figure 4.8 Universal Naming Utility results

This is an extremely powerful feature of ER/Studio as we can replace terms in attachments and throughout the entire model. You can even create a report of search results by clicking <Report>. RTF-formatted reports are ideal for print distribution, while HTML-formatted reports are better suited for browser viewing. More on reports in Chapter 13.

DELETING ENTITIES

Highlight the entity or entities you would like to delete and use one of the following options:

Menu	Toolbar	Explorer	Shortcut Key	Shortcut Menu
`Edit > Delete Entity`	Diagram toolbar:	Right-click on entity, `Delete Entity`	<DELETE> or <ALT + E>, then <D>	Right-click on entity, `Delete Entity`

Become an ER/Studio Hotshot:

- To select multiple entities for deletion, press and hold <CTRL> while clicking the entities or click and drag over the entities.
- Sometimes you will delete an entity and receive a message asking whether you would like to delete the entity from the entire data model or just the submodel. If you delete the entity just from the submodel, this entity will still exist in the model. More on submodels in the next chapter.

EXERCISE 4.1: CREATING ENTITIES

Technics Publications, the publisher we are modeling, publishes books and also organizes seminars and conferences. Create the following entities along with their definitions. Use the techniques taught in this chapter for resizing, coloring, font changing, moving, copying and pasting, etc., and also practice the undo feature (<CTRL + Z> for short).

Entity Name	Definition
Category	A subject that is of interest to a bookstore, wholesaler, reader, or attendee. For titles, categories are defined according to where the books should be placed on shelves (whether actual shelves or topics on a website). Examples include Database, Business Intelligence, and Data Modeling. For seminars and conferences, categories include the subject matter such as Agile Development or Data Modeling.
Language	The speech of a country, region, or group of people including its vocabulary, syntax, and grammar. Titles can be translated into different languages such as Japanese and Spanish, and training can be taught in different languages.
Speaker	The individual who will be teaching a seminar or presenting at a conference.
Conference	A forum for getting speakers and attendees together for discussing a topic of interest such as for data modeling and data warehousing.
Seminar	The training on a particular topic in a particular location on a particular date. Sometimes called a Class or Workshop such as the Advanced Data Modeling Workshop.
Offering	A generic way of referring to a title, conference, or seminar. An offering is a term for any product that Technics Publications sells.

Table 4.2 Create these entities

Each exercise builds on the prior one, so in the next chapter we will assign the entities from this exercise (plus the ones we created earlier in this chapter) to submodels.

Key Points

- An entity represents a collection of information about something that the business deems important and worthy of capture. An entity fits into one of several categories: who, what, when, where, why, or how. A noun or noun phrase identifies a specific entity. Entity instances are the occurrences or values of a particular entity.
- An entity can exist at the conceptual, logical, or physical level of detail.
- There are multiple ways to perform almost any action in ER/Studio.
- With the click of a button, you can arrange your entire diagram or a subset of entities using one of five types of layouts: circular, hierarchical, orthogonal, symmetric, and tree.
- Double-clicking on an entity brings up the edit window.
- Use text blocks to insert useful information into the diagram such as examples of an entity.
- Using the *Universal Naming Utility*, you can globally search (and replace, if desired) names, strings, and attachment value overrides for bound attachments.
- "Sticky buttons" are a great feature because we can create a lot of entities in very little time just by clicking. When you want to turn the sticky buttons feature off, just right-click on any white space and the cursor will return to its default selector symbol.

CHAPTER 5
Submodels

Model getting big?
Display in smaller pieces
Submodels make sense

Data models can be very large, so to maintain a useful communication tool, these large models need to be broken down into manageable chunks called submodels. This chapter will explain the submodel and show you how to work with submodels in ER/Studio.

SUBMODEL EXPLANATION

A submodel is a display of part of a data model. Submodels are used to make it easier to understand large complex data models. Someone may only be interested in seeing a subset of the model, so displaying the model in digestible pieces enhances communication. Just like we can create a folder on our computer and then add subfolders, we can create submodels within our larger model (and even submodels within submodels).

On the left side of Figure 5.1 is a typical Microsoft Windows file structure, and on the right side are ER/Studio submodels defined within a larger model. The submodel icon is a folder with a magnifying glass. Notice that in the submodel **Customers**, there are two nested submodels, **Direct** and **Indirect**.

When changing settings specific to a submodel such as the submodel's background color or model layout, only that submodel is impacted. When changing settings specific to an object on a submodel, such as changing an entity name, that entity name is changed everywhere (not just in the submodel). So for example, if we rename **Client** to **Customer** in one submodel, this entity will now be called **Customer** everywhere it appears and not just in that one submodel.

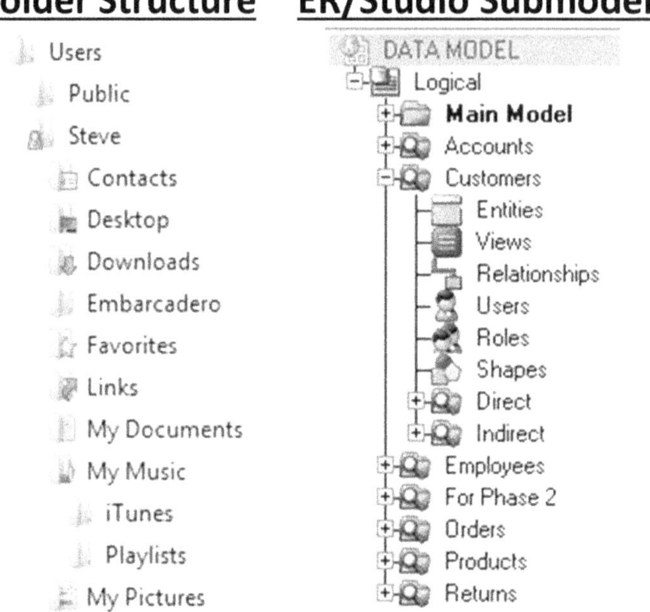

Figure 5.1 Comparing a folder structure with the submodel concept

SUBMODELS IN ER/STUDIO

When we create a data model, the **Main Model** submodel is also created. Think of the **Main Model** submodel as a holding area for everything that we create in our model. When we create a new submodel, only those objects we assign to that submodel will be displayed. When we create a new entity in that submodel, that entity will also exist in the **Main Model**.

CREATING SUBMODELS

Menu	Toolbar	Explorer	Shortcut Key	Shortcut Menu
`Model > Create Submodel…`		Right-click where submodel should be added, `Create Submodel…`	<ALT + M>, then <C>	Right-click on white space, `Create Submodel…`

Become an ER/Studio Hotshot:

- You can nest submodels within submodels. For example, we can have the **Transaction** submodel contain submodels **Order**, **Return**, and **Credit**. You can click and drag submodels to be included in another submodel just like dragging folders to create subfolders.
- A shortcut for creating a submodel with entities already in it is to highlight those entities you would like to have in the new submodel and then use one of the approaches above to create your submodel. You can highlight multiple entities by keeping the <CTRL> key depressed.
- ER/Studio automatically includes relationships between entities if related entities are part of the submodel. You can edit the submodel to include or exclude specific relationships.

Let's create the submodel **Title** by using one of these approaches. The *Create Submodel* screen should appear as in Figure 5.2.

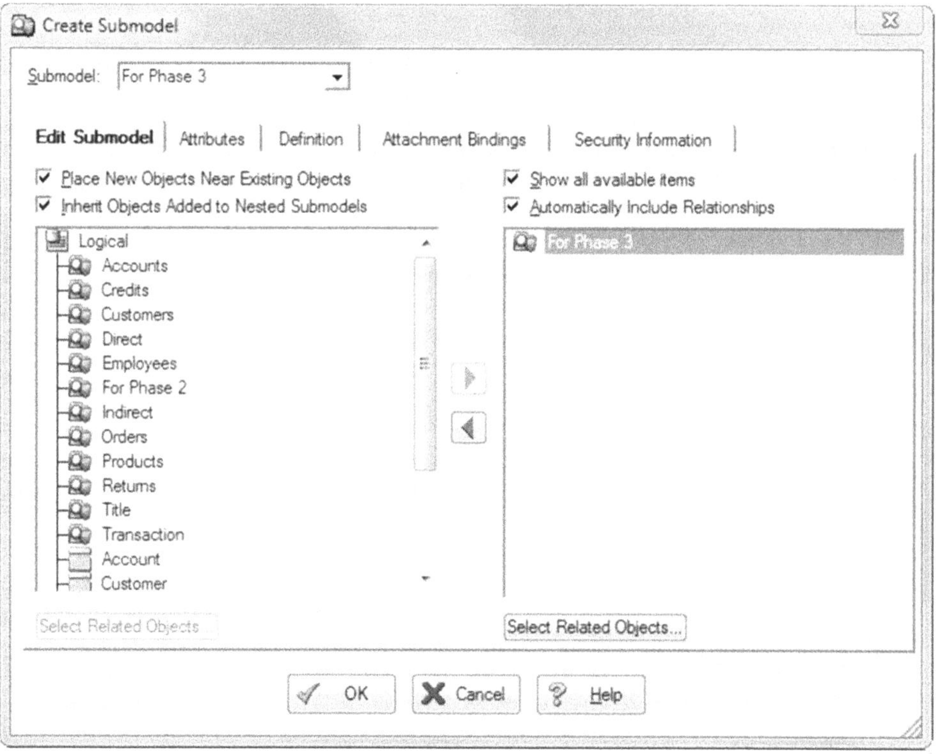

Figure 5.2 Create Submodel Screen

Note that this screen can be resized by clicking and dragging the lower right corner.

Choose the entities (or other submodels) you would like in the new submodel by highlighting in the left pane and clicking the icon. If you want to remove an item you have selected, highlight it in the right pane and click the icon. You can highlight multiple entities or submodels using the <SHIFT> or <CTRL> keys. There are several settings on this screen that are important to mention:

- `Place New Objects Near Existing Objects`, when checked, will place the entities you assign to the submodel near existing entities in this submodel (or towards the center of the submodel if there are no pre-existing entities in the submodel). If left unchecked, the entities will appear in the same positions they were in their source submodel.

- `Inherit Objects Added to Nested Submodels`, when checked, means if an entity is added to a nested submodel (the child), it will automatically be displayed in the parent submodel. So if the **Order** submodel is nested within the **Transaction** submodel, and we add the entity **Employee** to the **Order** submodel, the entity **Employee** will also be added to the **Transaction** submodel if this checkbox is selected.

- `Show all available items`, when checked, will show all possible submodels and entities that can be added to the submodel. When unchecked, only those entities and submodels that already have been assigned to the submodel will appear. That is, the source and target panes would contain the same objects when this feature is unchecked. Good idea to keep this one checked.

- `Automatically Include Relationships`, when checked, means all of the relationships associated with the entities you select will also be brought into the submodel. Good idea to leave this one checked too.

- `Select Related Objects...` allows you to bring in what is related to the entity in addition to the entity. I use this feature for a number of situations including when I want to see what is related to an entity or group of entities. It is also useful when I need to do a model review with a group of users in just one area, but I need to show the boundaries of that area. (That is, if I review the **Order** area, I would be interested in showing that orders connect to another area such as **Employee.**) The number `1` is set by default, meaning that only entities or submodels with direct relationships will be brought in. If you set this number to `2`, grandparents will be brought in as well as parents. For example, **if Order** is related to **Employee** and **Employee** is related to **Beneficiary**, both **Employee** and **Beneficiary** would be brought in. `Select Related Objects`... appears twice on this screen, so you have the option of selecting the parents, grandparents, etc., and then bringing them over using the left button. Alternately, you can first bring over the entities you need and then decide on the parents, grandparents, etc., using the right button.

There are four other tabs on the *Create Submodel* screen:

Tab	Here's what you need to know:
Attributes	Choose which attributes of the entities selected to include in the submodel. If you deselect an attribute, ER/Studio can display an ellipsis to indicate that not all attributes are displayed. I would advise using this feature only when the entity contains an extremely high number of attributes and, for readability, when displaying only a subset of attributes makes sense.
Definition	Enter a definition for the submodel.
Attribute Bindings	Bind an external piece of information, such as a Microsoft Word document or PDF file, to the submodel. Very useful for requirements documents, user stories, etc. Attachments are created in the Attachments folder of the Data Dictionary (discussed in Chapter 11) and must be added to the model before they will display on this tab.
Security Information	Change or view the current security information as defined in the Data Dictionary (discussed in Chapter 11).

Assign the entities **Title, Electronic Title,** and **Print Title** to the **Title** submodel. Click <OK> when done exploring each tab. The **Title** submodel is now created.

EDITING SUBMODELS

Menu	Toolbar	Explorer	Shortcut Key	Shortcut Menu
`Model > Edit Submodel…`	n/a	Right-click on submodel, `Edit Submodel…`	<ALT + M>, then <E>	Right-click on white space, `Edit Submodel…`

Become an ER/Studio Hotshot:

- You can also add a comment to a model or submodel by highlighting the model or submodel in Explorer and clicking on the Application toolbar. Comments can be used to capture the current state of the model, outstanding issues, the audience for the diagram, etc. If you are using the Repository, comments can be viewed by all ER/Studio users.

You can also easily change the background color on a submodel:

Menu	Toolbar	Explorer	Shortcut Key	Shortcut Menu
`Format > Colors & Fonts`	Diagram toolbar:	n/a	<ALT + O>, then <C>	Right-click on white space, `Colors & Fonts`

Choose `Model Background` from the drop-down list (or click anywhere in the white space within this window to bring up `Model Background` in the drop-down list) and click <Set Color> to select the color you would like. Click <OK> to exit this screen and apply your changes.

MOVING SUBMODELS

To assist you in analyzing your data model, you can move submodels from one model to another. You can also move submodels to nest them within other submodels. On the *Main* toolbar, click the *Selection* tool (the arrow). In the *Data Model Explorer*, click the submodel you want to move and then drag it to another model or submodel.

DELETING SUBMODELS

Menu	Toolbar	Explorer	Shortcut Key	Shortcut Menu
`Model > Delete Submodel…`	n/a	Right-click on submodel to delete and choose `Delete Submodel`	<ALT + M>, then <D>	n/a

EXERCISE 5.1: CHANGING SETTINGS IN SUBMODELS

Play with submodels and fill in the following spreadsheet, which captures which settings are specific to a given submodel and which settings apply to the model in its entirety. For each setting, put an 'x' in the "Applied to only submodel" column if changing this setting only impacts the submodel, and put an 'x' in the "Applied to entire model" column if changing this setting will impact the entire data model. See Appendix for answers.

Setting	Applied to only submodel	Applied to entire model
Changing submodel's background color		
Changing an entity's name		
Changing an entity's background color		
Resizing an entity		
Creating an entity		
Deleting an entity		
Rearranging entities		

EXERCISE 5.2: CREATING THREE MORE SUBMODELS

Create three more submodels for our publisher design: **Offerings**, **Conferences**, and **Seminars**. The **Offering** submodel will contain everything in our model, and the **Conferences** and **Seminars** submodels will contain subsets, as shown in Table 5.1.

Assign to this submodel...	These entities
Offerings	**Offering** **Title** **Electronic Title** **Print Title** **Category** **Conference** **Seminar** **Speaker**
Conferences	**Conference** **Speaker**
Seminars	**Seminar** **Speaker**

Table 5.1 Assignment of Entities to Submodels

EXERCISE 5.3: CREATING TITLE BLOCKS FOR EACH SUBMODEL

Create a *Title Block* for each of the four submodels (the **Title** submodel created earlier in this chapter and the three from the previous exercise). The *Title Block* provides important identification information about your model or submodel that by default includes the project name, file name, submodel, version, modification date, and copyright.

Menu	Toolbar	Explorer	Shortcut Key	Shortcut Menu
`Insert > Title Block`	Drawing Shapes toolbar:	n/a	<ALT + I>, then <B>	Right-click on white space, `Insert Title Block`

Become an ER/Studio Hotshot:
ER/Studio supports "sticky buttons," meaning you can create many occurrences of an object and then, when you are done, right-click on any white space to return the cursor to the default selector symbol.

Key Points

- A submodel is a display of part of a data model. Submodels are used to make it easier to understand large, complex data models.
- Submodels are organized very similar to the file structure in Microsoft Word.
- When changing model aesthetics in a submodel, such as the submodel's background color or model layout, only that submodel is impacted. When changing model content in a submodel, such as renaming an entity, that entity name is renamed everywhere (not just in the submodel).
- You can nest submodels within submodels.

CHAPTER 6
Attributes and Domains

Spreadsheets have columns
Similar to attributes
Measure and describe

This chapter defines an attribute and defines keys, distinguishing between candidate, primary, surrogate, foreign, and alternate keys. Domains are also discussed in this chapter. We will practice creating and editing attributes, keys, and domains in ER/Studio.

ATTRIBUTE EXPLANATION

An attribute is an elementary piece of information of importance to the business that identifies, describes, or measures instances of an entity. The attribute **Claim Number** identifies each claim. The attribute **Student Last Name** describes the last name of each student. The attribute **Gross Sales Amount** measures the monetary value of a transaction. Returning to our spreadsheet analogy from Chapter 4, the column headings on a spreadsheet are attributes. The cells beneath each column heading are the values for that column heading. Attributes can be thought of as the column headings in a spreadsheet, the fields on a form, or the labels on a report. **Author Last Name** and **Title ISBN** are examples of attributes from our publishing data model.

ATTRIBUTE TYPES

As with entities, attributes can exist at conceptual, logical, and physical levels. An attribute at the conceptual level must be a concept both basic and critical to the business. We do not usually think of attributes as concepts, but depending on the business need, they can be. When I worked for a telecommunications company, **Phone Number** was an attribute so important to the business that it was represented on a number of conceptual data models.

An attribute on a logical data model represents a business property. Each attribute shown contributes to the business solution and is independent of any technology including software and hardware. For example, **Author Last Name** is an attribute because it has business significance regardless of whether records are kept in a paper file or within the fastest database out there. An attribute on a physical data model represents a database column. The attribute **Author Last Name** might be represented as the column **AUTH_LAST_NM** within the RDBMS table **AUTH** or represented as the field name **AuthorLastName** in the MongoDB collection **LibraryCardCatalog**.

ATTRIBUTES IN ER/STUDIO

In this section we will practice creating and modifying attributes for the publishing data model.

CREATING ATTRIBUTES

Highlight the entity where you would like to create attributes and use one of these techniques:

Menu	Toolbar	Explorer	Shortcut Key	Shortcut Menu
`Edit > Edit Entity...`	n/a	Right-click on entity, `New Attribute`	<ALT + E>, then <E> Or Double-click on the entity	Right-click on entity, `Edit Entity`

Become an ER/Studio Hotshot:

- If you are using domains in your data model, you can click and drag a domain into an entity to create a new attribute. We will explain domains later in this chapter and show you how to create and manage them in Chapter 11, Data Dictionary.
- The status bar at the bottom of the screen shows the number of attributes in the model or submodel. You can hide or show this status bar using `View > Status Bar` or <ALT + V>, then <S>.

Any of these approaches brings up the *Entity Editor* screen. Make sure you are on the *Attributes* tab and click <Add> to create a new attribute. Figure 6.1

contains the most important section of the *Entity Editor* screen, followed by a description of each property.

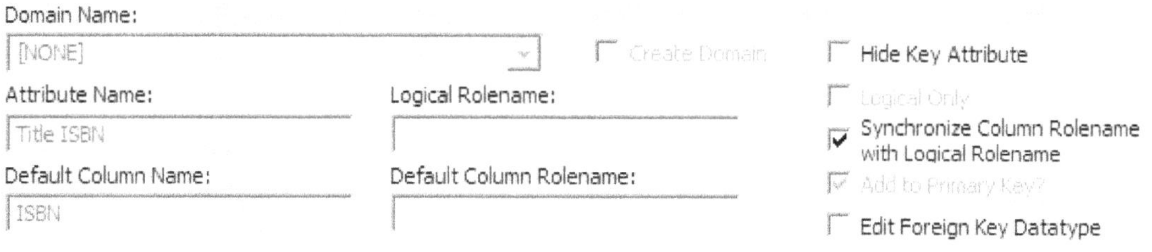

Domain Name: [NONE]
Create Domain
Hide Key Attribute
Attribute Name: Title ISBN
Logical Rolename:
Logical Only
Synchronize Column Rolename with Logical Rolename
Default Column Name: ISBN
Default Column Rolename:
Add to Primary Key?
Edit Foreign Key Datatype

Figure 6.1 New Attribute screen

- **Domain Name dropdown**. Lists all defined domains. You can assign any available domain to an attribute. More on domains later in this chapter.

- **Create Domain checkbox**. Allows you to create a new domain that is automatically added to the Data Dictionary. This checkbox will become active once a domain name is entered where it says `[NONE]`.

- **Attribute Name**. The full name that will appear on the data model for the attribute.

- **Logical Rolename**. Sometimes on a logical data model, there is a need to give a foreign key a different name than its primary key. The name you type in here will be the name of the foreign key. Foreign keys will be explained shortly in this chapter.

- **Default Column Name**. The column name on the physical data model is, by default, the same name as the attribute name on the logical data model (logical data models are discussed in Chapter 9, and physical data models are discussed in Chapter 10). If you want the physical column name to be different than the logical attribute name, type a new column name in the box. ER/Studio uses this name when generating the physical data model.

- **Default Column Rolename**. Sometimes on a physical data model, there is a need to give a foreign key a different name than the primary key it comes from. Primary and foreign keys will be explained shortly in this chapter. The name you type in here will be the name of the foreign key.

- **Hide Key Attribute checkbox**. Although not a recommended practice because it can impact the integrity of the database design, ER/Studio does give you the option of creating a partial key relationship. When a relationship is defined between two entities, the primary key of one of the entities (the parent) is propagated to the other entity (the child) as a foreign key. Sometimes these keys can be cumbersome in terms of size or complexity. A partial key relationship is when only part of the primary key (a subset of attributes) is propagated as the foreign key (instead of the whole primary key). By clicking this checkbox, the attribute will be hidden in the child entity. It will display as unavailable when editing the child table, but you can make it available again later by unclicking this checkbox.

- **Logical Only checkbox**. If selected, the attribute will not be implemented as a column when generating a physical data model. This can be useful when logically modeling future phases of a project.

- **Synchronize Column Rolename with Logical Rolename checkbox**. Available when the attribute selected is a foreign key. Allows you to change the role names of foreign attributes or columns to the same names as other attributes or columns in the same entity or table. Duplicates will be unified when the user ends the edit session.

- **Add to Primary Key? checkbox**. When chosen, adds the selected attribute to the entity's primary key.

- **Edit Foreign Key Datatype checkbox**. When selected for a child object, you can edit the datatype values of the foreign key. When this option is selected, changes made to this relationship in the parent are not propagated to the child until you deselect this option, preserving the foreign key overrides.

Figure 6.2 contains the tabs section of the Attributes section of the *Entity Editor* screen.

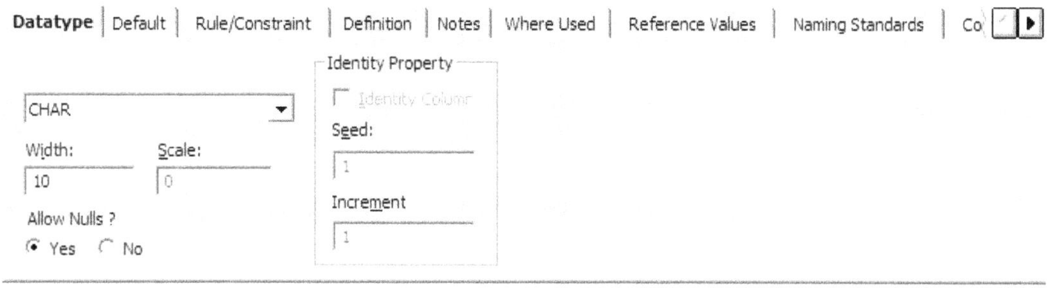

Figure 6.2 Attribute Tabs

Clicking the ▶ icon allows you to move the tabs to the right to navigate through all 14 tabs.

Tab	Here's what you need to know:
Datatype	Choose the format (e.g., character, date, decimal) and width (also called "length") of the attribute as well as whether the attribute is required (`Allow Nulls?` set to `No`) or optional (`Allow Nulls?` set to `Yes`). `Scale` is used for decimal formats to define how many places there should be to the right of the decimal point. The `Identity Property` settings is useful when you have a counter as the primary key. Click `Identity Column`; `Seed` then allows you to decide the starting number while `Increment` determines how much to add to that number each time an instance is created. For example, if **Customer** is identified by **Customer ID**, which you define as an identity column (click the `Identity Column` checkbox), by entering a `Seed` of `5` and an `Increment` of `15`, the first customer will have a **Customer ID** value of `5`, the second customer a value of `20`, the third a value of `35`, etc.
Default	We can assign a default value to this attribute that will be carried through to the data definition language to build the database. We can enter a default value here or use a default value as defined in the Data Dictionary, which will be discussed in Chapter 11.
Rule/Constraint	We can assign a constraint to this attribute that will be carried through to the data definition language to build the database. We can enter a constraint here or use a constraint as defined in the Data Dictionary.

Tab	Here's what you need to know:
Definition	This is where the full definition for the attribute is stored. If the target database supports it, ER/Studio adds this definition as an attribute comment when generating SQL code. The macro **Definition Editor** allows for easily entering definitions for multiple objects. More on macros in Chapter 16.
Notes	Use this for any other text outside the definition such as questions to ask business experts, known issues, or action items. HTML tags used in *Notes* will be applied as formatting in the HTML reports. The macro **Notes Editor** allows for easily entering notes for multiple objects. More on macros in Chapter 16.
Where Used	See which logical and physical data models and submodels contain the attribute. From this tab you can edit mappings and user-defined mappings.
Reference Values	Reference values are attributes that define allowed data. They represent look-up table columns, code-value ranges, or a rule or constraint applied to a column. Reference values can be defined as a range of values or as an itemized list. You can bind the attribute to a reference value on this tab.
Naming Standards	Allows you to apply different naming standards to different objects when portions of a model require different versions of a standard. For example, some objects already exist in the database and you may not want to apply a newer naming standard to them. The `Freeze Names` option, when selected, prevents any naming standards applied to the model from changing the name of the attribute selected. We'll talk more about this tab in Chapter 14, Naming Standards.
Compare Options	Select which, if any, properties (e.g., datatype, domain, nullability) of the attribute to ignore when comparing this attribute to another using the *Compare and Merge Utility*, which will be discussed in Chapter 15.
Data Lineage	Map the rules from source to target attributes in the model. We'll cover this tab in Chapter 12, Data Lineage.
Security Information	You can assign security settings that are defined in the Data Dictionary to this attribute. The Data Dictionary will be discussed in Chapter 11.

Tab	Here's what you need to know:
Attachment Bindings	Bind an external piece of information, such as a Microsoft Word document or PDF file, to the attribute. Very useful for requirements documents, user stories, etc. Attachments are created in the Attachments folder of the Data Dictionary and must be added to the model before they will display on this tab.
Data Movement Rules	We can assign a data movement rule to this attribute and it will be carried through to the data definition language to build the database. We can enter a data movement rule here or use a data movement rule as defined on the lineage tab, which will be discussed in Chapter 12.

EDITING ATTRIBUTES

Highlight the entity where you would like to edit attributes and use one of these techniques:

Menu	Toolbar	Explorer	Shortcut Key	Shortcut Menu
`Edit > Edit Entity…`	n/a	Right-click on entity, `Edit Entity…`	<ALT + E>, then <E> Or Double-click on the entity	Right-click on entity, `Edit Entity`

Any of these approaches brings up the *Entity Editor* screen. Make sure you are on the *Attributes* tab and highlight the attribute you would like to edit and click <Edit>.

MOVING ATTRIBUTES

Click on the attribute selection tool on the *Diagram Toolbar* and then click on and drag an attribute to move it to another location within that entity or to another entity. You can also move attributes up or down by using the Up and Down buttons in the *Entity Editor* on the *Attributes* tab.

The *Diagram and Object Display Options* screen (invoked either through `View > Diagram And Object Display Options` or on the `Diagram` toolbar) contains the *Logical Attribute Order* radio button. When selected, the primary key of the entity displays at the top. The other attributes display in the order designated in the *Entity Editor* of the corresponding entity.

DEFINING ATTRIBUTES

In the *Entity Editor* on the *Attributes* tab, there are a set of smaller tabs on the bottom of the screen. Click on the black right arrow to navigate over to the *Definition* tab. You can write your definition here.

The macro **Definition Editor** allows for easily entering definitions for multiple objects. More on macros in Chapter 16.

CHANGING THE APPEARANCE OF ATTRIBUTES

Using certain colors and fonts can help call attention to attributes. Highlight the entity where you would like to change the appearance of one or more attributes and use one of these commands:

Menu	Toolbar	Explorer	Shortcut Key	Shortcut Menu
`Format > Entity Color and Font Settings`	n/a	Right-click on entity, `Entity Color and Font Settings`	<ALT + O>, click on `Entity Color and Font Settings`	Right-click on entity, `Entity Color and Font Settings`

After applying one of the commands above, choose `Entity/Attributes Colors and Fonts`. From the *Category* section of this screen, you can choose types of attributes, such as primary keys, and then click <Set Color> and <Set Font>. Click <OK> to exit the screen.

There is a very quick way to change the color of all attributes at once:

Menu	Toolbar	Explorer	Shortcut Key	Shortcut Menu
`Format > Colors & Fonts`	Diagram toolbar:	n/a	<ALT + O>, then <C>	Right-click on white space, `Colors & Fonts`

Click on the type of attribute (e.g. `Key`, `Attribute`, `Trigger`) in the *Entity* box, or choose the appropriate type of attribute from the drop-down and click <Set Color> to select the color you would like. Click <OK> to exit this screen and apply your changes.

You can display various properties of the attributes (such as domain and nullability) under *Options*:

Menu	Toolbar	Explorer	Shortcut Key	Shortcut Menu
`Tools > Options`	n/a	n/a	<ALT + T>, then <P>	n/a

Then select the *Display* tab.

The *Display Mode:* drop-down allows you to select what should be displayed within the entity boxes. The options for attributes are:

- `Attribute (Model Order)`. Displays the entities and all their attributes in the default order according to the model type. In the logical data model, for example, the attributes appear as they normally would in a logical data model, primary keys first.

- `Attribute (Logical Order)`. Displays the entities and all their attributes in `Logical Order` regardless of whether you are viewing the logical or physical data model. When the attributes are in `Logical Order`, ER/Studio sequences the attributes so that the primary keys are always on top.

- `Attribute (Physical Order)`. Displays the entities and all their attributes in `Physical Order` regardless of whether you are viewing the logical or physical data model. When the attributes are in `Physical Order`, ER/Studio sequences the attributes to reflect their order in the physical data model without regard to whether the primary keys are on top or not.

COPYING ATTRIBUTES

Highlight the attribute you would like to copy using the attribute selection tool and then choose one of these commands:

Menu	Toolbar	Explorer	Shortcut Key	Shortcut Menu
`Edit > Copy`, then `Edit > Paste`	Diagram toolbar: (copy), then (paste)	Drag attributes to the desired entity in the *Data Model Window*	<CTRL + C> then <CTRL + V> **or** <ALT + E>, then <C> for copy, <ALT + E>, then <P> for paste	n/a

Become an ER/Studio Hotshot:

- An easy way to copy attributes is to click on the attribute selection tool on the *Diagram Toolbar* and then highlight the attribute you would like to copy from the source entity. Press the <CTRL> key while clicking and dragging the attribute to the target entity. Release the mouse button and you will see that the attribute was copied. If you would like to copy more than one attribute, you can highlight multiple attributes on the source entity by keeping the <CTRL> key pressed while you click on attributes, or to copy several attributes in a row, you can highlight the first attribute and then hold down the <SHIFT> key while pressing the last attribute. This will highlight several attributes at once.
- You can also cut and paste by using the icon on the Diagram toolbar.

A copy of the attribute is created with the same name as the original if the attribute has been copied to a different entity. If the attribute has been copied to the same entity, a number suffix will be added (such as **Title_Name_1** if **Title_Name** is copied to the same entity) to prevent duplicate attribute names from occurring in the same entity.

FINDING ATTRIBUTES

Recall our discussion on finding entities in Chapter 4 using the *Universal Naming Utility*. Using the *Universal Naming Utility*, you can globally search and replace, if desired, names, strings, and attachment value overrides for bound attachments. You define your search and then confine the search to specific attributes within your models.

Menu	Toolbar	Explorer	Shortcut Key	Shortcut Menu
`Tools > Universal Naming Utility`	Application toolbar:	n/a	<CTRL + F>	n/a

DELETING ATTRIBUTES

Highlight the attribute or attributes you would like to delete and use one of the following options:

Menu	Toolbar	Explorer	Shortcut Key	Shortcut Menu
`Edit > Delete Attribute`	Diagram toolbar:	Right-click on attribute, `Delete Attribute`	<DELETE> or <ALT + E>, then <D>	n/a

Become an ER/Studio Hotshot:

- You can also double-click the parent entity or table in the *Data Model Window* to bring up the entity or table editor. In the editor, you can select the attribute to delete and then click <Delete>.
- All of these options to delete an attribute will display a final warning message ("Are you sure you want to delete?"), with the exception of using the cut icon on the Diagram toolbar, which will delete the attribute without a final warning.

EXERCISE 6.1: CREATING ATTRIBUTES

In the previous chapter we assigned entities to submodels. For this exercise, add the following attributes to each of these entities as shown in Table 6.1.

Create in this entity...	These attributes
Offering	**Offering ID** **Offering Name** **Offering Price Amount**
Title	**ISBN** **Subtitle Name**

Electronic Title	**Title Instant Download Indicator**
Print Title	**Title Page Count**
Category	**Category Code** **Category Name**
Conference	**Conference Hotel Name** **Conference Start Date** **Conference End Date**
Seminar	**Seminar Start Date** **Seminar End Date**
Speaker	**Speaker Tax ID** **Speaker First Name** **Speaker Last Name**

Table 6.1 Assignment of Entities to Submodels

As an aside, on your data models you may notice bitmaps next to each attribute to the left of each name such as a diamond symbol. You can turn these bitmaps on and off through *Diagram and Object Display Options*. Choose *View > Diagram And Object Display Options* (or click on the icon) and click on or off `Attribute Bitmaps` on the *Entity* tab.

KEY EXPLANATION

There is a lot of data out there, but how do you sift through it all to find what you're looking for? That's where keys come in. A key is one or more attributes whose purposes include enforcing rules, efficiently retrieving data, and allowing navigation from one entity to another. This section defines candidate, primary, and alternate keys. Surrogate keys, foreign keys, and their importance are also explained. You will be creating and editing each type in ER/Studio.

CANDIDATE KEY

A candidate key is one or more attributes that uniquely identify an entity instance. An **ISBN** (International Standard Book Number) is assigned to every title. The **ISBN** uniquely identifies each title and is therefore the title's candidate key. When the **ISBN** for this title, `9781634620925`, is entered into many search engines and database systems, the book entity instance `Data Modeling Made Simple With Embarcadero ER/Studio` will be returned (try it!). **Tax ID** can be a candidate key for an organization in some countries such as the United States. **Account Code** can be a candidate key for an account. A **VIN** (Vehicle Identification Number) identifies a vehicle.

Sometimes a single attribute identifies an entity instance such as **ISBN** for a title. Sometimes it takes more than one attribute to uniquely identify an entity instance. For example, both a **Promotion Type Code** and **Promotion Start Date** may be necessary to identify a promotion. When more than one attribute makes up a key, we use the term *composite key*. Therefore, **Promotion Type Code** and **Promotion Start Date** together are a composite candidate key for a promotion.

A candidate key has four main characteristics:

- **Unique**. A candidate key value must not identify more than one entity instance (or one real-world thing).
- **Mandatory**. A candidate key may not be empty (also known as *nullable*). Each entity instance must be identified by exactly one candidate key value. Therefore, the number of distinct values of a candidate key is always equal to the number of distinct entity instances. If the entity **Title** has **ISBN** as its candidate key, and if there are 500 title instances, there will also be 500 unique ISBNs.
- **Non-volatile**. A candidate key value on an entity instance should never change.
- **Minimal**. A candidate key should contain only those attributes that are needed to uniquely identify an entity instance. If four attributes are listed as the composite candidate key for an entity, but only three are really needed for uniqueness, then only those three should make up the candidate key.

Figure 6.3 contains a data model before candidate keys have been identified.

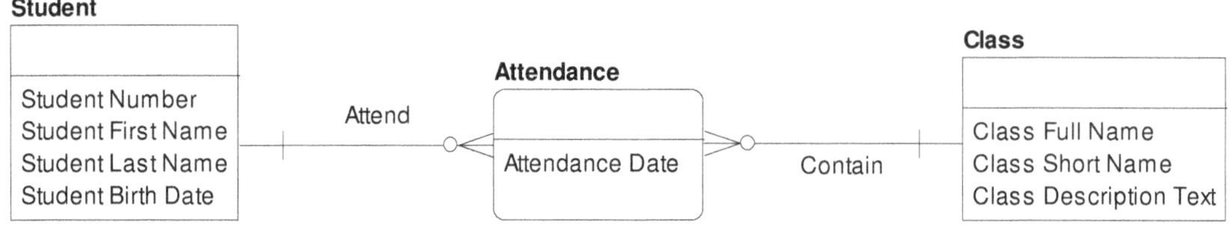

Each **Student** may attend one or many **Classes**.
Each **Class** may contain one or many **Students**.

Figure 6.3 Data model before candidate keys have been identified

Note that we have a many-to-many relationship between **Student** and **Class** that was replaced by the entity **Attendance** and two one-to-many relationships (more on this in our normalization section). In reading a many-to-many relationship, I have found it helpful to ignore the entity in the middle (**Attendance**, in this example) and just read the labels between the entities on either side. For example, each **Student** may attend one or many **Classes** and each **Class** may contain one or many **Students**. Table 6.2 contains sample values for each of these entities.

Student

Student Number	Student First Name	Student Last Name	Student Birth Date
SM385932	Steve	Martin	1/25/1958
EM584926	Eddie	Murphy	3/15/1971
HW742615	Henry	Winkler	2/14/1984
MM481526	Mickey	Mouse	5/10/1982
DD857111	Donald	Duck	5/10/1982
MM573483	Minnie	Mouse	4/1/1986
LR731511	Lone	Ranger	10/21/1949
EM876253	Eddie	Murphy	7/1/1992

Attendance

Attendance Date
5/10/2015
6/10/2015
7/10/2015

Class

Class Full Name	Class Short Name	Class Description Text
Data Modeling Fundamentals	Data Modeling 101	An introductory class covering basic data modeling concepts and principles.
Advanced Data Modeling	Data Modeling 301	A fast-paced class covering techniques such as advanced normalization and ragged hierarchies.
Tennis Basics	Tennis One	For those new to the game of tennis, learn the key aspects of the game.
Juggling		Learn how to keep three balls in the air at once!

Table 6.2 Sample values for Figure 6.3

Based on our definition of a candidate key and a candidate key's characteristics of being unique, non-volatile, and minimal, what would you choose as the candidate keys for each of these entities?

For **Student**, **Student Number** appears to be a valid candidate key. There are eight students and eight distinct values for **Student Number**. So unlike **Student First Name** and **Student Last Name**, which can contain duplicates like `Eddie Murphy`, **Student Number** appears to be unique. **Student Birth Date** can also contain duplicates such as `5/10/1982`, which is the **Student Birth Date** for both `Mickey Mouse` and `Donald Duck`. However, the combination of **Student First Name**, **Student Last Name**, and **Student Birth Date** may make a valid composite candidate key.

For **Attendance**, we are currently missing a candidate key. Although the **Attendance Date** is unique in our sample data, we will probably need to know which student attended which class on this particular date.

For **Class**, on first glance it appears that any of its attributes are unique, and would therefore qualify as a candidate key. However, `Juggling` does not have a **Class Short Name**. Therefore, because **Class Short Name** can be empty, we cannot consider it a candidate key. In addition, one of the characteristics of a candidate key is that it is non-volatile. I know, based on my teaching experience, that class descriptions can change. Therefore, **Class Description**

Text also needs to be ruled out as a candidate key, leaving **Class Full Name** as the best option for a candidate key.

PRIMARY AND ALTERNATE KEYS

Even though an entity may contain more than one candidate key, we can only select one candidate key to be the primary key for an entity. A primary key is the candidate key that has been chosen to be *the* unique identifier for an entity. An alternate key is a candidate key that, although unique, was not chosen as the primary key but still can be used to find specific entity instances.

We have only one candidate key in the **Class** entity, so **Class Full Name** becomes our primary key. We have to make a choice in **Student**, however, because we have two candidate keys. Which **Student** candidate key would you choose as the primary key?

In selecting one candidate key over another as the primary key, consider succinctness and privacy. Succinctness means if there are several candidate keys, choose the one with the fewest attributes or shortest length. In terms of privacy, it is possible that one or morc attributes within a candidate key will contain sensitive data whose viewing should be restricted. We want to avoid having sensitive data in our entity's primary key because the primary key can propagate as a foreign key and therefore spread this sensitive data throughout our database.

Considering succinctness and privacy in our example, I would choose **Student Number** over the composite **Student First Name**, **Student Last Name**, and **Student Birth Date**. It is more succinct and contains less sensitive data. Figure 6.4 shows our data model updated with primary and alternate keys.

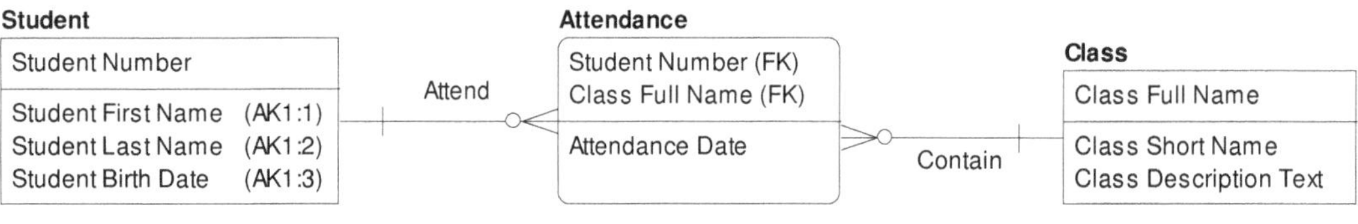

Figure 6.4 Data model updated with primary and alternate keys

In ER/Studio, primary key attributes are shown above the line in the rectangles. You will notice two numbers following the key abbreviations such as "AK." The first number is the grouping number for an alternate key, and the second number is the ordering of the attribute within the alternate key. So there are three attributes required for the **Student** alternate key: **Student First Name**, **Student Last Name**, and **Student Birth Date**. This is also the order in which the alternate key index will be created, because **Student First Name** has a "1" after the colon, **Student Last Name** a "2," and **Student Birth Date** a "3."

Attendance now has as its primary key **Student Number** and **Class Full Name**, which appear to make a valid primary key.

So to summarize, a candidate key consists of one or more attributes that uniquely identify an entity instance. The candidate key that is determined to be the best way to identify each unique record in the entity becomes the primary key. The other candidate keys become alternate keys. Keys containing more than one attribute are known as composite keys.

In the next chapter, on relationships, we will distinguish independent and dependent entities. In this student data model, we see examples of these two types of entities. Independent entities are rectangles that have in their primary key only attributes that they own (such as **Student** and **Class** in this example), and dependent entities are *bub-tangles* (rectangles with rounded corners) that have in their primary key at least one primary key from another entity. In the case of **Attendance**, the only way we can identify **Attendance Date** is by knowing which **Student** has attended a particular **Class**.

SURROGATE KEY

A surrogate key is a unique identifier for a table, often a counter and always system-generated without intelligence, meaning a surrogate key contains values whose meanings are unrelated to the entities they identify. (In other words, you can't look at a month identifier of `1` and assume that it represents the **Month** entity instance value of `January`.) Surrogate keys should not be visible to the business. They remain behind the scenes to help maintain uniqueness, allow for more efficient navigation across structures, and facilitate integration across applications.

Surrogate keys are also efficient. You've seen that a primary key may be composed of one or more attributes of the entity. A single surrogate key is more efficient to use than having to specify three or four (or five or six) attributes to locate the single record you're looking for. Surrogate keys are useful for integration, which is an effort to create a single, consistent version of the data. Applications such as data warehouses often house data from more than one application or system. Surrogate keys enable us to bring together information about the same entity instance that is identified differently in each source system.

When using a surrogate key, always make an effort to determine the natural key, which is what the business would consider to be the way to uniquely identify the entity, and then define an alternate key on this natural key. For example, assuming a surrogate key is a more efficient primary key than **Class Full Name**, we can create the surrogate key **Class ID** for **Class** and define an alternate key on **Class Full Name** as shown in Figure 6.5. Table 6.3 contains the values in **Class**.

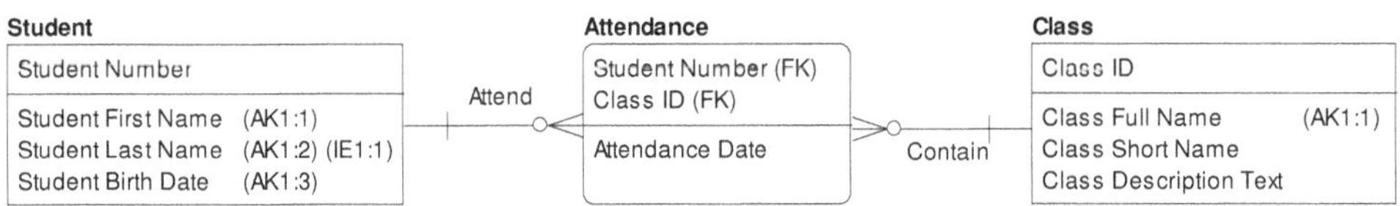

Figure 6.5 Data model updated with surrogate key on Class

Class ID	Class Full Name	Class Short Name	Class Description Text
1	Data Modeling Fundamentals	Data Modeling 101	An introductory class covering basic data modeling concepts and principles.
2	Advanced Data Modeling	Data Modeling 301	A fast-paced class covering techniques such as advanced normalization and ragged hierarchies.
3	Tennis Basics	Tennis One	For those new to the game of tennis, learn the key aspects of the game.
4	Juggling		Learn how to keep three balls in the air at once!

Table 6.3 Class values updated with a surrogate key

FOREIGN KEY

A foreign key is one or more attributes that provide a link to another entity. A foreign key allows a database management system to navigate from one structure to another. For example, if we need to know the customer who owns an account, we would want to include the **Customer ID** in the **Account** entity. The **Customer ID** in **Account** is the primary key for **Customer**. Using this foreign key back to **Customer** enables the database management system to navigate from a particular account or accounts to the customer or customers that own each account. Likewise, the database can navigate from a particular customer or customers to find all of their accounts. A foreign key is automatically created when we define a relationship between two entities (relationships will be covered in the next chapter).

In Figure 6.5, there are two foreign keys in **Attendance**. The **Student Number** foreign key points back to a particular student in the **Student** entity. The **Class ID** foreign key points back to a particular **Class** in the **Class** entity. Table 6.4 contains a few **Attendance** entity instances.

Student Number	Class ID	Attendance Date
SM385932	1	5/10/2015
EM584926	1	5/10/2015
EM584926	2	6/10/2015
MM481526	2	6/10/2015
MM573483	2	6/10/2015
LR731511	3	7/10/2015

Table 6.4 Attendance entity instances

By looking at these values and recalling the sample values from Table 6.4, we learn that `Steve Martin` and `Eddie Murphy` both attended the `Data Modeling Fundamentals` class on `5/10/2015`. `Eddie Murphy` also attended the `Advanced Data Modeling Class` with `Mickey` and `Minnie Mouse` on `6/10/2015`. `Lone Ranger` took `Tennis Basics` (by himself, as usual) on `7/10/2015`.

INVERSION ENTRY

Sometimes there is a need to retrieve data rapidly from a structure to answer a business query or meet a certain response time. An inversion entry (IE for short) is a key which allows quick access to those columns in the key. An IE is also known as a secondary key or non-unique index. For example, in Figure 6.5 we added an IE to **Student Last Name** in **Student** to allow for quick retrieval whenever any queries require **Student Last Name**.

EXERCISE 6.2: CLARIFYING CUSTOMER ID

During a recent training class, I was showing examples of both complete and incomplete definitions and shared the following incomplete definition for **Customer ID**: *A **Customer ID** is the unique identifier for a Customer.*

"What else can you say about **Customer ID** anyway?" a participant asked.

What else can you say about **Customer ID** (or any identifier) to add more meaning to its definition? See Appendix B for my answers.

KEYS IN ER/STUDIO

In this section we will practice creating and modifying keys for our publishing data model.

CREATING A KEY

Highlight the entity where you would like to create a key and use one of these commands:

Menu	Toolbar	Explorer	Shortcut Key	Shortcut Menu
`Edit > Edit Entity…`	n/a	Right-click on entity, `Edit Entity…`	<ALT + E>, then <E> Or Double-click on the entity	Right-click on entity, `Edit Entity`

> **Become an ER/Studio Hotshot:**
> There are two quick shortcuts for creating primary keys. In the *Attributes* tab there is an Add to Primary Key? checkbox. You can also use the attribute selection tool to click and drag attributes into (and out of) the primary key space.

Any of these approaches brings up the *Entity Editor* screen. Make sure you are on the *Keys* tab. Keys are defined only on existing attributes, so make sure there is at least one attribute in the entity we are editing. Click <Add> to create a new key. If creating alternate keys or inversion entries, use the radio buttons to decide which type of key it is, give it a name, and then select those attributes that should be part of the key as shown in Figure 6.6.

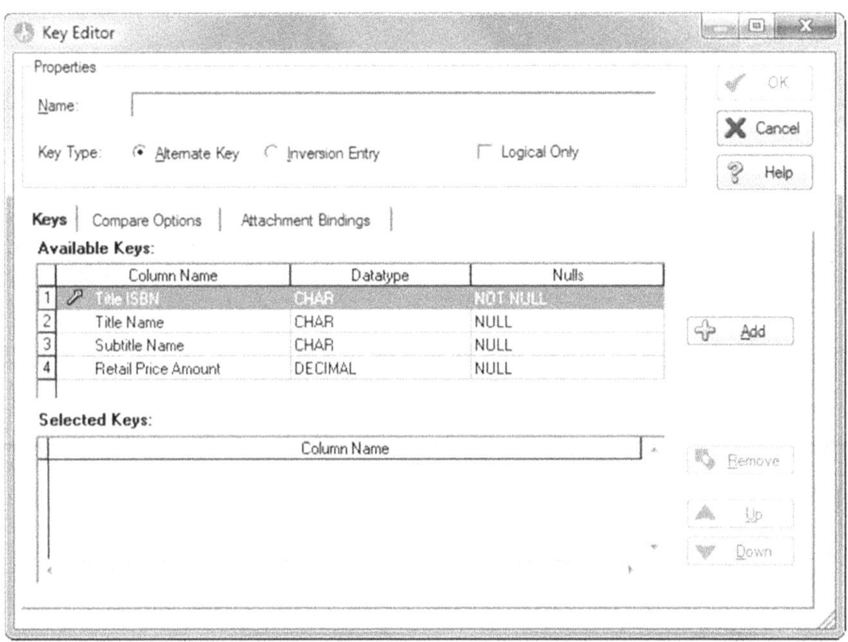

Figure 6.6 Key Editor screen

The `Key Type` section on this screen allows you to select whether you are creating an alternate key or inversion entry as well as if you would like to prevent a key from being implemented when generating a physical data model or SQL, done by selecting `Logical Only`. Then highlight those attributes you would like to be part of the key and click <Add>. You can sequence the attributes using the <Up> and <Down> buttons; when you're done, click <OK>.

There are two more tabs on this screen:

Tab	Here's what you need to know:
Compare Options	Select which, if any, properties (e.g., name, index options, attachments) of the key to ignore when comparing this key to another using the *Compare and Merge Utility*, which will be discussed in Chapter 15.
Attachment Bindings	Bind an external piece of information, such as a Microsoft Word document or PDF file, to the key. Very useful for requirements documents, user stories, etc. Attachments are created in the Attachments folder of the Data Dictionary (discussed in Chapter 11) and must be added to the model before they will display on this tab.

EDITING A KEY

Highlight the entity where you would like to edit the key and use one of these commands:

Menu	Toolbar	Explorer	Shortcut Key	Shortcut Menu
`Edit > Edit Entity…`	n/a	Right-click on entity, `Edit Entity…`	<ALT + E>, then <E> Or Double-click on the entity	Right-click on entity, `Edit Entity`

Any of these approaches brings up the *Entity Editor* screen. Highlight the attribute you would like to edit on the *Keys* tab and click <Edit>.

EXERCISE 6.3: CREATING KEYS

First, let's make sure the keys we create will be displayed. Open *Options*:

Menu	Toolbar	Explorer	Shortcut Key	Shortcut Menu
`Tools > Options`	n/a	n/a	<ALT + T>, then <P>	n/a

Under the *Display* tab, select `Attribute (Logical Order)` from the *Display Mode* drop-down. This will position all primary key columns before non-key columns. Select `Physical Order` to position the keys to mimic the order in the physical data model, meaning that primary keys can appear before or after non-key columns. Select `Logical Order` to prevent primary keys from being reordered in the *Entity Editor*.

Create the following keys for each of our entities:

Create in this entity…	These keys
Offering	Primary key on **Offering ID** Alternate key on **Offering Name**
Title	Primary key on **ISBN** Alternate key on **Subtitle Name**
Electronic Title	Inversion entry on **Title Instant Download Indicator**
Category	Primary key on **Category Code** Alternate key on **Category Name**
Speaker	Primary key on **Speaker Tax ID** Alternate key on both the **Speaker First Name** and **Speaker Last Name**
Conference	Alternate key on **Conference Hotel Name** Alternate key on both the **Conference Start Date** and **Conference End Date**
Seminar	Alternate key on both the **Seminar Start Date** and **Seminar End Date**

DOMAIN EXPLANATION

The complete set of all possible values that an attribute can be assigned is called a domain. A domain is a set of validation criteria that can be applied to more than one attribute; it provides a means of standardizing the characteristics of the attributes. For example, the domain **Date**, which contains all possible valid dates, can be assigned to any of these attributes:

Employee Hire Date
Order Entry Date
Claim Submit Date
Course Start Date

An attribute must never contain values outside of its assigned domain. The domain values are defined by specifying the actual list of values or a set of rules. **Employee Gender Code**, for example, may be limited to the domain of `female` and `male`. **Employee Hire Date** may initially be assigned the rule that its domain contain only valid dates. Therefore, this may include values such as:

```
February 15th, 2005
25 January 1910
20150410
March 10th, 2050
```

Because **Employee Hire Date** is limited to valid dates, it does not include `February 30th`. We can restrict a domain with additional rules. For example, by restricting the **Employee Hire Date** domain to dates earlier than today's date, we would eliminate `March 10th, 2050`. By restricting **Employee Hire Date** to YYYYMMDD (that is, year, month, and day concatenated), we would eliminate all the examples given except for `20150410`. Another way of refining this set of values is to restrict the domain of **Employee Hire Date** to dates that fall on a `Monday`, `Tuesday`, `Wednesday`, `Thursday`, or `Friday` (that is, the typical workweek).

There are three basic domain types:

- **Format.** Format domains specify the standard types of data one can have in a database. For example, Integer, Character(30), and Date are all format domains.

- **List.** List domains are similar to a drop-down list. They contain a finite set of values from which to choose. List domains are refinements of format domains. The format domain for **Order Status Code** might be Character(10). This domain can be further defined through a list domain of possible values `{Open, Shipped, Closed, Returned}`.

- **Range.** Range domains allow all values that are between a minimum and maximum value. For example, **Order Delivery Date** must be between today's date and three months in the future. As with list domains, range domains are a refined version of a format domain.

Domains are very useful for a number of reasons:

- **Improves data quality by checking against a domain before inserting data**. This is the primary reason for having a domain. By limiting the possible values of an attribute, the chances of bad data getting into the database are reduced. For example, if every attribute that represents money is assigned the **Amount** domain, consisting of all decimal numbers up to 15 digits in length including two digits after the decimal point, then there is a good chance that each of these attributes actually do contain currency. **Gross Sales Amount,** which is assigned the amount domain, would not allow the value `R2D2` to be added.

- **The data model communicates even more**. When we display domains on a data model, the data model communicates that a particular attribute has the properties of a particular domain, so the data model becomes a more comprehensive communication tool. We learn, for example, that **Gross Sales Amount**, **Net Sales Value Amount**, and **List Price Amount** all share the **Amount** domain and, therefore, share properties such that their valid values are limited to currency.

- **Greater efficiency in building new models and maintaining existing models.** When a data modeler embarks on a project, she can use a standard set of domains, thereby saving time by not reinventing the wheel. Any new attribute that ends in Amount, for example, would be associated with the standard **Amount** domain, saving analysis and design time.

Key Points

- An attribute is a property of importance to the business whose values contribute to identifying, describing, or measuring instances of an entity.
- A key is an attribute or set of attributes that helps us find entity instances.
- A candidate key consists of one or more attributes that uniquely identify an entity instance. The candidate key that is selected as the best way to identify each unique record in the entity becomes the primary key. The other candidate keys become alternate keys. Keys containing more than one attribute are known as composite keys.
- A surrogate key is a primary key with no embedded intelligence that is a substitute for a natural key. It is used by IT to facilitate integration and introduce database efficiencies.
- A foreign key points from one entity instance to another.
- A domain is a set of validation criteria that can be applied to more than one attribute.
- There are three basic domain types: format, list, and range.

CHAPTER 7
Relationships

Rules all around us
Relationships tell the tale
Connecting the dots

This chapter defines rules and relationships. Cardinality and labels are explained so that you can read any data model as easily as reading a book. Other types of relationships, such as recursive relationships and subtyping, are also discussed. Learn how to create and edit all of these different types of relationships in ER/Studio.

RELATIONSHIP EXPLANATION

A relationship is displayed as a line connecting two entities that captures the rule or navigation path between them. If the two entities are **Employee** and **Department**, the relationship can capture the rules "Each **Employee** must work for one **Department**" and "Each **Department** may contain one or many **Employees**."

RELATIONSHIP TYPES

Returning to our publishing data model, here are some rules that we can model as relationships:

Each author may write one or many titles.
Each title must be written by one or many authors.
Each title must belong to one or many categories.
Each category may contain one or many titles.

The three levels of granularity (conceptual, logical, and physical) that apply to entities and attributes also apply to the relationships that connect entities. Conceptual relationships are high-level rules that connect key concepts.

Logical relationships are detailed business rules that enforce the rules between the logical entities. Physical relationships are detailed technology-dependent rules between the physical structures (tables, views, or files) that the relationship connects.

In RDBMS, these physical relationships eventually become database constraints, which ensure that data adheres to the rules. A "constraint" is a physical term for a relationship, similar to an entity becoming a table and an attribute becoming a column. In NoSQL databases, these physical relationships become transformed into how the underlying technology views the relationship. For example, in MongoDB, a document-based database, these relationships can become containment relationships.

CARDINALITY

In a relationship between two entities, cardinality captures how many instances from one entity participate in the relationship with instances of the other entity. It is represented by the symbols that appear on both ends of a relationship line. It is through cardinality that the data rules are specified and enforced. Without cardinality, the most we can say about a relationship is that two entities are connected in some way through a rule. For example, **Employee** and **Department** have some kind of relationship, but we don't know more than this.

For cardinality, the choices are simple: zero, one, or many. *Many* (some people read it as *more*) means any number greater than zero. Each side of a relationship can have any combination of zero, one, or many. Specifying zero or one allows us to capture whether or not an entity instance is *required* in a relationship. Specifying one or many allows us to capture *how many* of a particular instance participates in a given relationship.

Because we have only three cardinality symbols, we can't specify an exact number (other than through documentation) as in "A **Car** contains four **Tires**." We can only say, "A **Car** contains many **Tires**."

Each of the cardinality symbols is illustrated in Figure 7.1, which contains **Author** and **Title**. The business rules are:

Each **Author** may write one or many **Titles**.
Each **Title** must be written by one **Author**.

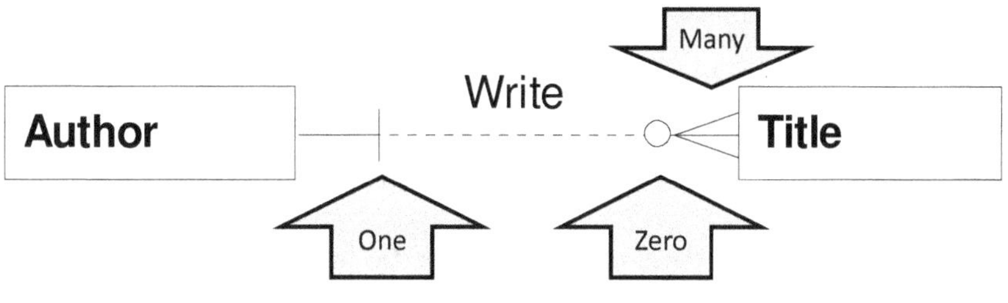

Figure 7.1 Author and Title, take 1

The small vertical line means *one*. (Looks like a 1, doesn't it?) The circle means *zero*. (Looks like a zero too!) The zero implies optionality and does not exclude the value *one*, so in the above example an author can write just one title too.

The triangle with a line through the middle means *many*. Some people call the *many* symbol a *crow's foot*. Relationship lines are frequently labeled to clarify the relationship and express the rule that the relationship represents. A data model is a communication tool, and if you think of the entities as nouns, the relationship label is a present tense verb. We are just reading a sentence:

Each **Author** may write one or many **Titles**.

Having a zero in the cardinality makes us use optional-sounding words such as *may* or *can* when reading the relationship. Without the zero, we use mandatory-sounding terms such as *must* or *have to*. So instead of being redundant and saying:

Each **Author** may write *zero*, one or many **Titles**.

We take out the word *zero* because it is expressed using the word *may*, which implies the zero:

Each **Author** may write one or many **Titles**.

Every relationship has a parent and a child. The parent entity appears on the *one* side of the relationship, and the child appears on the *many* side of the relationship. In Figure 7.1, the parent entity is **Author**, and the child entity is **Title**. When I read a relationship, I start with the entity on the *one* side of the relationship (the parent entity) first. "Each **Author** may write one or many **Titles**." It's then followed by reading the relationship from the many side: "Each **Title** must be written by one **Author**."

I also always use the word *each* in reading a relationship, starting with the parent side. The reason for the word *each* is that you want to specify, on average, how many instances of one entity relate to a different entity instance.

In Figure 7.1 we modeled that a **Title** must be written by one **Author**. Let's now allow a **Title** to be written by more than one **Author**. See Figure 7.2.

Figure 7.2 Author and Title, take 2

This is an example of a many-to-many relationship, in contrast to the previous example, which was a one-to-many relationship. The business rules here read as follows:

> Each **Author** may write one or many **Titles**.
> Each **Title** must be written by one or many **Authors**.

Write in Figure 7.2 is an example of a relationship label. Make sure relationship labels are as descriptive as possible. Here are some examples of good label names:

> contain
> work for
> own
> initiate
> categorize
> apply to

Always avoid the following words as label names as they provide no additional information to the reader. You can use these words in combination with other words to make a meaningful label name; just avoid using these words by themselves:

has
have
associate
participate
relate
be

A useful technique for checking whether relationship names make sense is to read them out aloud to a colleague who's not directly involved in creating the model. If they don't understand what you mean, you may need to reconsider your choice of verb. For example, replace the relationship sentence:

Each **Person** must be *associated* with one **Company**.

with

Each **Person** must be *employed* by one **Company**.

Fortunately, in ER/Studio, as you write the verb on the relationship label in the *Relationship Editor*, the sentence phrase is automatically written so you can check the meaningfulness of the label. ER/Studio uses the words *A* or *An* instead of *Each* at the beginning of the sentence and also prefers plural verbs over singular verbs for the relationship label. For example, in ER/Studio, "An **Author** writes one or many **Titles**" instead of "Each **Author** may write one or many **Titles.**" Either approach works fine, just remember to be consistent throughout the model. Many modelers capture labels on both sides of the relationship line instead of just one side as shown in this chapter. In weighing simplicity versus precision, I chose simplicity. The other label can often be inferred from the label that appears on the model. For example, if *write* is the verb phrase from **Author** to **Title**, then *written by* is assumed to be the verb phrase from **Title** to **Author**.

INDEPENDENT VS. DEPENDENT ENTITIES

Let's look at the two models in Figure 7.3. **Customer** and **Account** in the first example (and **Customer** in the second example) are rectangles, yet **Account** in the second example is a rectangle with rounded corners, called a *bub-tangle*.

The rectangles with straight, right-angle corners are independent, and those with rounded corners are dependent.

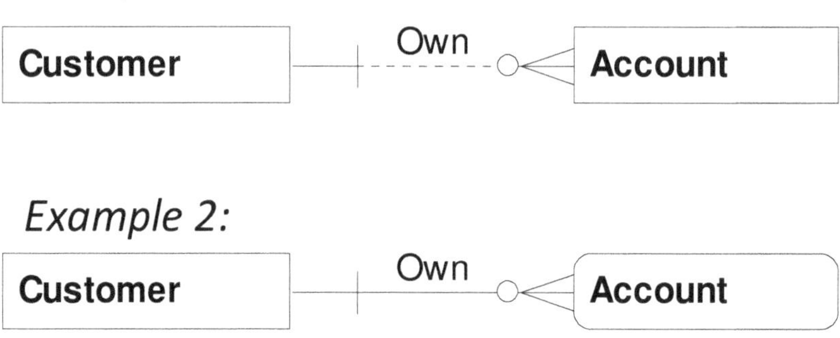

Figure 7.3 Independent and dependent entities

An independent entity, such as **Customer** in both examples and **Account** in the first example, is an entity where each occurrence (instance) can be found using only attributes that it owns like a **Customer ID**. A dependent entity, such as **Account** in the second example, can only be found by using at least one attribute from a different entity, such as **Customer ID** from **Customer**.

To make the explanation of independent and dependent clearer, Figure 7.4 contains the models from Figure 7.3 with example values for two attributes within **Account**, **Account Number,** and the foreign key back to **Customer**, **Customer ID**. (Making up actual values is always a good way to explain and validate a data model.)

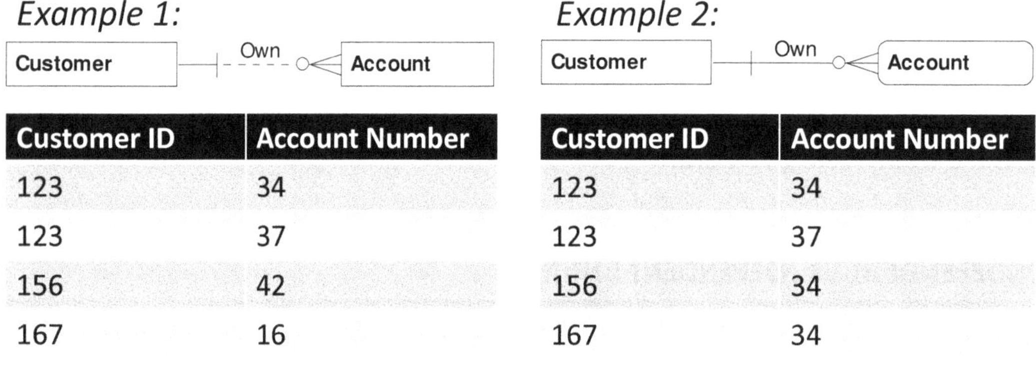

Example 1:

Customer ID	Account Number
123	34
123	37
156	42
167	16

Example 2:

Customer ID	Account Number
123	34
123	37
156	34
167	34

Figure 7.4 Independent and dependent entities with sample values

On the model in Example 1, we see that **Account Number** is unique, and therefore retrieving a specific **Account** requires only knowing the **Account Number** and not needing to know anything from **Customer**, making **Account** an independent entity. However, in Example 2, **Account Number** 34 repeats three times, so the only way to know to return a specific account is to know who the customer is. So the combination of **Customer ID** and **Account Number** is required to distinguish a particular account, making **Account** in Example 2 a dependent entity.

Notice also that the relationship line looks different when connecting to an independent verses dependent entity. The dotted line means *non-identifying* and the solid line means *identifying.* Identifying relationships mean that the entity on the many side (the child) is always going to be a dependent entity to the entity on the one side (the parent).

RECURSION

A recursive relationship is a rule that exists between instances of the same entity. A one-to-many recursive relationship describes a hierarchy, whereas a many-to-many relationship describes a network. In a hierarchy, an entity instance has at most one parent. In a network, an entity instance can have more than one parent. Let's illustrate both types of recursive relationships using **Employee**. See Figure 7.5 for a one-to-many recursive example and Figure 7.6 for a many-to-many example.

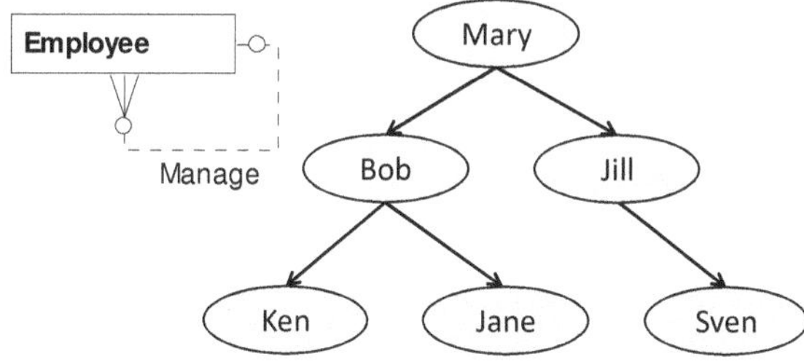

Each Employee may manage one or many Employees.
Each Employee may be managed by one Employee.

Figure 7.5 An Employee may work for one Manager

Using sample values such as Bob and Jill and sketching a hierarchy or network can really help understand, and therefore validate, cardinality. In Figure 7.5, for example, where the one-to-many captures a hierarchy, each employee may work for at most one manager. Yet in Figure 7.6, where the many-to-many captures a network, each employee may work for one or many managers such as Jane working for Bob, Ken, and Sven. (I would definitely update my resume if I were Jane.)

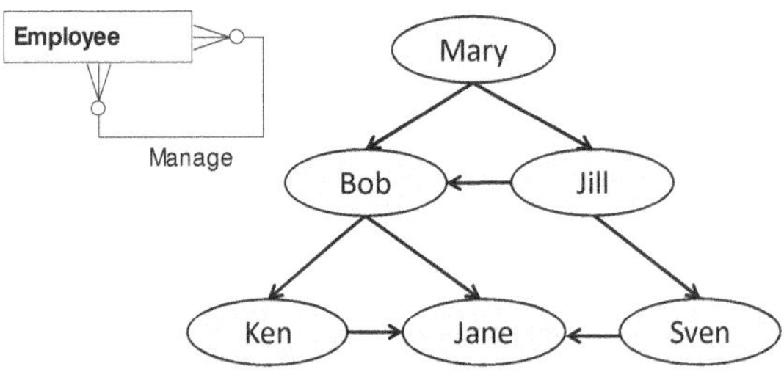

Figure 7.6 An Employee may work for one or many Managers

> Each Employee may manage one or many Employees.
> Each Employee may be managed by one or many Employees.

It is interesting to note that in both figures, there is optionality on both sides of the relationship. In these examples, it implies we can have an Employee who has no boss (such as Mary) and an Employee who is not a manager (such as Jane).

Data modelers have a love-hate relationship with recursion. On the one hand, recursion makes modeling a complex business idea very easy and leads to a very flexible modeling structure. We can have any number of levels in an organization hierarchy in Figure 7.5, for example. On the other hand, some consider using recursion to be taking the easy way out of a difficult modeling situation. There are many rules that can be obscured by recursion. For example, where is the Regional Management Level in Figure 7.6? It is hidden somewhere in the recursive relationship. Those in favor of recursion argue that you may not be aware of all the rules and that recursion protects you from having an incomplete model. Recursion adds a level of flexibility that ensures any rules not previously considered are also handled by the model. It is therefore wise to consider recursion on a case-by-case basis, weighing obscurity against flexibility.

CONTAINMENT

A containment relationship is used for nested objects within a supported database. For instance, if you have reverse engineered nested objects within MongoDB, these will be added with a containment relationship to the object they are nested within. Containment relationships will appear as an option only on the physical model when the target database is one that supports nesting such as MongoDB. For example, Figure 7.7 contains a logical data model for **Order** and **Order Line**.

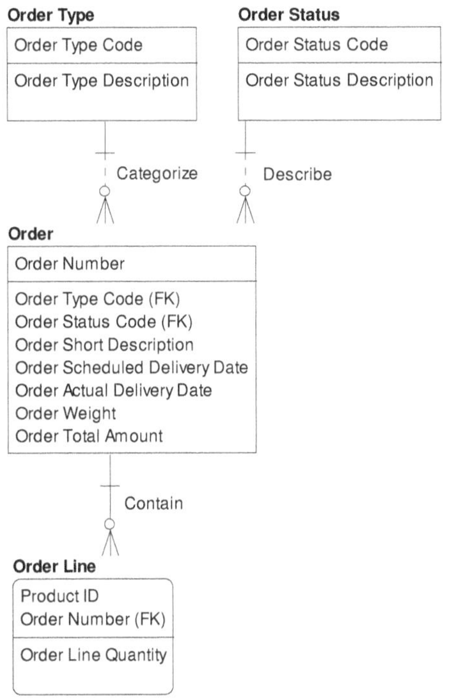

Figure 7.7 Order and Order Line LDM

Assume this will be implemented in MongoDB. The physical data modeler decides to denormalize **Order Type** and **Order Status** into **Order**, but she wants to treat **Order Line** as an array. An array in MongoDB (also known as a nested structure) is when the child (in this case **Order Line**) can appear any number of times in the parent (in this case **Order**). For example, here is a MongoDB **Order** document with three **Order Lines** (but it could also easily be ten lines or 100 lines):

```
Order:
{       orderNumber : "4839-02",
        orderShortDescription : "Professor review copies of titles",
        orderScheduledDeliveryDate : ISODate("2014-05-15"),
        orderActualDeliveryDate : ISODate("2014-05-17"),
        orderWeight : 8.5,
        orderTotalAmount : 19.85,
        orderTypeCode : "02",
        orderTypeDescription : "Universities Sales",
        orderStatusCode : "D",
        orderStatusDescription : "Delivered",
        orderLine :
                    [ {   productID : "9781935504375",
                          orderLineQuantity : 1
                    },
                    {     productID : "9781935504511",
                          orderLineQuantity : 3
                    },
                    {     productID : "9781935504535",
                          orderLineQuantity : 2
                    } ] }
```

We can show this as an array in ER/Studio using a containment relationship as shown in Figure 7.8.

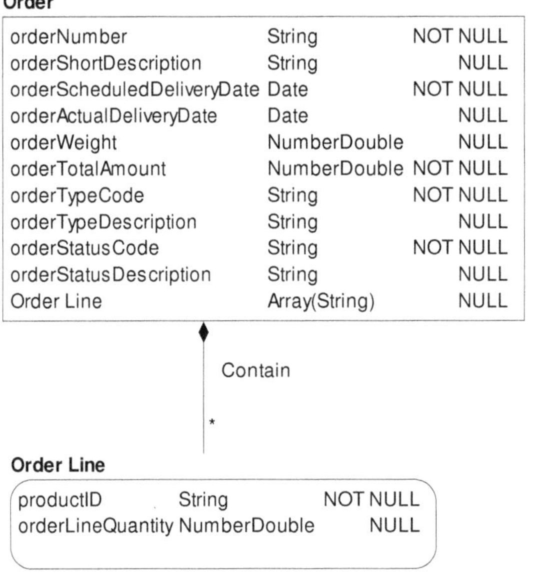

Figure 7.8 Order MongoDB collection

Order is the collection and **Order Line** is the nested object. Collections are displayed as rectangles, and nested objects are displayed as rectangles with rounded corners. Each **Order Line** must belong to one **Order**, and each **Order** may contain one or many **Order Lines**.

SUBTYPING

Subtyping groups the common attributes and relationships of entities while retaining what is special within each entity. Subtyping is an excellent way of communicating that certain concepts are very similar and for showing examples. For instance, the publishing data model in Figure 7.9 contains no subtyping.

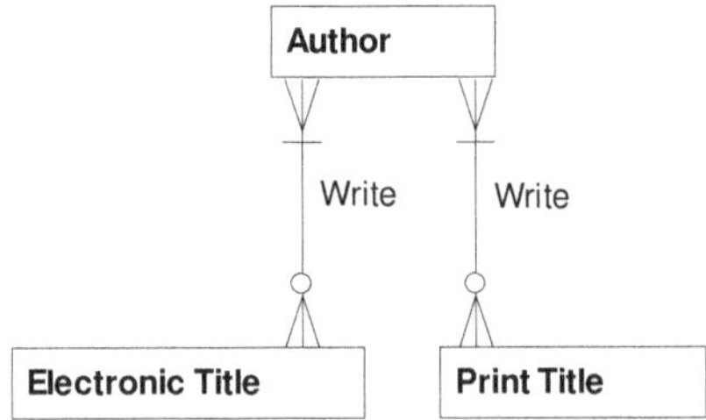

Each **Author** may write one or many **Electronic Titles**.
Each **Electronic Title** must be written by one or many **Authors**.
Each **Author** may write one or many **Print Titles**.
Each **Print Title** must be written by one or many **Authors**.

Figure 7.9 Publishing example before subtyping

Rather than repeat the relationship to **Author**, we can introduce subtyping as shown in Figure 7.10. The subtyping relationship implies that all of the properties from the supertype are inherited by the subtype. Therefore, there is an implied relationship from **Author** to **Electronic Title** as well as from **Author** to **Print Title**. Not only does subtyping reduce redundancy on a data model, but it makes it easier to communicate similarities across what otherwise would appear to be distinct and separate concepts. A subtype cluster can be either complete or incomplete. Complete means all possible subtype entities are included in the subtype cluster. An example of a complete subtype cluster is one in which **Person** is the supertype and **Male** and **Female** are the subtypes. An example of an incomplete subtype cluster is one in which

Account is the supertype and **Checking Account** and **Savings Account** are subtypes. There could be other types of accounts as well, such as **Brokerage Account**, making this subtype incomplete.

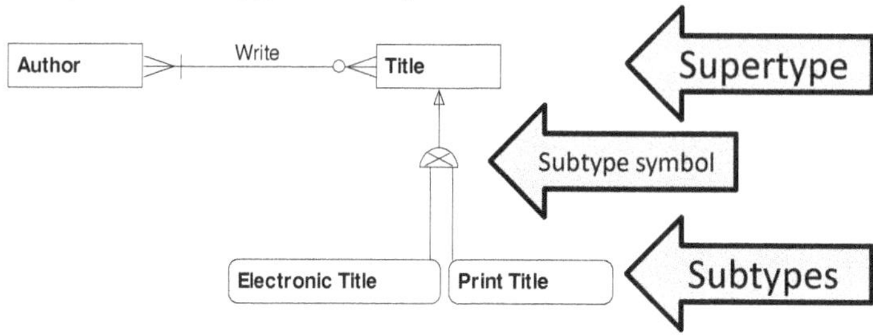

Each **Author** may write one or many **Titles**.
Each **Title** must be written by one or many **Authors**.
Each **Title** may be either an **Electronic Title** or **Print Title**.
Each **Electronic Title** is a **Title**.
Each **Print Title** is a **Title**.

Figure 7.10 Publishing example after subtyping

A subtype cluster can be either exclusive or inclusive. Exclusive or non-overlapping means that each supertype can be only one subtype at a time. A **Person** is either a **Male** or **Female** but not both. Inclusive or overlapping means that each supertype can be more than one subtype at the same time. An **Account** can be both a **Checking Account** and a **Savings Account**.

EXERCISE 7.1: READING A MODEL

Practice reading the relationships in this model. See Appendix B for the sentences you can read from this model.

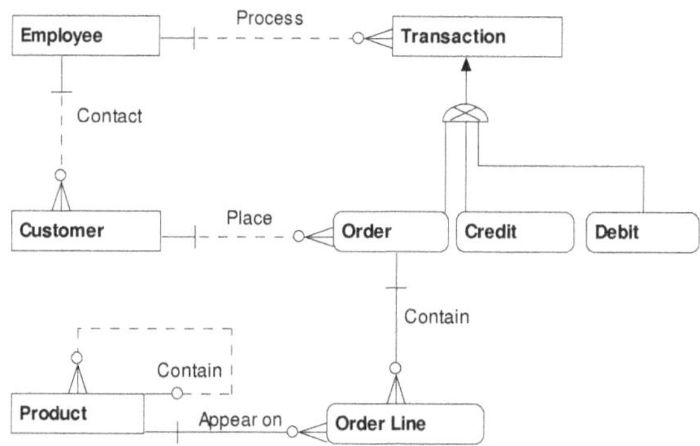

DATA MODELING NOTATIONS

Now that you are comfortable reading relationships, you can read relationships in any data modeling notation. There are a number of different data modeling notations that are popular, and in general, once you are comfortable with the concepts of zero, one, and many, you just need to know the symbols used to show these in any data modeling notation. The two most popular data modeling notations are Information Engineering (IE) and Integration Definition for Information Modeling (IDEF1X). IE notation is being used throughout this book. Figure 7.11 contrasts IE with IDEF1X notation using the prior examples from Figure 7.10.

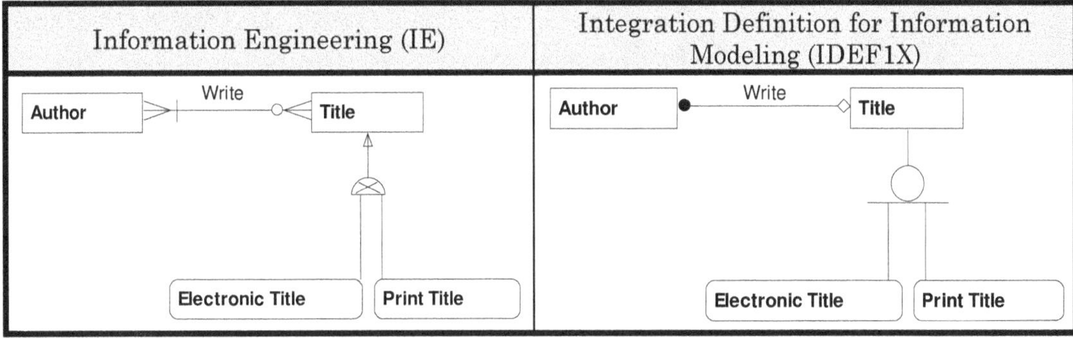

Figure 7.11 Comparing IE with IDEF1X

To change the data modeling notation, Choose `View > Diagram And Object Display Options`, or click on the icon and then click the *Relationship* tab. In *Display Preferences* section, choose the desired notation and then click <OK>. ER/Studio supports two different variations of IE (Martin/Finkelstein and Crows Foot), and also has a notation where foreign keys are hidden. I am using the IE Crows Foot notation throughout the book.

RELATIONSHIPS IN ER/STUDIO

In this section we will practice creating and modifying relationships for the publishing data model.

CREATING RELATIONSHIPS

Menu	Toolbar	Explorer	Shortcut Key	Shortcut Menu
`Insert > Relationship`	Modeling toolbar:	Right-click on `Relationships, New Relationship...`	<ALT + I>, then <R>	Right-click on white space, `Insert Relationship`

Become an ER/Studio Hotshot:

- Are you a "drop-downer" or a "clicker"? When you create a relationship in *Data Model Explorer*, you can choose which entities the relationship should connect via drop-downs. For the other four techniques, the cursor has changed into a relationship symbol. Click first on the parent entity and then the child entity, and the relationship line appears.
- Note that the cursor will stay in the relationship symbol, allowing you to create many relationships easily. When you want to turn this sticky buttons feature off, just right-click on any white space and the cursor returns to its default selector symbol.
- ER/Studio supports sound design practices by automatically propagating the primary key from the parent to the child entity as a foreign key. In the *Relationship Editor,* you have the option of propagating alternate keys from parent to child entity as well.
- The status bar at the bottom of the screen shows the number of relationships in the model or submodel. You can hide or show this status bar using `View > Status Bar` or <ALT + V>, then <S>.

Practice creating relationships between **Author** and **Title** using each of these five techniques. Click <CTRL + Z>, which is your faithful undo button, after each technique except for the last technique so that you have something similar to the model in Figure 7.12.

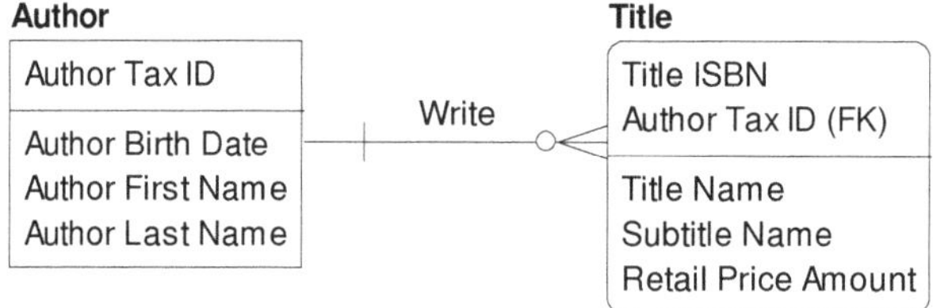

Each **Author** may write one or many **Titles**.
Each **Title** must be written by one **Author**.

Figure 7.12 Each Author may write one or many Titles

There are five types of relationships that can be created, and we'll illustrate each using **Author** and **Title**. See Table 7.1.

Symbol	Name	Example
	Identifying	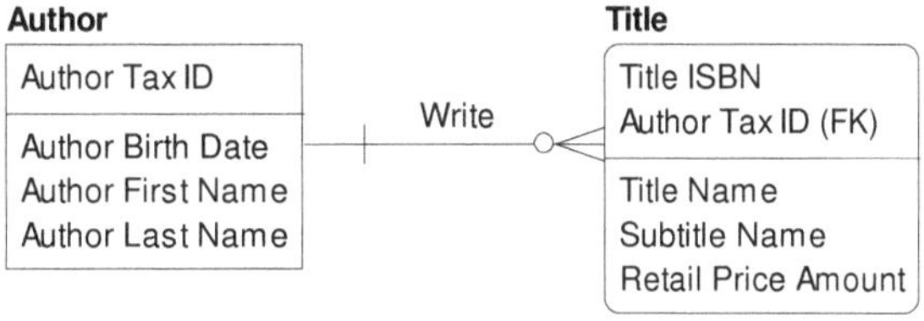 Author: Author Tax ID; Author Birth Date, Author First Name, Author Last Name — Write — Title: Title ISBN, Author Tax ID (FK); Title Name, Subtitle Name, Retail Price Amount Each **Author** may write one or many **Titles**. Each **Title** must be written by one **Author**.
	Non-identifying, mandatory	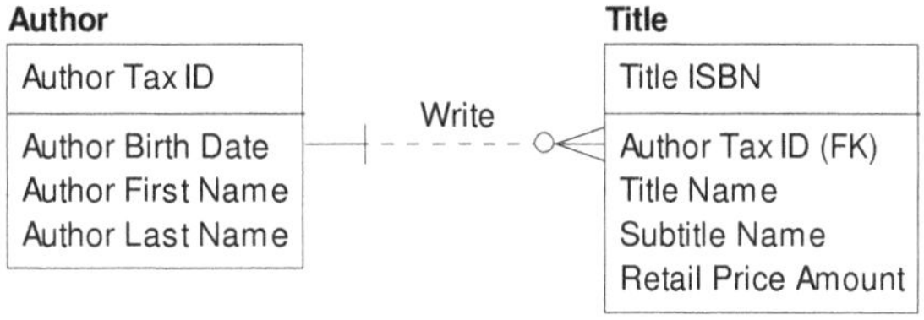 Author: Author Tax ID; Author Birth Date, Author First Name, Author Last Name — Write — Title: Title ISBN; Author Tax ID (FK), Title Name, Subtitle Name, Retail Price Amount Each **Author** may write one or many **Titles**. Each **Title** must be written by one **Author**.
	Non-identifying, optional	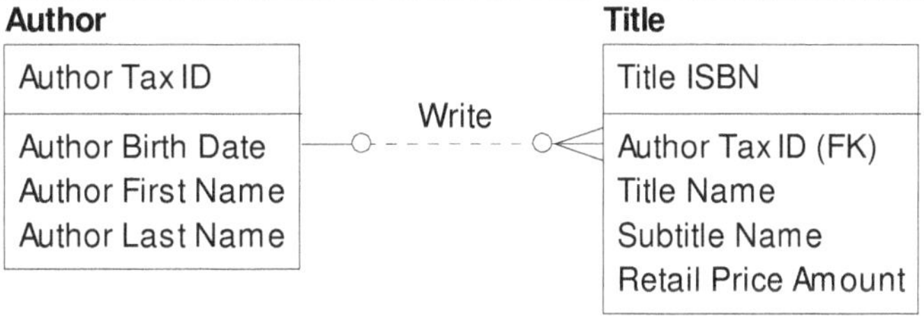 Author: Author Tax ID; Author Birth Date, Author First Name, Author Last Name — Write — Title: Title ISBN; Author Tax ID (FK), Title Name, Subtitle Name, Retail Price Amount Each **Author** may write one or many **Titles**. Each **Title** may be written by one **Author**.
	One-to-one	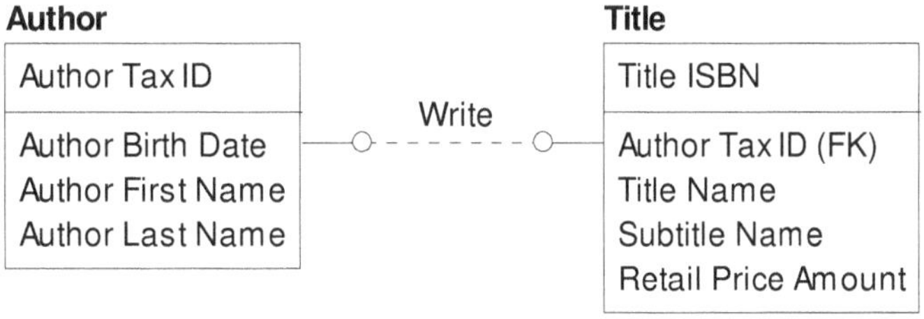 Author: Author Tax ID; Author Birth Date, Author First Name, Author Last Name — Write — Title: Title ISBN; Author Tax ID (FK), Title Name, Subtitle Name, Retail Price Amount Each **Author** may write one **Title**. Each **Title** may be written by one **Author**.

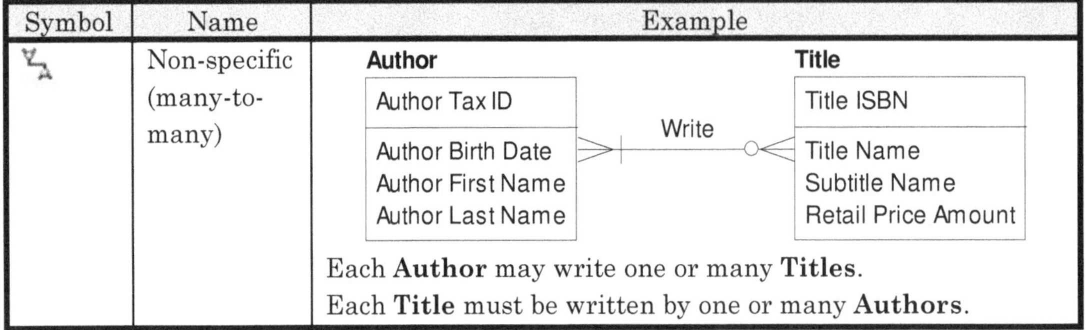

Symbol	Name	Example
	Non-specific (many-to-many)	**Author**: Author Tax ID; Author Birth Date, Author First Name, Author Last Name — Write — **Title**: Title ISBN; Title Name, Subtitle Name, Retail Price Amount Each **Author** may write one or many **Titles**. Each **Title** must be written by one or many **Authors**.

Table 7.1 Example of each relationship type

CREATING SUBTYPES

Menu	Toolbar	Explorer	Shortcut Key	Shortcut Menu
`Insert > Subtype Cluster > Complete or Incomplete`	Modeling toolbar:	n/a	n/a	Right-click on white space, `Insert > Subtype Cluster > Complete or Incomplete`

Become an ER/Studio Hotshot:

- To create a subtype relationship, make sure you are on a logical data model as subtype structures do not exist in a physical data model. Click an entity to designate it as the parent (supertype) and then click the child (subtype).
- You can add multiple entities to the subtype cluster by pressing <CTRL> while clicking the desired entities.
- The subtype discriminator is an attribute that distinguishes each of the subtype entities from one another. For example, **Gender Code** would be the subtype discriminator in the gender subtype cluster.
- You can add an entity to a subtype cluster by choosing the identifying or subtype relationship, clicking the subtype cluster symbol next to the supertype you want to associate the entity with, and then clicking the entity you want to add to the subtype cluster.

CREATING RECURSIVE RELATIONSHIPS

A recursive relationship is when an entity is related to itself. For example, let's say there are relationships between titles, such as the second edition of a particular title replaces the first edition. We would therefore want to create a relationship from the **Title** entity to the **Title** entity. When we do this in ER/Studio, the *Recursive Relationship* screen appears as shown in Figure 7.13.

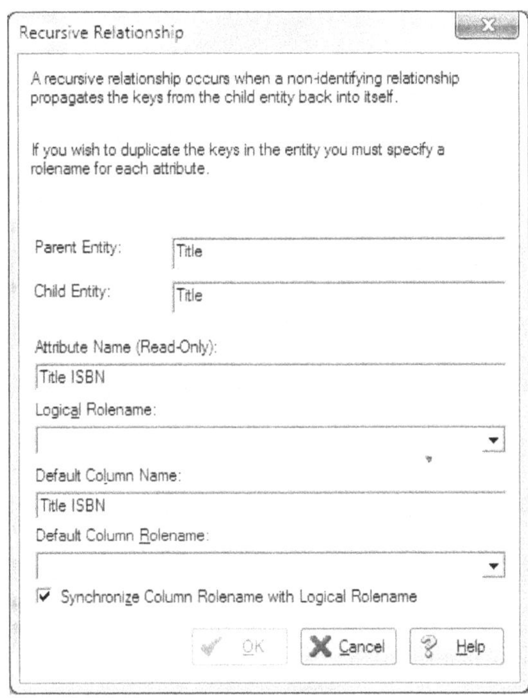

Figure 7.13 Recursive Relationship screen

Using this editor you can assign rolenames to any duplicate keys to differentiate the native and foreign key. Recall from an earlier discussion that a rolename is another name given to a foreign key. The rolename cannot be the same as an existing attribute or column name.

Duplicate Relationships

If there is already a relationship between two entities and we create an additional relationship between these same two entities, the *Duplicate Relationship* screen appears. When we created a second relationship from **Author** to **Title**, the screen in Figure 7.14 appeared.

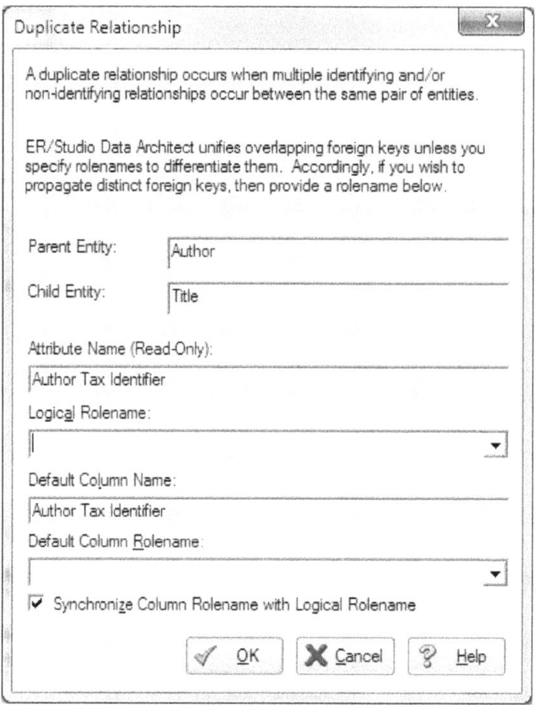

Figure 7.14 Duplicate Relationship screen

Using this editor you can assign rolenames to any duplicate foreign keys.

Duplicate Attributes

Let's say we have the model in Figure 7.15 and want to create a relationship from **Author** to **Title**.

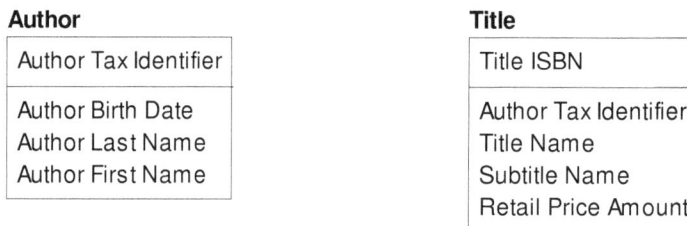

Figure 7.15 Author Tax Identifier already present in Title

Notice that **Title** already contains the **Author Tax Identifier**. This would be the foreign key from **Author** after we create our relationship. Therefore, when we draw the relationship from **Author** to **Title**, the **Duplicate Attribute Editor** screen appears as in Figure 7.16.

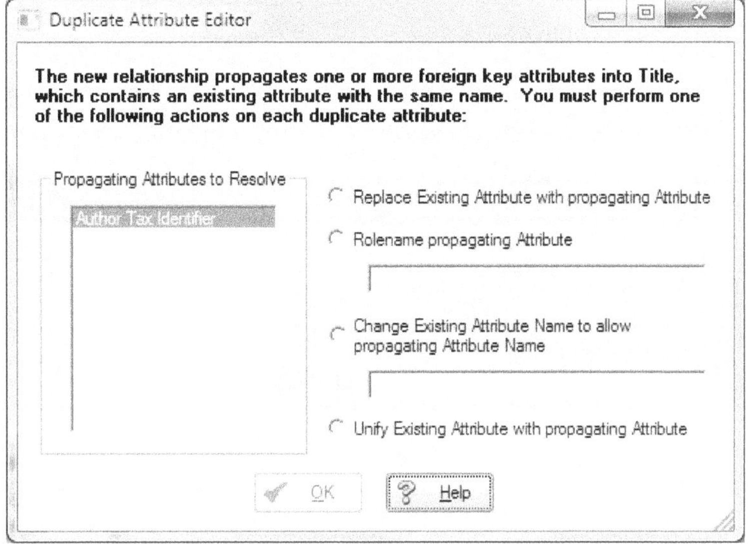

Figure 7.16 Duplicate Attribute Editor screen

We have several choices on this screen:

- `Replace Existing Attribute with propagating Attribute`. If selected, ER/Studio replaces the attribute in the child with the propagated foreign key attribute.
- `Rolename propagating Attribute`. If selected, you can rename the foreign key so that the native attribute in the child entity can still exist with its original name. After propagation, both attributes will exist in the child entity.
- `Change Existing Attribute Name to allow propagating Attribute Name`. If selected, you can rename the original native attribute in the child entity so that the attribute name from the parent entity can be used for the foreign key. After propagation, both attributes will exist in the child entity.
- `Unify Existing Attribute with propagating Attribute`. If selected, ER/Studio unifies the propagating foreign key with the native

attribute in the child table. If the relationship is later deleted, ER/Studio leaves the native child attribute.

CREATING CONTAINMENT RELATIONSHIPS

To create a containment relationship, make sure you are in a physical data model where the target database supports nested objects (such as MongoDB).

Menu	Toolbar	Explorer	Shortcut Key	Shortcut Menu
`Insert > Containment relationship`	Modeling toolbar:	n/a	n/a	n/a
Become an ER/Studio Hotshot: A containment relationship can only be created from a Collection to a Nested Object.				

EDITING RELATIONSHIPS

The *Relationship Editor* screen will allow you to enter additional information about the relationship. If you created the relationship via *Data Model Explorer*, this screen automatically appears. If you created the relationship using one of the other techniques, double-click on the relationship line to bring up the *Relationship Editor*. See Figure 7.17.

This screen can be resized by clicking and dragging the lower right corner. This screen can also become maximized by clicking the square symbol in the upper right corner (to the left of the 'x' which closes the window), and then returned back to its original size by clicking the two square symbols in the upper right corner.

Notice the *Relationship Editor* contains parent and child entity and primary key information followed by a series of tabs. The `Logical Only` checkbox if checked will not copy this relationship to the physical—the relationship will only exist on the logical data model.

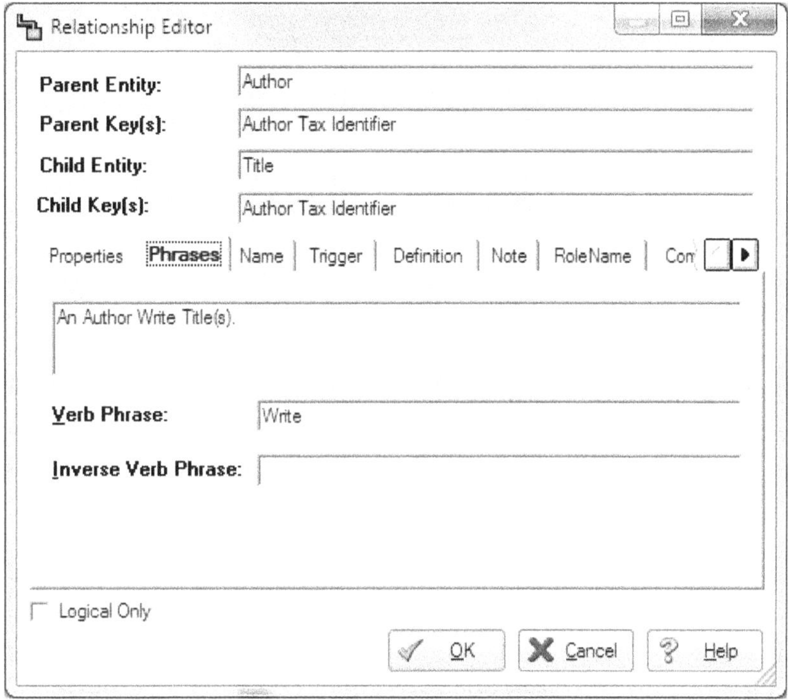

Figure 7.17 Relationship Editor

There are 9 tabs on this screen:

Tab	Here's what you need to know:
Properties	Change the type of relationship, including existence and cardinality.
Phrases	Write the business reason for the relationship. You can add verb phrases on both sides of the relationship. I really like that ER/Studio creates sentences based on these verb phrases. If you write a verb phrase that does not appear on the model, most likely you will need to turn on the verb phrase through `View > Diagram And Object Display Options`, or click on the icon and then click the *Relationship* tab. Click on `Verb Phrases` and then click <OK>.
Name	If you feel it is useful you can create both business and physical (constraint) names for the relationship.

Tab	Here's what you need to know:
Trigger	Set the actions to take when a parent or child instance is deleted.
Definition	This is where the full definition for the relationship is stored.
Note	Use this for any other text outside the definition such as questions to ask business experts, known issues, or action items. HTML tags used in *Notes* will be applied as formatting in the HTML reports. The macro **Notes Editor** allows for easily entering notes for multiple objects. More on macros in Chapter 16.
RoleName	Rename a foreign key attribute. This is useful when the same foreign key could appear more than once in the same entity and we need to therefore avoid duplicates. (For example, **Country of Residence** and **Country of Citizenship**.)
Compare Options	Select which, if any, properties (e.g., cardinality, definition, notes) of the relationship to ignore when comparing this relationship to another using the *Compare and Merge Utility* as discussed in Chapter 15.
Attachment Bindings	Bind an external piece of information, such as a Microsoft Word document or PDF file, to the relationship. Very useful for requirements documents, user stories, etc. Attachments are created in the Attachments folder of the Data Dictionary (discussed in Chapter 11) and must be added to the model before they will display on this tab.

When you are done making your changes, click <OK> to exit the editor.

MOVING RELATIONSHIPS

You can click and drag on a relationship line to move it to a new location. You can also click and drag on the relationship label to position it in a different place. As you move your cursor over the relationship line, you will notice that the cursor shape changes into a two-directional arrow indicating you can click and drag to move the relationship line. As you move your cursor over the relationship label, the cursor changes into a four-directional arrow indicating you can click and drag to move the relationship label.

You can also move a relationship by right-clicking on the relationship line and choosing one of the following options:

- **Layout Relationship**. Choose `Elbowed` if you would like the option to have the relationship line go around other entities or relationships, or choose `Straight` if would like the relationship line to be as short and direct as possible.

- **Straighten Relationship Line**. Sometimes the relationship line is slightly misaligned, and choosing this option takes out the jaggedness. After choosing this option, it is also easier to click and drag and have the resulting line still be straight.

- **Reset To Default Docking Position**. Redraws the relationship line to what it looked like when it was first created.

- **Remove All Bends**. This option takes out all of the 90-degree relationship line direction changes, sometimes resulting in a diagonal line.

You can select all the relationship lines in the data model by pressing <CTRL + A> and then apply one of these options as well.

CHANGING THE APPEARANCE OF RELATIONSHIPS

You can decide whether hovering on a relationship line brings up a description of the relationship:

Menu	Toolbar	Explorer	Shortcut Key	Shortcut Menu
`View > Cursor Popup Help Options > Display Relationship Help`	n/a	n/a	n/a	n/a

You can also apply auto layouts. When you use the auto layouts, ER/Studio organizes the data model objects according to the specifications of that particular layout. Each layout has different specifications for the way relationships bend and how relationships dock or intersect with entities and attributes. You can move the docking positions of relationship lines on parent or child entities.

There are two kinds of bends in ER/Studio, N bends and Orthogonal bends. N Bends are relationship lines that bend at any angle, while Orthogonal bends only bend at a 90-degree angle. Both Hierarchical and Orthogonal auto layouts use only Orthogonal relationship lines. All other auto layouts use straight relationship lines. You can also create straight relationship lines that are vertical or horizontal.

You can also change the colors of relationships. Using certain colors and fonts can help highlight portions of the model and distinguish sections of the model from other sections:

Menu	Toolbar	Explorer	Shortcut Key	Shortcut Menu
`n/a`	n/a	Right-click on relationship, `Relationship Color`	n/a	Right-click on relationship, `Relationship Color`

After applying one of the commands above, you are given two options:

- `Edit Settings.` Choose the color you would like for the highlighted relationship and click <OK>. If you would like to change this relationship color everywhere this relationship appears, click `Apply to all submodels.`
- `Set Relationship(s) to Use Submodel Defaults.` This will reset the colors and fonts to the submodel defaults.

There is a very quick way to change the color of all of the relationships at once:

Menu	Toolbar	Explorer	Shortcut Key	Shortcut Menu
`Format > Colors & Fonts`	Diagram toolbar:	n/a	<ALT + O>, then <C>	Right-click on white space, `Colors & Fonts`

Click on the relationship symbol, or choose `Relationships` from the drop-down and click <Set Color> to select the color you would like. Click <OK> to exit this screen and apply your changes.

To change the style of relationship lines in all new data models, open *Options*:

Menu	Toolbar	Explorer	Shortcut Key	Shortcut Menu
`Tools > Options`	n/a	n/a	<ALT + T>, then <P>	n/a

The Model Display area also contains other display options for relationships such as displaying cardinality and verb phrases.

FINDING RELATIONSHIPS

Relationship Navigation highlights relationships, making it easier to see which entities a relationship connects as well as providing a method for you to walk someone through the model. That is, the relationships become highlighted one at a time as you right-click on entities, so you can discuss a relationship. When finished, right-click again to move on to the next relationship. To bring up *Relationship Navigation*, use one of these options:

Menu	Toolbar	Explorer	Shortcut Key	Shortcut Menu
`Insert > Relationship Navigation`	Diagram toolbar:	n/a	<ALT + I>, then <G>	n/a

DELETING RELATIONSHIPS

Highlight the relationship (or relationships) you would like to delete and use one of the following options:

Menu	Toolbar	Explorer	Shortcut Key	Shortcut Menu
`Edit > Delete Relationship`	n/a	Right-click on relationship, `Delete Relationship`	<DELETE> or <ALT + E>, then <D>	Right-click on relationship, `Edit > Delete Relationship`

Become an ER/Studio Hotshot:

- To select multiple relationships, press and hold <CTRL> while clicking the entities, or click and drag over the relationships.
- Sometimes you will delete a relationship and receive a message asking whether you would like to delete the relationship from the entire data model or just the submodel. If you delete the relationship from just the submodel, this relationship will still exist in the model. We covered submodels in Chapter 5.

You can delete a subtype if you no longer want to include it in your data model. You can also add or remove entities from a subtype cluster in much the same way you add or delete relationships between entities. Delete a subtype by selecting the subtype and then choosing `Edit > Delete Subtype Cluster`. Deleting a subtype cluster deletes all relationships between the parent entity (supertype) and the child entities (subtypes).

EXERCISE 7.2: CREATING RELATIONSHIPS

In previous chapters, we created entities, submodels, attributes, and keys for our publishing example. Now let's relate the entities to each other. Convert the following business assertions into relationships on our data model (remember to add the verb phrase and make sure it appears on the diagram):

Each **Offering** can be a **Title**, **Conference**, or **Seminar**.
Each **Title** is an **Offering**.
Each **Conference** is an **Offering**.
Each **Seminar** is an **Offering**.
Each **Author** may write one or many **Titles**.
Each **Title** must be written by one or many **Authors**.
Each **Title** can be an **Electronic Title** or a **Print Title**.
Each **Electronic Title** is a **Title**.
Each **Print Title** is a **Title**.
Each **Category** may contain one or many **Offerings**.
Each **Offering** may belong to one or many **Categories**.
Each **Speaker** may present at one or many **Conferences**.
Each **Conference** must contain one or many **Speakers**.
Each **Speaker** may teach at one or many **Seminars**.
Each **Seminar** must contain one or many **Speakers**.

Key Points

- A rule is visually captured on a data model by a line connecting two entities, called a relationship.
- Cardinality is represented by the symbols on both ends of a relationship that define the number of instances of each entity that can participate in the relationship. The three simple choices are zero, one, or many.
- Labels are the verbs that appear on the relationship lines. Labels should be as descriptive as possible to retain data model precision.
- A recursive (reflexive) relationship is a rule that exists between instances of the same entity.
- Subtyping groups the common attributes and relationships of entities while retaining what is special within each entity. Subtyping is an excellent way of communicating that certain concepts are very similar and for showing examples.

SECTION III
Conceptual, Logical, and Physical Data Models

Section III explores the three different levels of models: conceptual, logical, and physical. A conceptual data model (CDM) represents the business need within a defined scope, a logical data model (LDM) the detailed business solution, and a physical data model (PDM) the detailed technical solution. Chapter 8 focuses on the CDM, Chapter 9 the LDM, and Chapter 10 the PDM.

In addition to these three levels of detail, there are also two different modeling mindsets: relational and dimensional. Relational data modeling is the process of capturing how the business *works* by precisely representing business rules, while dimensional data modeling is the process of capturing how the business is *monitored* by precisely representing navigation.

The major difference between relational and dimensional data models is in the meaning of the relationship lines. On a relational data model a relationship communicates a business rule, and on dimensional data model the relationship communicates a navigation path. On a relational data model, for example, we can represent the business rule "A **Customer** must have at least one **Account**". On a dimensional data model we can display the measure **Gross Sales Amount** along with all of the navigation paths that a user needs to see

Gross Sales Amount at such as by day, month, year, region, account, and customer. The dimensional data model is all about viewing measures at different levels of granularity.

The following table summarizes these three levels of detail and two modeling mindsets, leading to five different types of models:

Types of models	Mindset: Relational	Mindset: Dimensional
CDM	Key concepts and their business rules, such as a "Each Customer may place one or many Orders."	Key concepts focused around one or more measures, such as "I want to see Gross Sales Amount by Customer."
LDM	All attributes required for a given application or business process, neatly organized into entities according to strict business rules and independent of technology such as "Each Customer ID value must return at most one Customer Last Name."	All attributes required for a given reporting application, focused on measures and independent of technology such as "I want to see Gross Sales Amount by Customer and view the customer's first and last name."
PDM	The LDM modified for a specific technology such as database or access software. For example, "To improve retrieval speed, we need a non-unique index on Customer Last Name." Or "To improve retrieval speed, we need to embed this MongoDB collection within that MongoDB collection."	

By the end of this section you will be able to create relational and dimensional conceptual, logical, and physical data models in ER/Studio.

CHAPTER 8
Conceptual Data Models

Need the Big Picture?
No common definitions?
Build a CDM!

The highlighted row in Table 8.1 shows the focus of this chapter: the conceptual data model (CDM).

	Relational	Dimensional
Conceptual Data Model (CDM)	**"One-pager" on business rules**	**"One-pager" on navigation**
Logical Data Model (LDM)	Detailed business solution on business rules	Detailed business solution on navigation
Physical Data Model (PDM)	Detailed technical solution	

Table 8.1 The Conceptual Data Model is the focus of this chapter

A CDM shows the key concepts in a particular area and how these concepts interact with each other. This chapter defines a concept, followed by an explanation of the importance of the conceptual data model and concept definitions. Then both relational and dimensional CDMs will be discussed. Then we provide a summary of the five-step approach to building a conceptual data model. We conclude this chapter with a description of the support provided by ER/Studio for CDMs and a couple of exercises to reinforce what you've learned.

CONCEPTUAL DATA MODEL EXPLANATION

A concept is a key idea that is both *basic* and *critical* to your audience. "Basic" means this term is probably mentioned many times a day in conversations with the people who are the audience for the model. "Critical" means the business would be very different or non-existent without this concept.

The majority of concepts are easy to identify and include ideas that are common across industries, such as **Customer**, **Employee**, and **Product**. An airline may call a **Customer** a **Passenger**, and a hospital may call a **Customer** a **Patient**, but in general they are all people who receive goods or services. Each concept will be shown in much more detail at the logical and physical phases of design. For example, the **Customer** concept might encompass the logical entities **Customer**, **Customer Association**, **Customer Demographics**, **Customer Type**, and so on.

Many concepts, however, can be more challenging to identify, as they may be concepts to your audience but not to others in the same department, company, or industry. For example, **Account** would most likely be a concept for a bank and for a manufacturing company. However, the audience for the bank conceptual data model might also require **Checking Account** and **Savings Account** to be on their model, whereas the audience for the manufacturing conceptual data model might, instead, require **General Ledger Account** and **Accounts Receivable Account** to be on the model.

In our publishing data model, for example, an audience that needs to see the entire company on a conceptual may just require the entity **Order**, yet in communicating with the sales department, the Sales Conceptual Data Model will have more details, showing not only **Order** but also **Order Line** and **Order Adjustment**.

Concepts such as those in the preceding discussion are represented on a conceptual data model. A conceptual data model is a one-page data model that captures the business need and project scope, designed for a particular audience. Limiting the conceptual data model to one page is important because it forces the modeler and participants to select only key concepts. We can fit 20 concepts on one page but not 500 concepts. A good rule of thumb, therefore, is to ask yourself if the audience for this model would include this concept as one of the top 20 concepts in their business. This will rule out concepts that are at too low a level of detail; they will appear in the more detailed logical data model. If you're having trouble limiting the number of concepts, think about whether or not there are other concepts into which the ones you're discussing could be grouped, such as grouping **Order Line** into **Order**. These higher concepts are the ones you should be including in the conceptual data model.

The conceptual data model includes concepts, their definitions, and the relationships that show how these concepts interact with each other. Unlike the logical and physical data models, as we will see, conceptual data models may contain many-to-many relationships. A sample conceptual data model appears in Figure 8.1.

In this diagram, the display preferences in ER/Studio have been changed to display the concept definitions. To display definitions on the model, choose `View > Diagram And Object Display Options`, or click on the icon and then choose `Definition` as the display level.

Note: The ER/Studio Business Architect application provides conceptual modeling capabilities which can be exported into Data Architect. However, in this example we are building a conceptual model in Data Architect.

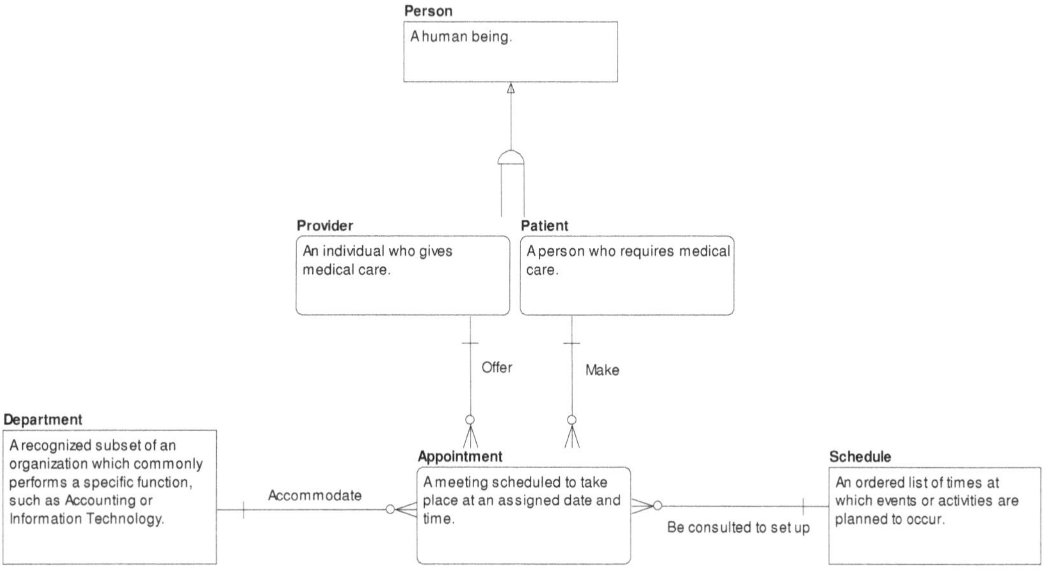

Figure 8.1 Healthcare Facility Appointment Conceptual Data Model

Business Rules (listed in the order we would typically walk someone through the model):

> Each **Person** may be a **Provider**, a **Patient**, or both a **Provider** and a **Patient**. Note that when the subtyping symbol does *not* have an 'X' in its center (as shown in Figure 8.1), it indicates that a member of

the supertype can play more than one subtype role. This is called an inclusive (overlapping) subtype. Here, a particular person can be both a provider and a patient.

Each **Provider** is a **Person**.

Each **Patient** is a **Person**.

Each **Provider** may offer one or many **Appointments**.

Each **Patient** may make one or many **Appointments**.

Each **Schedule** may be consulted to set up one or many **Appointments**.

Each **Department** may accommodate one or many **Appointments**.

Each **Appointment** must involve one **Provider**, one **Patient**, one **Department**, and one **Schedule**.

Notice on the model in Figure 8.1 that concepts such as **Provider** and **Patient** are likely to be considered concepts throughout the healthcare industry. There are also slightly more detailed concepts on this model, such as **Schedule** and **Appointment**, which are considered basic and critical and are therefore concepts for the particular audience for this conceptual data model. Yet these more detailed concepts may not be considered concepts within a different department, such as accounting and marketing, in this same healthcare company.

During the conceptual data modeling phase, documenting clearly and completely what each concept means is critical. All too often, we wait until it is too late in the development process to get definitions. Waiting too long usually leads to not writing definitions at all or doing a rush job by writing quick definition phrases that have little or no usefulness. If the definitions behind the terms on a data model are nonexistent or poor, multiple interpretations of the concept become a strong possibility. Imagine a business rule on our model that states that an **Employee** must have at least one **Benefits Package**. If the definition of **Employee** is lacking, we may wonder, for example, whether this business rule includes job applicants and retired employees.

By agreeing on definitions at the conceptual level, the more detailed logical and physical analysis will go more smoothly and take less time. For example, definitions can address the question, "Does **Customer** include potential customers or only existing customers?"

When the conceptual data model is complete, which includes concept definitions, it is a powerful tool that can provide a number of important business benefits:

- **Provides broad understanding**. We can capture extremely complex and encompassing business processes, application requirements, and even entire industries on a single piece of paper. This enables people with different backgrounds and roles to understand and communicate with each other on the same concepts, agreeing on or debating issues.
- **Defines scope and direction**. By visually showing concepts and their business rules, we can more easily identify a subset of the model to analyze. For example, we can model the entire Logistics department and then scope out of this a particular logistics application that we would like to build. The broad perspective of a conceptual data model can help us determine how planned and existing applications will coexist. It can provide direction and guidance on what new functionality the business will need next.
- **Offers proactive analysis**. By developing a high-level understanding of the application, there is a strong chance we will be able to identify important issues or concerns, saving substantial time and money later on. Examples include term definition differences and different interpretations of project scope.
- **Builds rapport between IT and the business**. A majority of organizations have some issues of internal communication between the business and IT departments. Building a conceptual data model together is a great way to remove or reduce these communication barriers. On one occasion, a key business user and I sketched out a Consumer Affairs CDM, which not only increased my business understanding, but also led to a strong relationship with this key user.

Relational and Dimensional Conceptual Data Models

Recall from this section's introduction that relational data modeling is the process of capturing how the business *works* by precisely representing business rules, while dimensional data modeling is the process of capturing how the business is *monitored* by precisely representing navigation. There are both relational and dimensional conceptual data models.

RELATIONAL CDM EXAMPLE

The relational conceptual model includes concepts, their definitions, and the relationships that capture the business rules binding these concepts. Unlike the logical and physical data models, as we will see, conceptual models may contain many-to-many relationships. For example, Figure 8.2 contains part of a financial relational CDM.

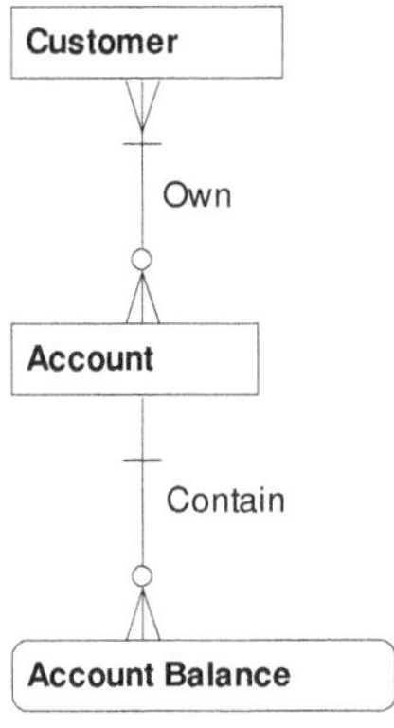

Figure 8.2 Financial relational CDM subset

Following is a full list of the concept definitions we arrived at from our meetings with the project sponsor:

Customer	A customer is a person or organization who obtains our product for resale. A person or organization must have obtained at least one product from us to be considered a customer. That is, prospects are not customers. Also, once a customer, always a customer, so even customers that have not obtained anything in 50 years are still considered customers. The customer is different than the consumer, who purchases the product for consumption as opposed to resale.
Account	An account is a contractual arrangement by which our bank holds funds on behalf of a customer.
Account Balance	An account balance is a financial record of how much money a customer has with our bank at the end of a given time period such as someone's checking account balance at the end of a month.

Business Rules (listed in the order we would typically walk someone through the model):

> Each **Customer** may own one or many **Accounts**.
> Each **Account** must be owned by one or many **Customers**.
> Each **Account** may contain one or many **Account Balances**.
> Each **Account Balance** must belong to one **Account**.

Notice that in this example definitions were not displayed directly on the diagram as on the model in Figure 8.1. I find that if the data model is small enough (and the definitions are short enough), it can be a valuable communication tool to display the definitions on the diagram. I also choose to display the definitions when I need to highlight poor or lacking definitions or definitions that I know will spur debate.

DIMENSIONAL CDM EXAMPLE

To understand and document our reporting requirements, we can also build a dimensional CDM such as the example in Figure 8.3.

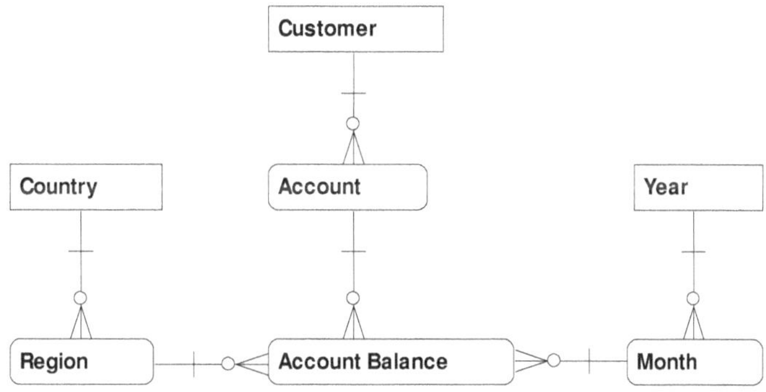

Figure 8.3 Financial dimensional CDM using the same notation as the relational CDM

In this case, we'd like to see certain measures around account balances (such as **Account Balance Amount**) at a **Region**, **Account**, and **Month** level and then have the ability to navigate to higher levels (e.g., viewing **Account Balance Amount** at a **Country** level). We take measures such as **Account Balance Amount** up and down hierarchies. A hierarchy is when an entity instance is a child of at most one other entity instance such as the month `January 2016` belonging to only the year `2016`.

Concept definitions:

Account Balance	An account balance is a financial record of how much money a customer has with our bank at the end of a given time period such as someone's checking account balance at the end of a month.
Country	A country is a recognized nation with its own government, occupying a particular territory, which is included in the ISO country code listing.
Region	A region is our bank's own definition of dividing a country into smaller pieces for branch assignment or reporting purposes.
Customer	A customer is a person or organization who obtains our product for resale. A person or organization must have obtained at least one product from us to be considered a customer. That is, prospects are not customers. Also, once a customer, always a customer, so even customers that have not obtained anything in 50 years are still considered customers. The customer is different than the consumer, who purchases the product for consumption as opposed to resale.
Account	An account is a contractual arrangement by which our bank holds funds on behalf of a customer.
Year	A year is a period of time containing 365 days, consistent with the Gregorian calendar.
Month	A month is each of the twelve named periods into which a year is divided.

The model in Figure 8.3 was created using the same symbols we used for the relational, which is called Information Engineering (IE) notation. ER/Studio contains a separate set of symbols we can use to build the dimensional model as shown in Figure 8.4.

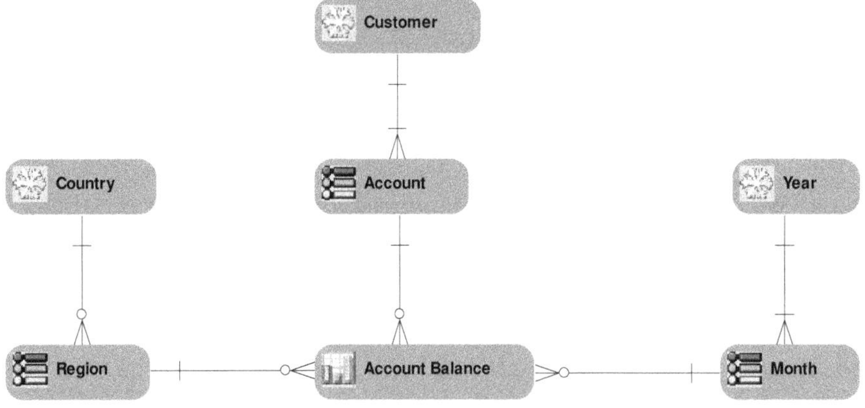

Figure 8.4 Financial dimensional CDM using dimensional notation

The relationship lines have the same appearance as in Figure 8.3, yet the entities appear as bub-tangles. There are several different types of entities on a dimensional model, each type distinguished with a different icon.

Account Balance is an example of a fact table (on a conceptual and logical data model often called a "meter"). The icon for a meter in ER/Studio is the graph symbol because we are measuring the health of a business process. A meter is an entity containing a related set of measures. It is not a person, place, event, or thing, as we find on the relational model. Instead, it is a bucket of common measures. As a group, common measures address a business process such as Profitability, Employee Satisfaction, or Sales. The meter is so important to the dimensional model that the name of the meter is often the name of the application: the **Sales** meter, the Sales Data Mart.

Region, **Account**, and **Month** are examples of dimensions, distinguished by the three horizontal lines icon. A dimension is a subject whose purpose is to add meaning to the measures. All of the different ways of filtering, sorting, and summing measures make use of dimensions.

Country, **Customer**, and **Year** are examples of snowflakes, distinguished by the snowflake icon. These are higher levels in a hierarchy. A hierarchy is when a higher level can contain many lower levels but a lower level can belong to, at most, one higher level. These higher levels indicate that we can view the measures in the meter at these levels as well. For example, we can view **Account Balance Amount** at the **Country**, **Customer**, and **Year** level.

We will explain additional dimensional terminology in Chapter 9, Logical Data Models. When I build a dimensional data model, I use the notation I think my audience will best understand. I will use the IE notation when my audience is already very familiar with this modeling notation from the relational data models but often use the dimensional data modeling notation when my audience is less familiar with data modeling.

Creating a Conceptual Data Model

There are five steps to conceptual data modeling as illustrated in Figure 8.5.

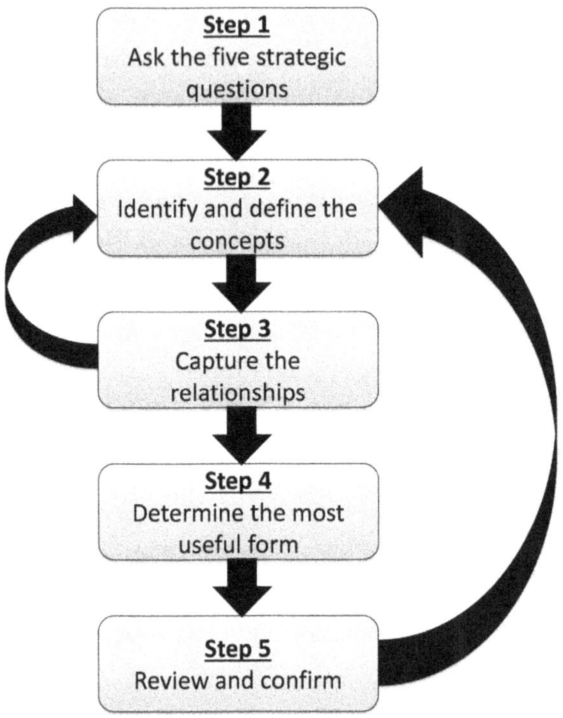

Figure 8.5 Five steps to conceptual data modeling

Before you begin any project, there are five strategic questions that must be asked (Step 1). These questions are a prerequisite to the success of any application effort. Next, identify all of the concepts within the scope of the application you are building (Step 2). Make sure each concept is clearly and completely defined. Then determine how these concepts are related to each other (Step 3). Often, you will need to go back to Step 2 at this point because in capturing relationships you often come up with new concepts—and then there are new relationships between these new concepts. Next, decide the most useful form for making sure your work during this phase is put to good use (Step 4). Someone will need to review your work and use your findings during development, so deciding on the most useful form is an important step. As a final step, review your work to get approval to move on to the logical data modeling phase (Step 5).

STEP 1: ASK THE FIVE STRATEGIC QUESTIONS

There are five questions that need to be asked (refer to the example in Figure 8.6):

1. **What is the application going to do?** Precisely and clearly document the answer to this question in a few sentences. Make sure to include whether you are replacing an existing system, delivering new functionality, integrating several existing applications together, etc. Always "begin with the end in mind," and so you know exactly what you are going to deliver. This question helps determine the scope of the application.

2. **"As is" or "to be"?** You need to know if there is a requirement to understand and model the current business environment (that is, the "as is" view) or to understand and model a proposed business environment (that is, the "to be" view).

3. **Is analytics a requirement?** Analytics, in informal terms, is the field of playing with numbers. That is, taking measurements such as **Gross Sales Amount** or **Inventory Count** and viewing them at different levels of granularity such as by day or year. If there is a requirement for analytics, at least part of your solution needs to be dimensional. Relational modeling focuses on business rules, and dimensional modeling focuses on business questions.

4. **Who is the audience?** That is, who is the person or group who is the validator and can confirm your understanding of the CDM, and who will be the users of the CDM? It is a good policy with anything you produce to determine early on who will check your work (the validators) and who will be the recipient or users of your work. This question will ensure you choose the ideal display format for your conceptual data model. Note that if the validators and users vary considerably in their technical expertise, you may need more than one form for the CDM.

5. **Flexibility or simplicity?** In terms of design, there is always a balancing act between flexibility and simplicity. If you are leaning more towards flexibility, you will most likely use some generic terms such as **Event** instead of **Order** or **Person** instead of **Employee**.

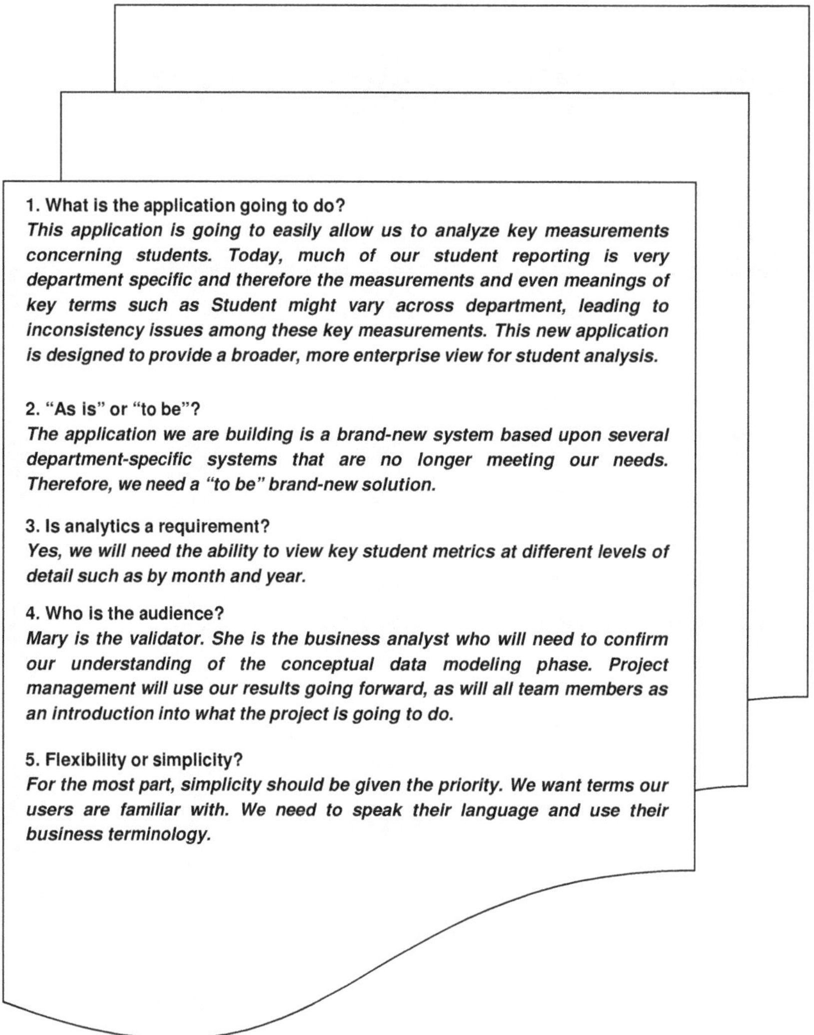

1. What is the application going to do?
This application is going to easily allow us to analyze key measurements concerning students. Today, much of our student reporting is very department specific and therefore the measurements and even meanings of key terms such as Student might vary across department, leading to inconsistency issues among these key measurements. This new application is designed to provide a broader, more enterprise view for student analysis.

2. "As is" or "to be"?
The application we are building is a brand-new system based upon several department-specific systems that are no longer meeting our needs. Therefore, we need a "to be" brand-new solution.

3. Is analytics a requirement?
Yes, we will need the ability to view key student metrics at different levels of detail such as by month and year.

4. Who is the audience?
Mary is the validator. She is the business analyst who will need to confirm our understanding of the conceptual data modeling phase. Project management will use our results going forward, as will all team members as an introduction into what the project is going to do.

5. Flexibility or simplicity?
For the most part, simplicity should be given the priority. We want terms our users are familiar with. We need to speak their language and use their business terminology.

Figure 8.6 Sample answers to the five strategic questions for a student application

STEP 2: IDENTIFY AND DEFINE THE CONCEPTS

Now that we have direction, we can work with the business experts to identify the concepts within the scope of the application and come up with an agreed-upon definition for each concept.

For Relational

To identify and define the relational concepts, recall our definition of an entity as a noun or noun phrase that fits into one of six categories: who, what, when, where, why, or how. We can use these six categories to create a Concept Template for capturing the entities on our conceptual data model. See Table 8.2.

Who?	What?	When?	Where?	Why?	How?
1.	1.	1.	1.	1.	1.
2.	2.	2.	2.	2.	2.
3.	3.	3.	3.	3.	3.
4.	4.	4.	4.	4.	4.
5.	5.	5.	5.	5.	5.

Table 8.2 Concept template

Table 8.3 contains a completed concept template for an Account System.

Account Project Concepts

Who?	What?	When?	Where?	Why?	How?
1. Customer	1. Account	1. Account Open Date	1. Branch	1. Check Debit	1. Check
2.	2.	2.	2.	2. Deposit Credit	2. Deposit Slip
3.	3.	3.	3.	3. Interest Credit	3. Withdrawal Slip
4.	4.	4.	4.	4. Monthly Statement Fee	4. Bank Account Statement
5.	5.	5.	5.	5. Withdrawal Debit	5. Account Balance

Table 8.3 Completed concept template for an account application

Here are some of the concept definitions:

Account	An account is an arrangement by which our bank holds funds on behalf of a customer. This arrangement includes the amount of funds we hold on behalf of a customer as well as a historical perspective of all of the transactions that have impacted this amount such as deposits and withdrawals. An account is structured for a particular purpose such as for stock investing, which is called a "brokerage account"; for interest-bearing, which is called a "savings account"; and for check writing, which is called a "checking account." An account can only be one of these types. That is, an account cannot be both checking and savings.
Account Balance	An account balance is a financial record of how much money a customer has with our bank at the end of a given time period such as someone's checking account balance at the end of a month. The account balance is impacted by many types of transactions including deposits and withdrawals. The account balance amount is restricted to just a single account. That is, if we wanted to know Bob the customer's net worth to our bank, we would need to sum the account balances for all of Bob's accounts.
Account Open Date	The day, month, and year that a customer first opens their account. This is the date that appears on the new account application form and is often not the same date as when the account first becomes active and useable. It may take 24-48 hours after the application is submitted for the account to be useable. The account open date can be any day of the week including a date when the bank is closed (if the customer submits the application using our website off hours).
Bank Account Statement	A periodic record of the events that have impacted the account. Events include withdrawals, deposits, etc. The bank account statement is usually issued monthly and includes the beginning account balance, a record of all events, and the ending account balance. Also listed are bank fees and, if applicable, any interest accrued.

For Dimensional

For dimensional, we need to determine the specific business questions that must be answered. For example, imagine that we work with the business analysts for a university and identify the following four questions:

1. Show me the number of students receiving financial aid by department and semester for the last five years. [From Financial Aid Office]

2. Show me the number of students on full or partial scholarship by department and semester for the last four years. [From Accounting Department]

3. How many students graduated by department and semester over the last three years? [From Alumni Affairs]

4. How many students applied to the university over the last ten years? I want to compare applications from high school students vs. other universities. [From Admissions Department]

STEP 3: CAPTURE THE RELATIONSHIPS

For Relational

Relational is all about capturing the business rules, so our objective at the relational conceptual level is to determine which entities relate to each other and then articulate the rules. For each relationship line on our model, we find ourselves asking up to eight questions: two on participation, two on optionality, and up to four questions on subtyping. See Table 8.4.

Question	Yes	No
Can an Entity A be related to more than one Entity B?		
Can an Entity B be related to more than one Entity A?		
Can an Entity A exist without an Entity B?		
Can an Entity B exist without an Entity A?		
Are there examples of Entity A that would be valuable to show?		
Are there examples of Entity B that would be valuable to show?		
Does an Entity A go through a lifecycle?		
Does an Entity B go through a lifecycle?		

Table 8.4 Eight questions to ask for each conceptual relationship

The first two questions are on participation, and the answers to these questions will determine whether there is a one or many symbol on the relationship line next to each entity. For example, if "Yes" Entity A can be related to more than one Entity B then there will be a many symbol on the relationship line next to Entity B.

The next two questions are on optionality, and the answers to these questions will determine whether there is a zero symbol on the relationship line next to either entity. For example, if "Yes" Entity A can exist without Entity B, then there will be a zero symbol on the relationship line next to Entity B.

The answers to the next four questions will determine where we introduce subtyping on the conceptual data model. When examples will aid communication or if it is important to explain the lifecycle of a concept, then subtyping needs to be added to the model.

Table 8.5 shows an example for our Account application.

Question	Yes	No
Can a Customer own more than one Account?	✓	
Can an Account be owned by more than one Customer?	✓	
Can a Customer exist without an Account?	✓	
Can an Account exist without a Customer?		✓
Are there examples of Customer that would be valuable to show?		✓
Are there examples of Account that would be valuable to show?	✓	
Does a Customer go through a lifecycle?	✓	
Does an Account go through a lifecycle?		✓
Can a Branch contain more than one Account?	✓	
Can an Account belong to more than one Branch?		✓
Can a Branch exist without an Account?	✓	
Can an Account exist without a Branch?		✓
Are there examples of Branch that would be valuable to show?		✓
Does a Branch go through a lifecycle?		✓

Table 8.5 Partial set of answers to the eight questions for an account application

Shading was used in the above table as a way to group the questions for each relationship together. That is, the unshaded rows answer the questions on the relationship between **Customer** and **Account** and the shaded rows answer the questions on the relationship between **Branch** and **Account**. Notice also since we answered the example and lifecycle questions for **Account** for

Account's relationship with **Customer**, we did not need to ask these questions again when **Account** is related with **Branch**.

For Dimensional

For dimensional, we need to take the business questions we identified in the prior step and then create a Grain Matrix. A grain matrix is a spreadsheet where the measures from the business questions become columns and the dimensional levels from the business questions become rows. The purpose of a grain matrix is to efficiently scope analytic applications. It is possible to elicit hundreds of business questions, and after plotting these questions on a grain matrix, we make the observation that questions from different departments can actually be very similar to each other. By consolidating questions, we can scope applications that address the needs for more than one department. Table 8.6 contains a completed grain matrix for our Student Application.

	Student Count
Financial Aid Indicator	1
Semester	1, 2, 3
Year	1, 2, 3, 4
Department	1, 2, 3
Scholarship Indicator	2
Graduation Indicator	3
High School Application Indicator	4
University Application Indicator	4

Table 8.6 Completed grain matrix for a student application

In this grain matrix, we took each of the four questions from Step 2 and parsed them so that the measure from each question (**Student Count**) became a column and the levels of detail in each question became rows. The numbers in the grain matrix refer back to the question numbers.

STEP 4: DETERMINE THE MOST USEFUL FORM

Someone will need to review your work and use your findings during development, so deciding the most useful form is an important step. We know the users for the model after getting an answer to Strategic Question #4 from

Step 1: *Who is our audience?* What person or group is the validator and can confirm our understanding of the CDM, and who will be the users of the CDM?

For Relational

If the validator and users are already familiar with data modeling notation, the decision is an easy one: use the traditional data modeling notation they are comfortable with such as this example in Figure 8.7. Refer back to the answers from Step 3 to see how these answers impacted the cardinality on this model. Subtyping has been introduced for **Account** because there was a need to show examples of **Account** and subtyping was introduced for **Customer** because **Customer** goes through a lifecycle.

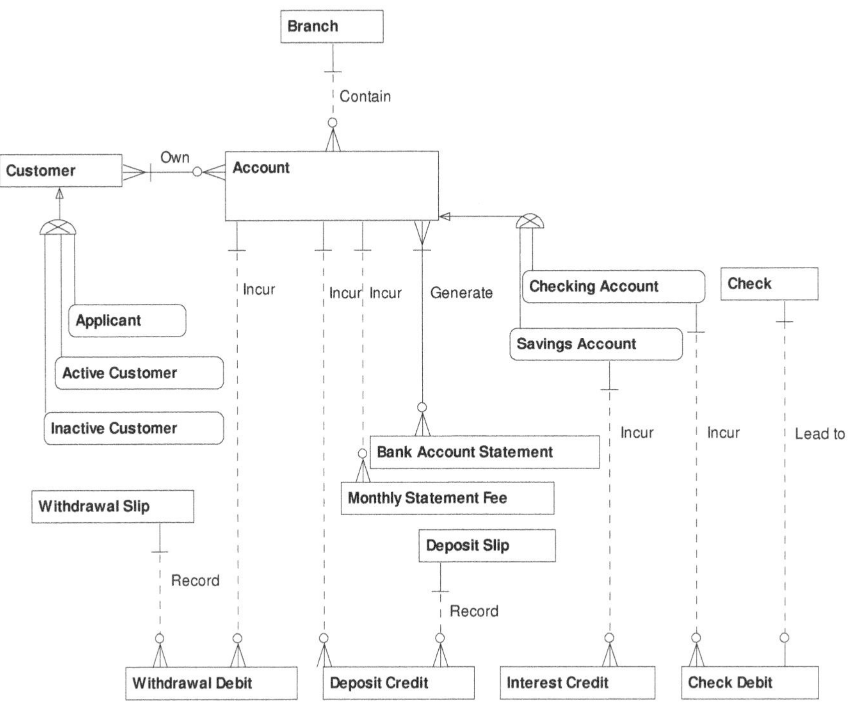

Figure 8.7 Traditional data modeling notation

However, very frequently at the conceptual level, the validator (and sometimes the users too) is not familiar with traditional data modeling notation or simply doesn't want to see a data model. In these situations, be creative with how you display the model, coming up with a visual that the audience for the model would understand. For example, Figure 8.8 contains a business sketch that can be used instead of the traditional data modeling notation.

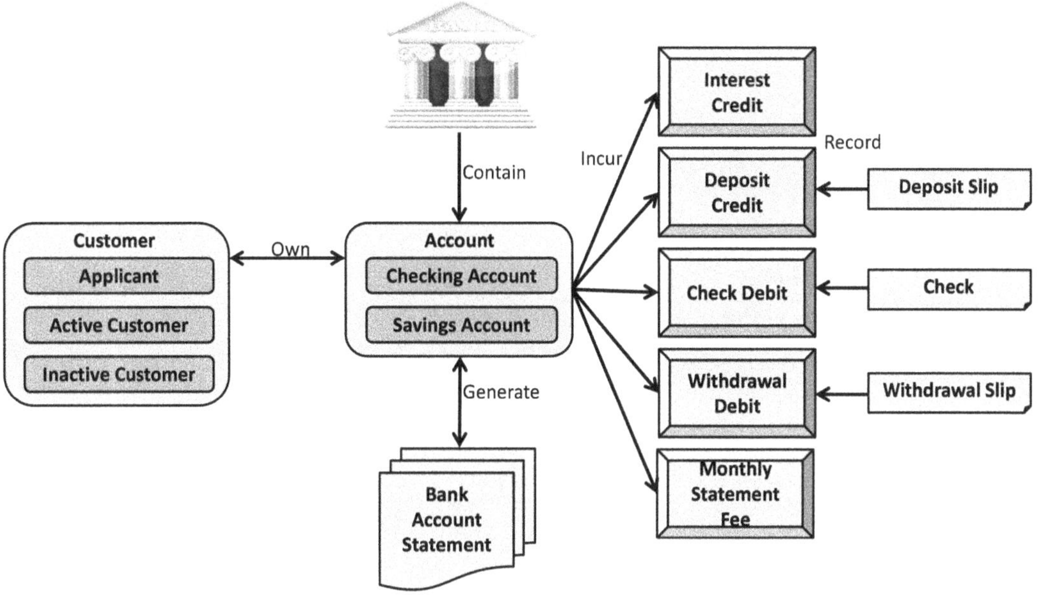

Figure 8.8 Business sketch instead of the traditional data model

Instead of the word "Branch" inside a rectangle, this model contains a picture of a branch. Instead of subtyping symbols, the subtypes are shown inside the supertype. Instead of the word "Bank Account Statement" inside a rectangle, a shape which represents a large document is used. Different shapes are used for smaller documents such as a **Withdrawal Slip** and button shapes are used to represent transactions such as an **Interest Credit**.

For Dimensional

Figure 8.9 shows the dimensional model with the traditional notation and Figure 8.10 shows my favorite conceptual dimensional form, the Axis Technique.

The axis technique is when you put the business process you are measuring in the center (e.g. **Student Attrition**) with each axis representing a dimension. The notches on each axis represent the levels of detail that are required to see the measures in the meter. This form works very well when the audience has limited exposure to data modeling.

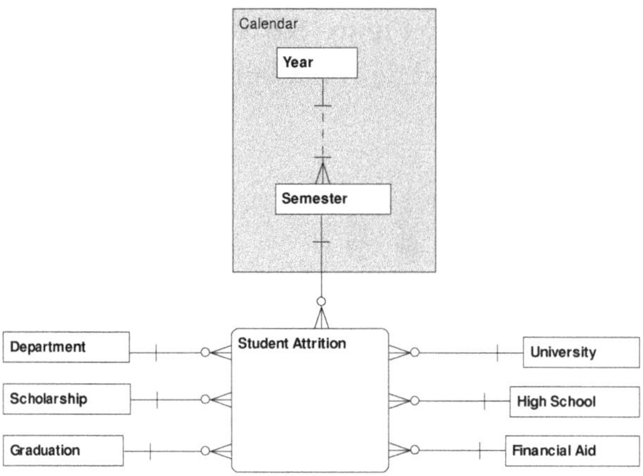

Figure 8.9 Traditional data modeling notation

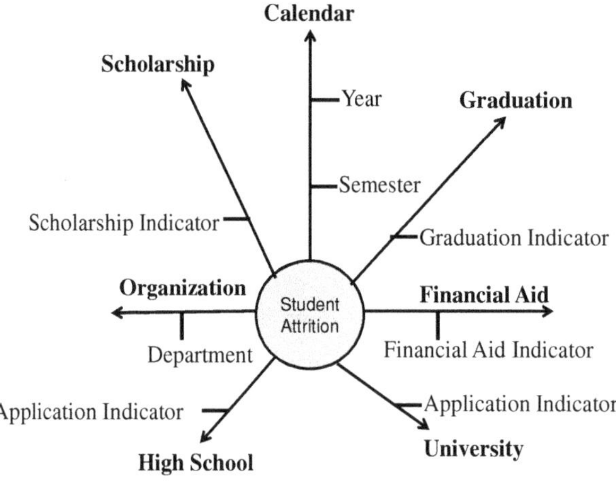

Figure 8.10 Axis technique data modeling notation

STEP 5: REVIEW AND CONFIRM

The validators will need to review our data model and frequently during this step there are changes that require us to go back to Step 2 and refine the concepts. Most likely (and hopefully) the validators were involved during the process of building the conceptual, and therefore in many cases this review step becomes a formality.

EXERCISE 8.1: CREATING A CONCEPTUAL DATA MODEL

Technics Publications needs a reporting application to track book sales. The data models we build through this chapter and the next two will be used as the design for a book sales analytics system where book sales can be tracked by different parameters.

For this exercise, create a dimensional CDM to track book sales at the level of month, region, and title. Then allow navigation from month to quarter and year, from region to country, and from title to category.

Create two separate data models in ER/Studio, one built using information engineering notation and the other dimensional notation. Recall that when we create a new data model, we are given a choice from a drop-down whether to select `Relational` or `Dimensional`. So build two data models for the same example, one relational, the other dimensional. See Appendix B for my models to compare when you're done.

As an aside (and outside the scope of this exercise), ER/Studio Business Architect offers process modeling functionality, which is extremely useful at the conceptual modeling stage, and it also maps process with data concepts. If you are not familiar with Business Architect, you can download a trial at http://www.embarcadero.com/downloads.

EXERCISE 8.2: Adding Definitions to a Data Model

Add the following definitions to one of the data models you created in the prior exercise and then display the model so that the definitions appear on the screen. (HINT: Choose `View > Diagram And Object Display Options` or click on the icon and then choose `Definition` as the display level.)

If you are looking for a quick way to enter these definitions, use the macro **Definition Editor**, which can be run by clicking the *Macros* tab in *Explorer*, right-clicking on the *Definition Editor*, and choosing `Run`. See Appendix B for my model when you're done.

Concept definitions:

Title Sales	A collection of measures that determine how our book sales are doing such as **Title Sales Quantity** and **Title Gross Sales Amount**.
Country	A country is a recognized nation with its own government, occupying a particular territory, and which is included in the ISO country code listing.
Region	A region is our own definition of dividing a country into smaller pieces for reporting purposes.
Category	A category is a grouping of like titles, commonly grouped by a subject so one knows which section to assign the book on a shelf at a bookstore or library.
Title	A title is a work for publication, distinguished by the Library of Congress by an ISBN (International Standard Book Number).
Year	A year is a period of time containing 365 days, consistent with the Gregorian calendar.
Quarter	A quarter is each of the four named periods into which a year is divided.
Month	A month is each of the twelve named periods into which a year is divided.

EXERCISE 8.3: SEGMENTING THE PUBLISHER CDM INTO SUBMODELS

Create a separate submodel for each dimension in one of the models you created in Exercise 8.1. There should be a separate submodel for **Calendar**, **Geography**, and **Title**.

EXERCISE 8.4: CREATING A CONCEPTUAL DATA MODEL FOR YOUR ORGANIZATION

Identify an area within your organization that is in need of a CDM and build it for them in ER/Studio using the approach from this chapter. Don't forget the definitions!

Key Points

- A concept is a key term that is both basic and critical to your audience.
- A conceptual data model (CDM) is a set of symbols and text that represents key concepts and the rules binding these key concepts for a specific business or application scope and for a particular audience.
- The relational CDM includes concepts, their definitions, and the relationships that show how these concepts interact with each other. The dimensional CDM includes concepts, their definitions, and the navigation paths required to analyze measures at different levels of detail.
- To create a CDM in ER/Studio, choose View > Diagram And Object Display Options or click on the icon and then choose `Entity` or `Definition` as the display level.

CHAPTER 9
Logical Data Models

What does business need?
Forget the technology
Enter logical

The highlighted row in Table 9.1 shows the focus of this chapter, which is the logical data model (LDM).

	Relational	Dimensional
Conceptual Data Model (CDM)	'One-pager' on business rules	'One-pager' on navigation
Logical Data Model (LDM)	**Detailed business solution on business rules**	**Detailed business solution on navigation**
Physical Data Model (PDM)	Detailed technical solution	

Table 9.1 The Logical Data Model is the focus of this chapter

A LDM takes the business need defined on a conceptual data model down to the next level of a business solution. That is, once you understand at a broad level the scope of an effort and what business people require to solve their problem, the next step is to come up with a solution for them in the form of a LDM. In this chapter, the logical data model is explained along with a comparison of relational and dimensional mindsets. We explain the relational techniques of normalization and abstraction, and dimensional terminology such as meters and dimensions. We will also practice building logical data models in ER/Studio.

Logical Data Model Explanation

A logical data model (LDM) is a business solution to a business problem. It is how the modeler captures the business requirements without complicating the model with implementation concerns such as software and hardware.

On the conceptual data model, we might learn, for example, what the terms, business rules, and scope would be for a new order entry system. After understanding the requirements for the order entry system, we create a LDM containing all of the attributes and business rules needed to deliver the application. For example, the conceptual data model will show that a **Customer** may place one or many **Orders**. The LDM will capture all of the details behind **Customer** and **Order** such as the customer's name, their address, the order number, and what is being ordered.

RELATIONAL AND DIMENSIONAL LOGICAL DATA MODELS

Recall from this section's introduction that relational data modeling is the process of capturing how the business *works* by precisely representing business rules, while dimensional data modeling is the process of capturing how the business is *monitored* by precisely representing navigation. There are both relational and dimensional logical data models.

You have seen examples of both relational and dimensional conceptual data models (recall Figures 8.3 and 8.4 from the chapter on conceptual data modeling); Figures 9.1 and 9.2 show these two examples at a logical level. Let's go through how each of these are built, starting with relational.

RELATIONAL LDM EXAMPLE

The relational logical data model includes entities along with their definitions, relationships, and attributes. For example, Figure 9.1 contains part of a financial relational LDM.

Business Rules (listed in the order we would typically walk someone through the model):

> Each **Customer** may own one or many **Accounts**.
> Each **Account** must be owned by one or many **Customers**.
> Each **Account** may contain one or many **Account Balances**.
> Each **Account Balance** must belong to one **Account**.

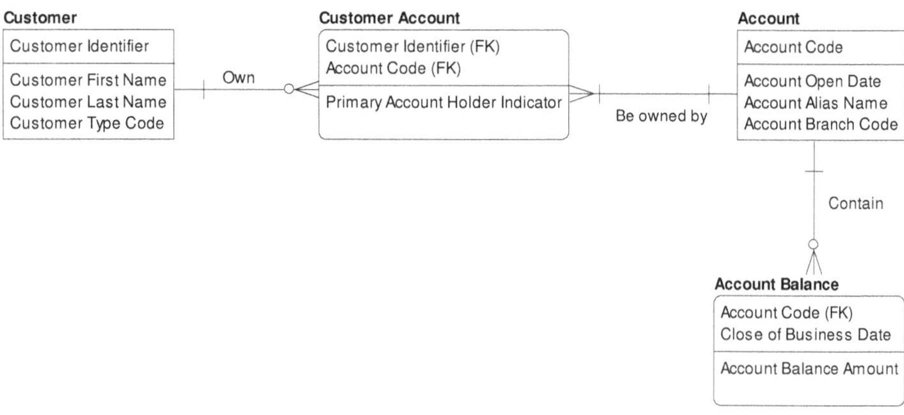

Figure 9.1 Financial relational LDM subset

DIMENSIONAL LDM EXAMPLE

Figure 9.2 shows a dimensional LDM.

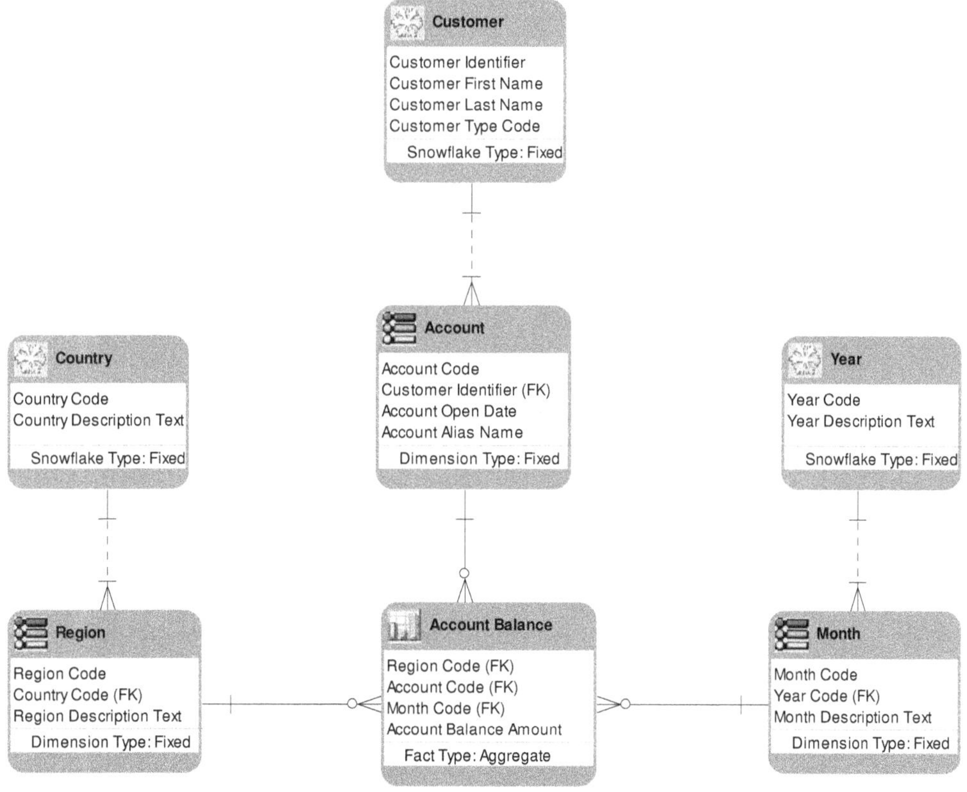

Figure 9.2 Financial dimensional LDM

We take measures such as **Account Balance Amount** up and down hierarchies. In this case, we'd like to see Account Balance Amount at a Region, Account, and Month level and then have the ability to navigate to higher levels such as viewing Account Balance Amount at a Country level instead of the more granular Region level.

Region is an interesting level to discuss. Often when building a dimensional data model, we trace back the measures and ways of looking at these measures to a relational data model that will eventually be the source for the dimensional data. On our relational data model in Figure 9.1, we have an **Account Branch Code** in the **Account** entity. On the corresponding dimensional data model, however, there is no need to know what the branch code is—only the higher level of **Region**. Therefore, each **Region** has to be derived from the corresponding **Branch Code** because in this case, **Region** was requested as an easier level to navigate than **Branch**.

CREATING A RELATIONAL LOGICAL DATA MODEL

The two techniques used to build the relational logical data model are normalization and abstraction.

NORMALIZATION

When I turned 12, I received a trunk full of baseball cards as a birthday present from my parents. I was delighted, not just because there may have been a Hank Aaron or Pete Rose buried somewhere in that trunk, but because I loved to organize the cards. I categorized each card according to year and team. Organizing the cards in this way gave me a deep understanding of the players and their teams. To this day, I can answer many baseball card trivia questions.

Normalization, in general, is the process of applying a set of rules with the goal of organizing *something*. I was normalizing the baseball cards according to year and team. We can also apply a set of rules and normalize the attributes within our organizations. Just as those baseball cards lay unsorted in that trunk, our companies have huge numbers of attributes spread throughout departments and applications. The rules applied to normalizing the baseball cards entailed first sorting by year and then by team within a year. The rules for normalizing our attributes can be boiled down to a single sentence:

> Make sure every attribute is single-valued and provides a fact completely and only about its primary key.

The underlined terms require more of an explanation.

Single-valued means an attribute must contain only one piece of information. If **Consumer Name** contains both the consumer's first and last name, for example, we must split **Consumer Name** into two attributes: **Consumer First Name** and **Consumer Last Name**.

Provides a fact means that a given primary key value will always return no more than one of every attribute that is identified by this key. If a **Customer Identifier** value of `123` for example, returns three customer last names (`Smith`, `Jones`, and `Roberts`), it violates this part of the normalization definition.

Completely means that the minimal set of attributes that uniquely identify an instance of the entity is present in the primary key. If, for example, there are two attributes in an entity's primary key, but only one is needed for uniqueness, the attribute that is not needed for uniqueness should be removed from the primary key.

Only means that each attribute must provide a fact about the primary key and nothing else. That is, there can be no hidden dependencies. For example, assume an **Order** is identified by an **Order Number**. Within **Order**, there are many attributes including **Order Scheduled Delivery Date**, **Order Actual Delivery Date**, and **Order On Time Indicator**. **Order On Time Indicator** contains either a `Yes` or a `No`, providing a fact about whether the **Order Actual Delivery Date** is less than or equal to the **Order Scheduled Delivery Date**. **Order On Time Indicator**, therefore, provides a fact about **Order Actual Delivery Date** and **Order Scheduled Delivery Date**, not directly about **Order Number**. **Order On Time Indicator** is an example of a derived attribute, meaning it is calculated. Derived attributes are removed from a normalized model.

So a general definition for normalization is that it is a series of rules for organizing something. As mentioned, the series of rules can be summarized as: *Every attribute is single-valued and provides a fact completely and only about its primary key*. An informal definition I frequently use for normalizing is "A formal process of asking business questions." We cannot determine if every attribute is single-valued and provides a fact completely and only about its primary key unless we understand the data. To understand the data, we usually need to ask lots of questions. Even for an apparently simple attribute such as **Phone Number,** for example, we can ask many questions:

- Whose phone number is this?
- Do you always have to have a phone number?
- Can you have more than one phone number?
- Do you ever recognize the area code as separate from the rest of the phone number?
- Do you ever need to see phone numbers outside a given country?
- What type of phone number is this? That is, is it a fax number, mobile number, etc.?
- Does the time of day matter? For example, do we need to distinguish between the phone numbers to use during working hours and outside working hours? Of course, that would lead to a discussion on what we mean by "working hours."

To ensure that every attribute is single-valued and provides a fact completely and only about its primary key, we apply a series of rules in small steps, where each step (or level of normalization) checks something that moves us towards our goal. Most data professionals would agree that the full set of normalization levels is the following:

first normal form (1NF)
second normal form (2NF)
third normal form (3NF)
Boyce/Codd normal form (BCNF)
fourth normal form (4NF)
fifth normal form (5NF)

Each level of normalization includes the lower levels of rules that precede it. If a model is in 5NF, it is also in 4NF, BCNF, and so on. Even though there are higher levels of normalization than 3NF, many interpret the term *normalized* to mean 3NF. This is because the higher levels of normalization (that is, BCNF, 4NF, and 5NF) cover specific situations that occur much less frequently than the first three levels. Therefore, to keep things simple, this chapter focuses only on first through third normal forms.

Initial Chaos

I would describe the trunk of baseball cards I received as being in a chaotic state because there was no order to the cards. Just a bunch of cards thrown in a large box. I removed the chaos by organizing the cards. The term *chaos* can be applied to any unorganized pile, including attributes. We may have a strong understanding of each of the attributes, such as their name and definition, but we lack knowledge as to which entity the attribute should be assigned. When I pick out a 1978 Pete Rose from the box and put this card in the 1978 pile, I start bringing order were there was chaos—similar to assigning **Customer Last Name** to the customer pile (called the **Customer** entity).

Let's walk through an example. Figure 9.3 contains a bunch of what appears to be employee attributes.

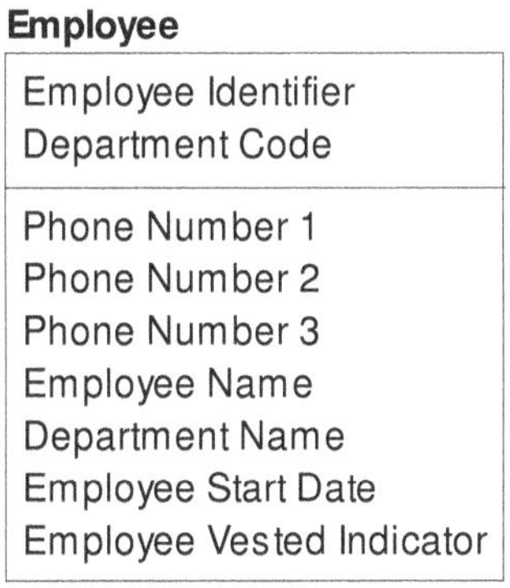

Employee

Employee
Employee Identifier Department Code
Phone Number 1 Phone Number 2 Phone Number 3 Employee Name Department Name Employee Start Date Employee Vested Indicator

Figure 9.3 Initial chaotic state

Often definitions are of poor quality or missing completely, and let's assume that this is the case with this **Employee** entity. We are told, however, that **Employee Vested Indicator** captures whether an **Employee** is eligible for retirement benefits (a value of `Y` for "yes" means the employee is eligible, and a value of `N` for "no" means the employee is not eligible) and this indicator is derived from the employee's start date. For example, if an employee has worked for the company for at least five years then this indicator contains the value Y.

What is lacking at this point, and what will be solved though normalization, is putting these attributes into the right entities.

It is very helpful to have some sample values for each of these attributes, so let's assume the spreadsheet in Table 9.2 is a representative set of employee values.

Emp Id	Dept Cd	Phone 1	Phone 2	Phone 3	Emp Name	Dept Name	Emp Start Date	Emp Vested Ind
123	A	973-555-1212	678-333-3333	343-222-1111	Henry Winkler	Data Admin	4/1/2012	N
789	A	732-555-3333	678-333-3333	343-222-1111	Steve Martin	Data Admin	3/5/2007	Y
565	B	333-444-1111	516-555-1212	343-222-1111	Mary Smith	Data Warehouse	2/25/2006	Y
744	A	232-222-2222	678-333-3333	343-222-1111	Bob Jones	Data Admin	5/5/2011	N

Table 9.2 Sample employees

First Normal Form (1NF)

Recall that the series of rules can be summarized as: *Every attribute is single-valued and provides a fact completely and only about its primary key*. First Normal Form (1NF) is the "single-valued" part. It means that for a given primary-key value, we can find, at most, one of every attribute that depends on that primary key.

Ensuring each attribute provides a fact about its primary key includes correcting the more blatant issue shown in Table 9.2 as well as addressing repeating groups and multi-valued attributes. Specifically, the modeler needs to:

- **Move repeating attributes to a new entity**. When there are two or more of the same attribute in the same entity, they are called repeating attributes. The reason repeating attributes violate 1NF is that for a given primary key value, we are getting more than one value back for the same attribute. Repeating attributes often take a sequence number as part of their name such as phone number in this employee example. We can find ourselves asking many questions just to determine if there are any repeating attributes we need to address. We can have a question template like this: "Can a [[insert entity name here]] have more than one [[insert attribute name here]]?" So these are all valid questions in our employee example:

  - Can an **Employee** have more than one **Employee Identifier**?
  - Can an **Employee** have more than one **Department Code**?
  - Can an **Employee** have more than one **Phone Number**?
  - Can an **Employee** have more than one **Employee Name**?
  - Can an **Employee** have more than one **Department Name**?
  - Can an **Employee** have more than one **Employee Start Date**?
  - Can an **Employee** have more than one **Employee Vested Indicator**?

- **Separate multi-valued attributes**. *Multi-valued* means that within the same attribute we are storing at least two distinct values. In other words, there are at least two different business concepts hiding in one attribute. For example, **Employee Name** may contain both a first name and last name. **Employee First Name** and **Employee Last Name** can be considered distinct attributes; and therefore, `Henry Winkler` stored in Name, is multi-valued because it contains both `Henry` and `Winkler`. We may find ourselves asking many questions just to determine if there are any multi-valued attributes we need to identify. We can use another question template: "Does a [[insert attribute name here]] contain more than one piece of business information?" So these are all valid questions in our employee example:

  - Does an **Employee Identifier** contain more than one piece of business information?
  - Does a **Department Code** contain more than one piece of business information?
  - Does a **Phone Number** contain more than one piece of business information?
  - Does an **Employee Name** contain more than one piece of business information?

- Does a **Department Name** contain more than one piece of business information?
- Does an **Employee Start Date** contain more than one piece of business information?
- Does an **Employee Vested Indicator** contain more than one piece of business information?

After talking with a business expert and answering these questions based on the sample data from Table 9.2, we update the model which appears in Figure 9.4.

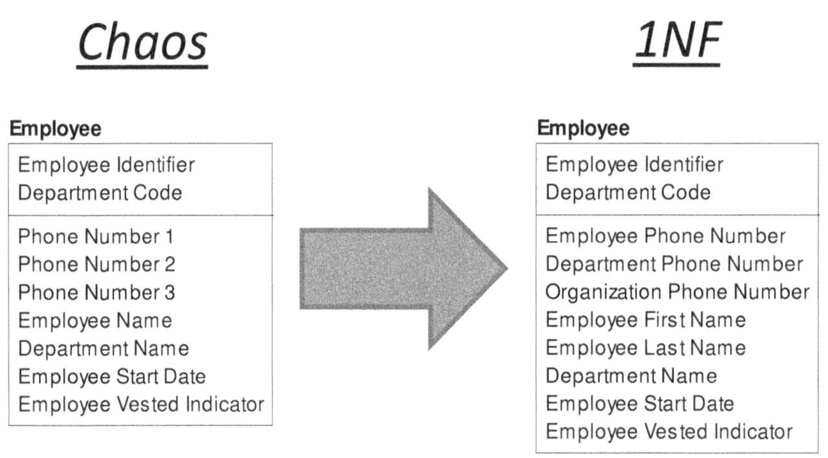

Figure 9.4 From Chaos to 1NF

We learned that although **Phone Number 1**, **Phone Number 2**, and **Phone Number 3** appear as repeating attributes, they are really three different pieces of information based upon the sample values we were given. **Phone Number 3** contained the same value for all four employees, and we learned after validating with the business expert that this is the organization's phone number. **Phone Number 2** varied by department, so this attribute was renamed to **Department Phone Number**. **Phone Number 3** is different for each employee, and we learned that this is the **Employee Phone Number**. We also were told that **Employee Name** does contain more than one piece of information and therefore should be split into **Employee First Name** and **Employee Last Name**.

Second Normal Form (2NF)

Recall that the series of rules can be summarized as: *Every attribute is single-valued and provides a fact completely and only about its primary key.* First Normal Form (1NF) is the "single-valued" part. Second Normal Form (2NF) is the "completely" part. This means each entity must have the minimal set of attributes that uniquely identifies each entity instance.

As with 1NF, we will find ourselves asking many questions to determine if we have the minimal primary key. We can use another question template: "Are all of the attributes in the primary key needed to retrieve a single instance of [[insert attribute name here]]?" In the Employee example shown in Figure 9.4, the "minimal set of primary key instances" are **Employee Identifier** and **Department Code.**

So these are all valid questions for our employee example:

- Are both **Employee Identifier** and **Department Code** needed to retrieve a single instance of **Employee Phone Number**?
- Are both **Employee Identifier** and **Department Code** needed to retrieve a single instance of **Department Phone Number**?
- Are both **Employee Identifier** and **Department Code** needed to retrieve a single instance of **Organization Phone Number**?
- Are both **Employee Identifier** and **Department Code** needed to retrieve a single instance of **Employee First Name**?
- Are both **Employee Identifier** and **Department Code** needed to retrieve a single instance of **Employee Last Name**?
- Are both **Employee Identifier** and **Department Code** needed to retrieve a single instance of **Department Name**?
- Are both **Employee Identifier** and **Department Code** needed to retrieve a single instance of **Employee Start Date**?
- Are both **Employee Identifier** and **Department Code** needed to retrieve a single instance of **Employee Vested Indicator**?

Normalization is a process of asking business questions. In this example, we could not complete 2NF without asking the business "Can an Employee work for more than one Department at the same time?" If the answer is "Yes" or "Sometimes," then the first model in Figure 9.5 on the left is accurate. If the answer is "No," then the second model prevails.

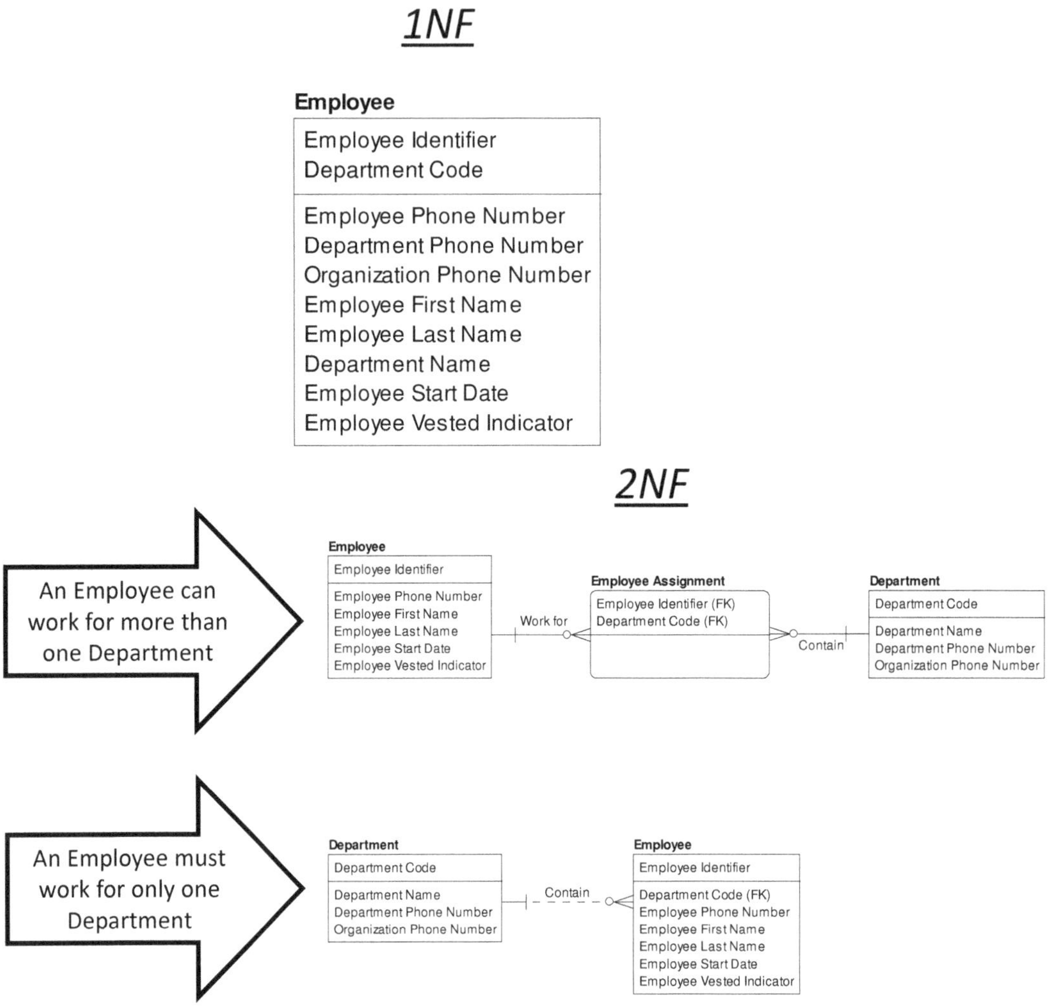

Figure 9.5 Employee example in 2NF

Third Normal Form (3NF)

Recall that the series of rules can be summarized as: *Every attribute is single-valued and provides a fact completely and only about its primary key.* First Normal Form (1NF) is the "single-valued" part. Second Normal Form (2NF) is the "completely" part. Third Normal Form (3NF) is the "only" part.

3NF requires the removal of hidden dependencies. Each attribute must be directly dependent on the primary key and not directly dependent on any other attributes within the same entity.

The data model is a communication tool. The relational logical data model communicates which attributes are facts about the primary key and only the primary key. Hidden dependencies complicate the model and make it difficult to determine how to retrieve values for each attribute.

To resolve a hidden dependency, you will either need to remove the attribute that is a fact about non-primary key attribute(s) from the model or you will need to create a new entity with a different primary key for the attribute that is dependent on the non-primary key attribute(s).

As with 1NF and 2NF, we will find ourselves asking many questions to uncover hidden dependencies. We can use another question template: "Is [[insert attribute name here]] a fact about any other attribute in this same entity?"

So these are all valid questions for our contact example:

- Is **Employee Phone Number** a fact about any other attribute in **Employee**?
- Is **Organization Phone Number** a fact about any other attribute in **Department**?
- Is **Department Phone Number** a fact about any other attribute in **Department**?
- Is **Employee First Name** a fact about any other attribute in **Employee**?
- Is **Employee Last Name** a fact about any other attribute in **Employee**?
- Is **Department Name** a fact about any other attribute in **Department**?
- Is **Employee Start Date** a fact about any other attribute in **Employee**?
- Is **Employee Vested Indicator** a fact about any other attribute in **Employee**?

Note that **Employee Vested Indicator** may be a fact about **Employee Start Date** as **Employee Vested Indicator** can be calculated `Y` or `N` based upon the employee's start date. Figure 9.6 shows the model now in 3NF after removing the derived attribute, **Employee Vested Indicator.**

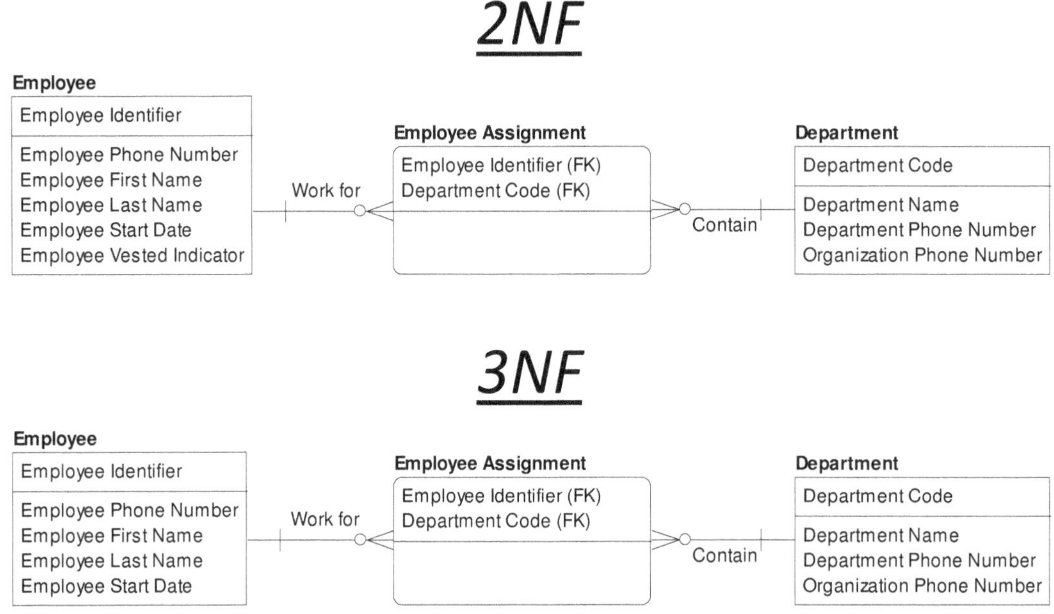

Figure 9.6 Employee example in 3NF

You will find that the more you normalize, the more you go from applying rules sequentially to applying them in parallel. For example, instead of first applying 1NF to your model everywhere, then when you are done applying 2NF, and so on, you will find yourself looking to apply all levels at once. This can be done by looking at each entity and making sure the primary key is correct and contains a minimal set of attributes and that all attributes are facts about only the primary key.

ABSTRACTION

Normalization is a mandatory technique on the relational logical data model. Abstraction is an optional technique. Abstraction brings flexibility to your data models by redefining and combining some of the attributes, entities, and relationships within the model into more generic terms.

For example, we can take our normalized data model and abstract **Employee** into **Party** and **Role**, as shown in Figure 9.7.

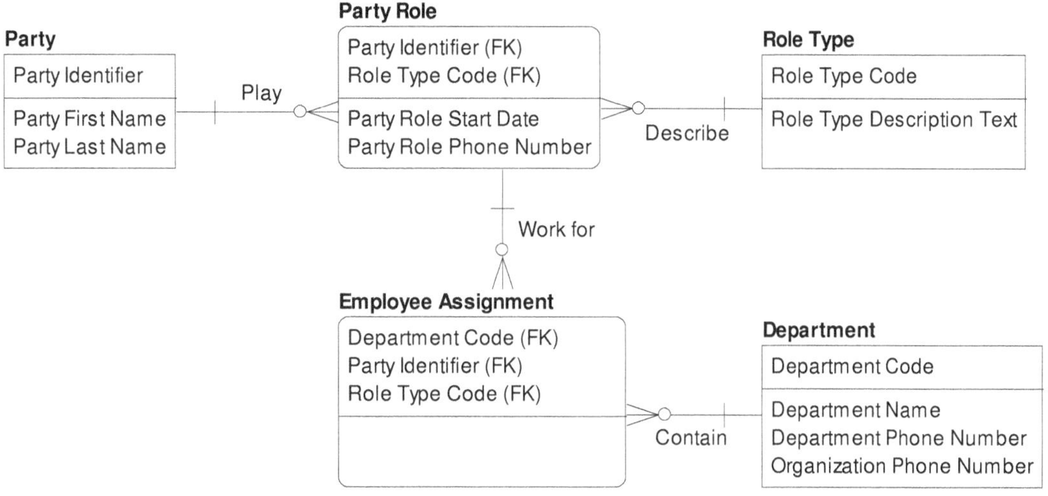

Figure 9.7 Employee abstracted

Notice the extra flexibility we gain with abstraction. By abstracting **Employee** into the **Party Role** concept, we can accommodate additional roles without changes to our model and most likely without changes to our application. Roles such as **Contractor** and **Consumer** can be added gracefully without updates to our model. However, this extra flexibility does come with a price. Actually, three high prices:

- **Loss of communication**. The concepts we abstract are no longer represented explicitly on the model. That is, when we abstract, we often convert column names to entity instances. For example, **Employee** is no longer an explicit entity but is instead an entity instance of **Party Role**, with a **Role Type Code** value of `03` for `Employee`. One of the main reasons we model is to aid communication, but abstracting can definitely hinder communication.

- **Loss of business rules**. When we abstract, we can also lose business rules. To be more specific, the rules we enforced on the data model before abstraction now need to be enforced through other means such as through programming code. If we wanted to enforce that an **Employee** must have a **Start Date,** for example, we can no longer enforce this rule through the abstracted data model in Figure 9.7.

- **Additional development complexity**. Abstracting requires sophisticated development techniques to turn attributes into values when loading an abstract structure, or to turn values back into attributes when populating a structure from an abstract source. Imagine the work to populate **Party Role** from the source **Employee**. It would be much easier for a developer to load data from an entity called **Employee** into an entity called **Employee**. The code would be simpler and it would be very fast to load.

So although abstraction provides flexibility to an application, it does come with a cost. It makes the most sense to use abstraction when the modeler or analyst anticipates additional *types* of something coming in the near future. In the example from Figure 9.7, additional types of people might include **Contractor** and **Consumer**.

Creating a Dimensional Logical Data Model

Recall the dimensional data model from earlier in this chapter, repeated here in Figure 9.8.

In a dimensional model, each structure is assigned a *Table Model* type, which is distinguished by an icon displayed in the upper left corner of the entity box. You can further describe the structure in the *Table Editor* by assigning it a *Table Type* that displays at the bottom of the entity (e.g., Fixed). The *Table Type* does not change how the data is handled but provides information to the reader about the data in the structure. It is purely for documentation purposes.

Account Balance is an example of a fact table (on a conceptual and logical data model, this is often called a "meter"). The icon for a meter in ER/Studio is the graph symbol because we are measuring something. A meter is an entity containing a related set of measures. It is not a person, place, event, or thing, as we find on the relational model. Instead, it is a bucket of common measures; in this case, just the measure **Account Balance Amount**. As a group, common measures address a business process such as **Profitability**, **Employee Satisfaction**, or **Sales**.

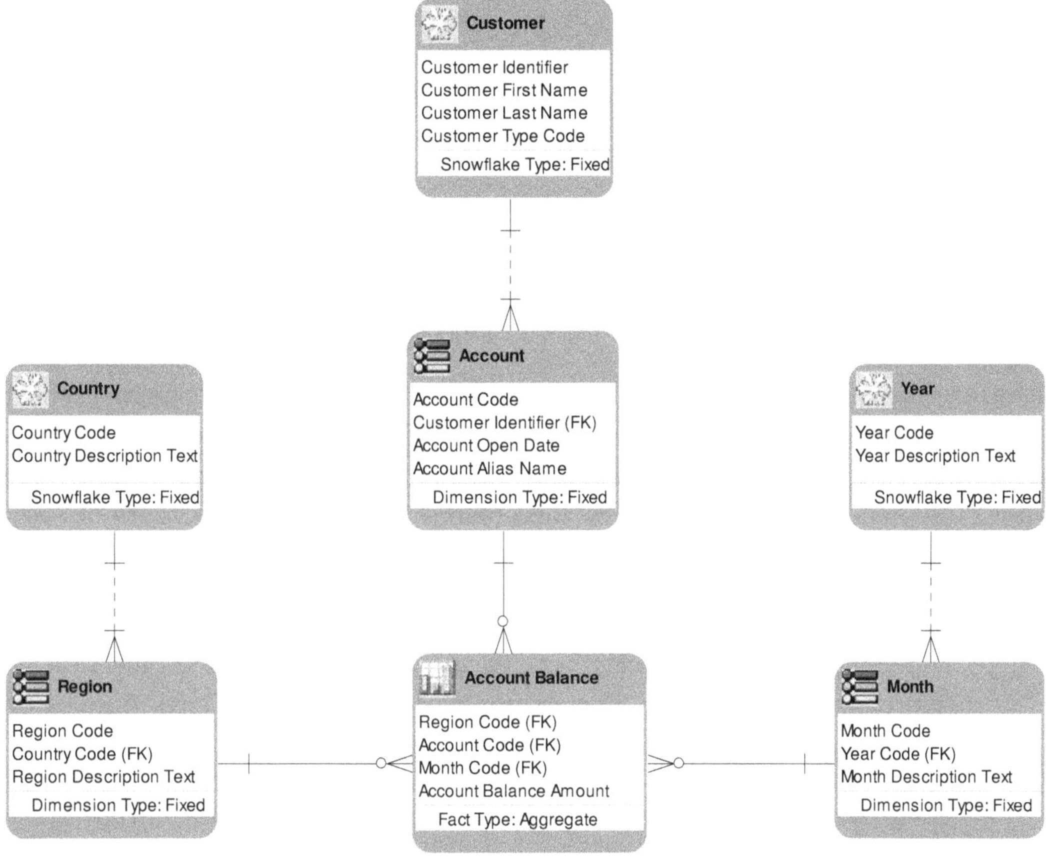

Figure 9.8 Financial dimensional LDM

A fact table can be further classified into one these four types:

- **Aggregate**. Also known as a summarization, an aggregate contains information that is stored at a higher level of granularity than translation level details. Aggregates provide quick access to data and can be very user-friendly structures for users and reporting tools. **Account Balance** is an aggregate.

- **Atomic**. Contains the lowest level of detail available in the business, often the same level of detail that exists in operational systems such as order entry systems. An example of an atomic fact in the account balance subject area would be the individual bank account withdrawal and deposit transactions.

- **Cumulative**. Also known as accumulating, cumulative captures how long it takes to complete a business process. For example, tracking how long it takes from application through completion of a home mortgage application would be represented in a cumulative fact.

- **Snapshot**. Contains time-related information that details specific steps in the life of the entity. For example, snapshot information for a sale could contain information such as when the order was created, confirmed, shipped, delivered, and paid for.

Region, **Account**, and **Month** are examples of dimensions, distinguished by the three horizontal lines icon. A dimension is a subject whose purpose is to add meaning to the measures. All of the different ways of filtering, sorting, and summing measures make use of dimensions. Dimensions have their own attributes. A dimension can be further classified into one these six types:

- **Fixed Dimension**. Also known as a Type 0 Slowly Changing Dimension (SCD for short), a fixed dimension contains values that do not change over time. For example, **Gender** is a fixed dimension containing the values `Male` and `Female`.

- **Degenerate**. A dimension whose attribute(s) have been moved to the fact table. A degenerate dimension is most common when the original dimension contained only a single data attribute such as a transaction identifier like an **Order Number**.

- **Multi-Valued**. A multi-valued dimension can help you model a situation where there are multiple values for an attribute or column. For example, a health care bill can have a line item of **Diagnosis** for which there could be multiple values. Best practice modeling dictates that there should be a single value for each line item. To model this multi-valued situation, you could create a multi-valued structure that captures the diagnosis information and weighs each diagnosis so that the total adds up to one.

- **Ragged**. In a ragged dimension, the parent of at least one member is missing from the level immediately above the member. Ragged dimensions allow for hierarchies of indeterminate depth such as organizational charts and parts explosions.

- **Shrunken**. A shrunken table is a version of the fact table often containing attributes that are not measures. It is often used when there are large text strings that are at the same level of detail as the fact table and are stored in a separate structure for space or query efficiency reasons.

- **Slowly Changing Type 0 through 6**. Slowly Changing Dimension (SCD) Type 0 is equivalent to the fixed dimension concept where values do not change over time. SCD Type 1 means we are only storing the current view and ignoring history. SCD Type 2 means we want all history (Type 2 is the Time Machine). SCD Type 3 means we want only some history such as the most current state and the previous state or the most current state and the original state. SCD Type 6 is when we have a complex dimension with varying history needs; for example, if part of the dimension is a Type 1, part is a Type 2, and part is a Type 3 (1 + 2 + 3 = 6). Types 0, 1, 2, and 3 are the building blocks for more advanced history requirements such as the Type 6.

Country, **Customer**, and **Year** are examples of snowflakes, distinguished by the snowflake icon. These are higher levels in a hierarchy. A hierarchy is when a higher level can contain many lower levels, but a lower level can belong to at most one higher level. These higher levels indicate that we can view the measures in the meter at these levels as well. For example, we can view **Account Balance Amount** at the **Country**, **Customer**, and **Year** level. Snowflakes can also have their own attributes. Snowflakes can be further classified using the same descriptors as just mentioned with dimensions.

EXERCISE 9.1: CREATING A DIMENSIONAL LOGICAL DATA MODEL

Save your dimensional conceptual data model from Exercise 8.1 as a new model and add at least three attributes to each of the entities. Remember to change the display level so that attributes appear on the model. (HINT: Choose `View > Diagram And Object Display Options` or click on the icon and under the *Entity* tab choose the `Logical Attribute Order` display level.)

Key Points

- A logical data model (LDM) represents a detailed business solution.
- A relational logical data model represents how the business works. A dimensional logical data model represents what the business is monitoring.
- Normalizing is a formal process of asking business questions. Normalization ensures that every attribute is a fact about the key (1NF), the whole key (2NF), and nothing but the key (3NF).
- Abstraction brings flexibility to your logical data models by redefining and combining some of the attributes, entities, and relationships within the model into more generic terms.
- There are a number of important terms unique to dimensional modeling including meters and dimensions.
- There are different types of meters including aggregate, atomic, cumulative, and snapshot.
- There are different types of dimensions including fixed dimension, degenerate, multi-valued, ragged, shrunken, and slow changing.

CHAPTER 10
Physical Data Models

Let's get Physical
Compromise the Logical
Efficiency rules

The highlighted row in Table 10.1 shows the focus of this chapter, which is the physical data model (PDM).

	Relational	Dimensional
Conceptual Data Model (CDM)	"One-pager" on business rules	"One-pager" on navigation
Logical Data Model (LDM)	Detailed business solution on business rules	Detailed business solution on navigation
Physical Data Model (PDM)	**Detailed technical solution**	

Table 10.1 The Physical Data Model is the focus of this chapter

A PDM takes the business solution defined on a logical data model to the next level of a technical solution. That is, once you solve the problem independent of software and hardware concerns, you can then make adjustments for software and hardware. This chapter will explain the most popular techniques for making adjustments to a business solution (LDM) to create an efficient technical solution (PDM). I will explain the PDM and then discuss the techniques of denormalization, views, indexing, and partitioning. Although these techniques apply to relational, dimensional, and NoSQL models, their names may differ depending on which type of model they are applied to. I will explain these terminology differences in this chapter as well. As with the conceptual and logical data modeling chapters, be prepared to practice everything in ER/Studio!

PHYSICAL DATA MODEL EXPLANATION

The physical data model (PDM) is the logical data model compromised for specific software or hardware. On the CDM, we learn what the terms, business rules, and scope would be for a new order entry system. After understanding the need for an order entry system, we create a LDM representing the business solution. It contains all of the attributes and business rules needed to deliver the system. For example, the conceptual data model will show that a **Customer** may place one or many **Orders**. The LDM will capture all of the details behind **Customer** and **Order** such as the customer's name, their address, and the order number. After understanding the business solution, we move on to the technical solution and build the PDM. We may make some modifications to the **Customer** and **Order** structures, for example, for factors such as performance or storage.

While building the PDM, we address the issues that have to do with specific hardware or software such as:

- We have a big data scenario, so how can we process a lot of data very quickly and then afterwards analyze it very quickly?
- How can we make this information secure?
- How can we answer this business question in less than two seconds?

Note that in the early days of data modeling, when storage space was expensive and computers were slow, there were major modifications made to the PDM to make it work efficiently. In some cases, the PDM looked like it was for an entirely different application than the LDM. As technology improved, the PDM started looking more like the LDM. Faster and cheaper processors, cheaper and more generous disc space and system memory, and also specialized hardware have all played their part to make the physical look more like its logical counterpart. However, with big data processing and analytical tools becoming more mainstream, there is now (at least temporarily) a large difference again between physical and logical. Physical big data designs can even be file- or document-based to allow for fast loading and analyzing of data. So be aware of physical data models that are all in one table (or file); it may be the optimal design depending on the database technology.

RELATIONAL AND DIMENSIONAL PHYSICAL DATA MODELS

Recall from this section's introduction that relational data modeling is the process of capturing how the business *works* by precisely representing business rules, while dimensional data modeling is the process of capturing how the business is *monitored* by precisely representing navigation. There are both relational and dimensional physical data models.

You have seen examples of both relational and dimensional conceptual and logical data models (recall Figures 8.3 and 8.4 from the chapter on conceptual data modeling and Figures 9.1 and 9.2 from the chapter on logical data modeling). Figures 10.1 and 10.2 show these two examples at a physical level. Let's go through how each of these are built, starting with relational.

RELATIONAL PDM EXAMPLE

The relational PDM includes entities with their definitions, relationships, and columns along with their definitions. Note that in RDBMS the term *table* is used instead of the term *entity* and *column* instead of *attribute* on the physical data model. Figure 10.1 contains part of a financial relational PDM. Compromises such as combining **Customer** and **Account** into one structure were made to this model, most likely to improve data retrieval performance or to make it easier for developers to extract, transform, and load (ETL) data.

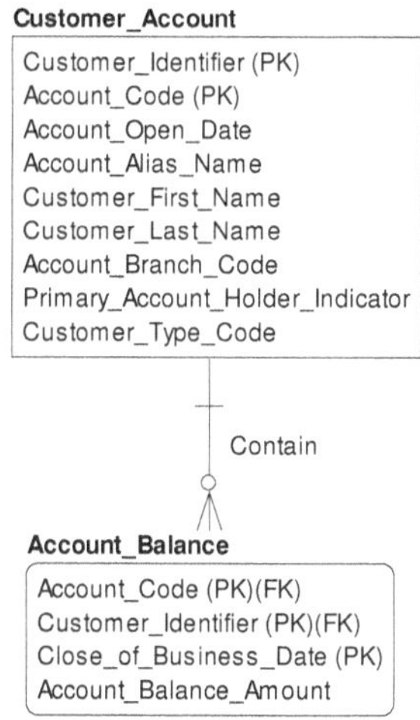

Figure 10.1 Financial relational PDM subset

DIMENSIONAL PDM EXAMPLE

To understand and document our reporting requirements, we can also build a dimensional PDM such as the example in Figure 10.2. This model, called a star schema (which we'll cover shortly), is similar to its logical counterpart except that each dimension from the dimensional LDM has been flattened on the model from Figure 9.2 into one structure.

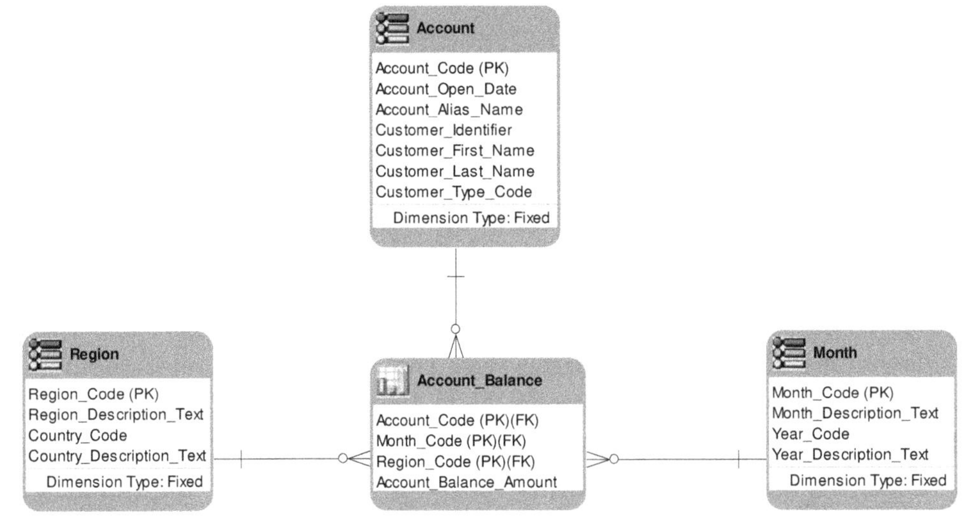

Figure 10.2 Financial dimensional PDM

CREATING A PHYSICAL DATA MODEL IN ER/STUDIO

In ER/Studio, it is wisely assumed that a physical data model cannot be created from scratch but instead must be based upon an existing logical data model or reverse engineered from an existing database (such as the actual database or a data definition language like SQL). We'll go into both approaches in this section.

GENERATING A PHYSICAL DATA MODEL FROM A LOGICAL DATA MODEL

To design the most effective data model possible, create the logical design before the physical design. The logical data modeling process will bring up important inputs to design that will lead to a more efficient and supportable physical data model and therefore database.

The *Generate Physical Model Wizard* in ER/Studio automatically creates a relational or dimensional physical data model based on a logical data model, freeing you to focus on performance tuning during the physical model design phase. The wizard can assist you by ensuring conformance with the basic naming and syntax rules of the target database platform and by enforcing logical rules such as keys and relationships.

To generate a physical data model from a logical data model, use one of these commands:

Menu	Toolbar	Explorer	Shortcut Key	Shortcut Menu
`Model > Generate Physical Data Model…`	Application toolbar:	Right-click on model, `Generate Physical Data Model…`	<ALT + M>, then <G>	`Model > Generate Physical Data Model…`

Let's generate a physical data model from our publisher relational logical data model. The first page of the *Generate Physical Model* screen appears, as shown in Figure 10.3.

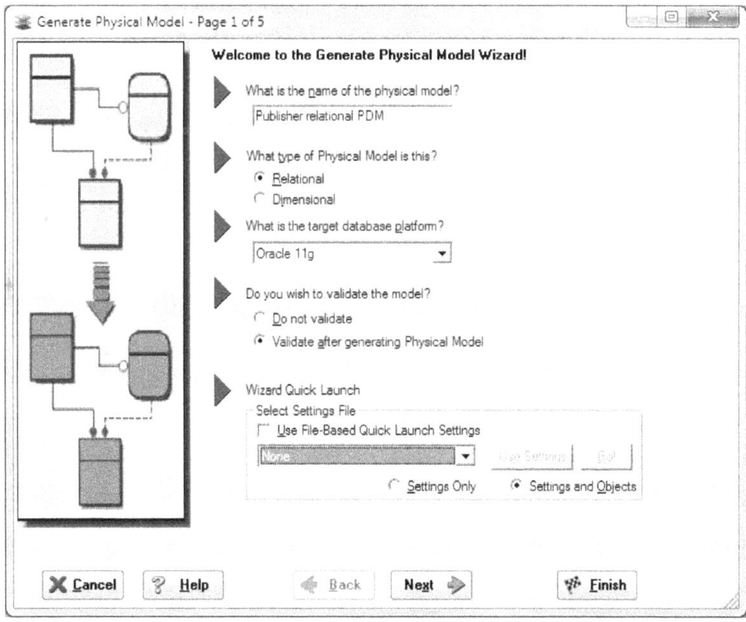

Figure 10.3 Generate Physical Model Page 1 of 5

Make sure you give your PDM a name, select whether the PDM will be a relational or dimensional PDM, and select the correct target database platform from that drop-down. I chose Oracle 11g for this example. With every new release of ER/Studio comes new features that are supported for each database platform. For example, ER/Studio 11 includes the ability to suppress index names for Teradata, Partition by Growth for Universal Table Space (UTS) for DB2, and Advanced Compression for Oracle Database 11g.

As an aside, you can always change the database platform at a later time. Make sure you are in the physical data model whose platform you would like to change and then follow these steps:

Menu	Toolbar	Explorer	Shortcut Key	Shortcut Menu
`Database > Change Database Platform...`	Application toolbar:	Right-click on physical data model, `Change Database Platform...`	<ALT + B>, then <C>	n/a

Choosing `Validate after generating Physical Model` means a number of checks will be made against standards defined in the data dictionary. The **Wizard Quick Launch** allows you to load a file that contains your preferred settings whenever you generate a physical data model. This can be a real timesaver if you generate physical data models often and can also increase consistency across the physical data models. On the last page of the wizard (Page 5), you are given the option of saving your settings for generating future physical data models.

Click <Next> to advance to Page 2 of 5. See Figure 10.4.

On this screen you can choose which entities you would like converted into physical structures for your PDM as well as customize certain settings on keys and indexes. An important radio button to consider is *How do you wish to resolve external FKs in this Submodel?* Checking `Delete Attributes` means that if you bring in a subset of tables and some of these tables contain foreign keys back to other tables that were not brought in, these foreign keys with hidden relationships will be deleted.

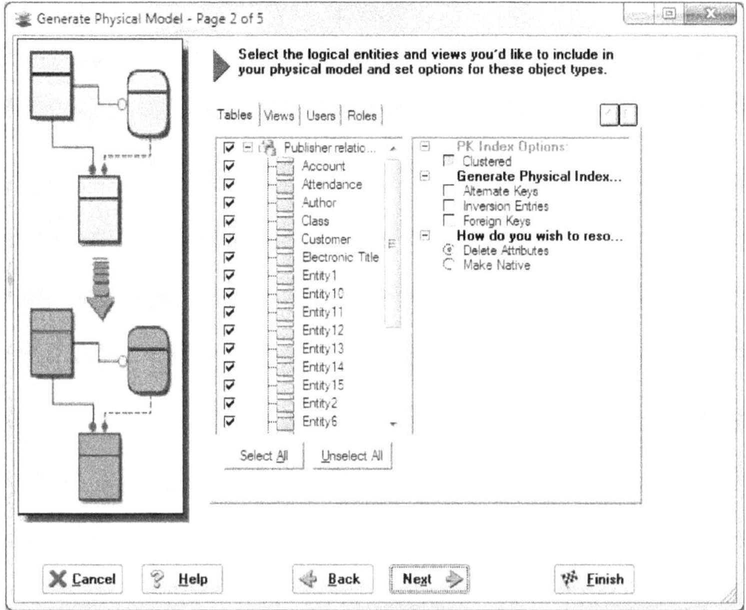

Figure 10.4 Generate Physical Model Page 2 of 5

Click <Next> to advance to Page 3 of 5. See Figure 10.5.

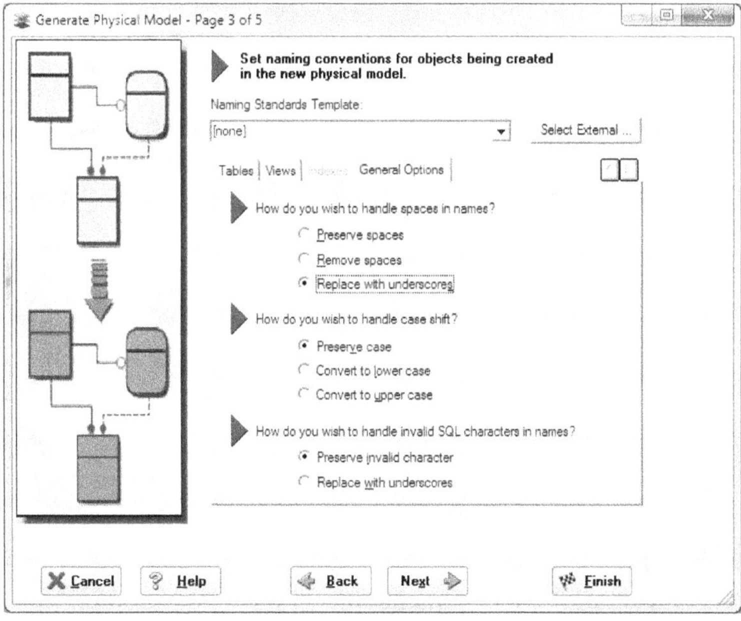

Figure 10.5 Generate Physical Model Page 3 of 5

Notice there are four tabs on the Page 3 of 5 screen. I went to the General Options tab and selected the radio button to `Replace with underscores`, which will replace spaces between entity and attribute terms on the logical with underscores on the physical.

Click <Next> to advance to Page 4 of 5. See Figure 10.6. This screen is useful if you know details on how much space each table will use initially or grow over time. Just leave blank if you don't know.

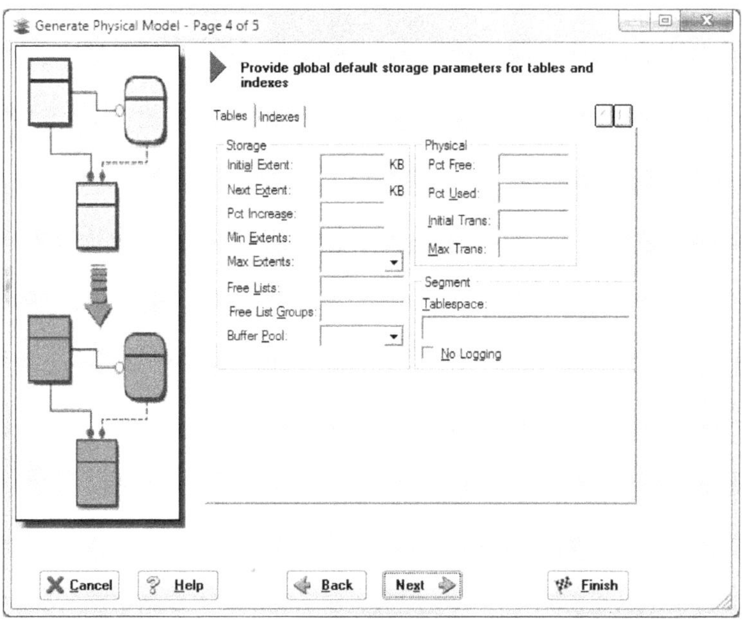

Figure 10.6 Generate Physical Model Page 4 of 5

Click <Next> to advance to Page 5 of 5. See Figure 10.7.

On this screen you can decide how to resolve many-to-many relationships (called *non-specific*) as well as select which logical modeling components to forward engineer such as submodels, text blocks, and drawing shapes. The *Quick Launch* can store common settings so that an operation can be reused on this model or on any other models. You can reuse the settings on another model by choosing the `Use File-Based Quick Launch Setting` option when saving the *Quick Launch* information on this page of the wizard.

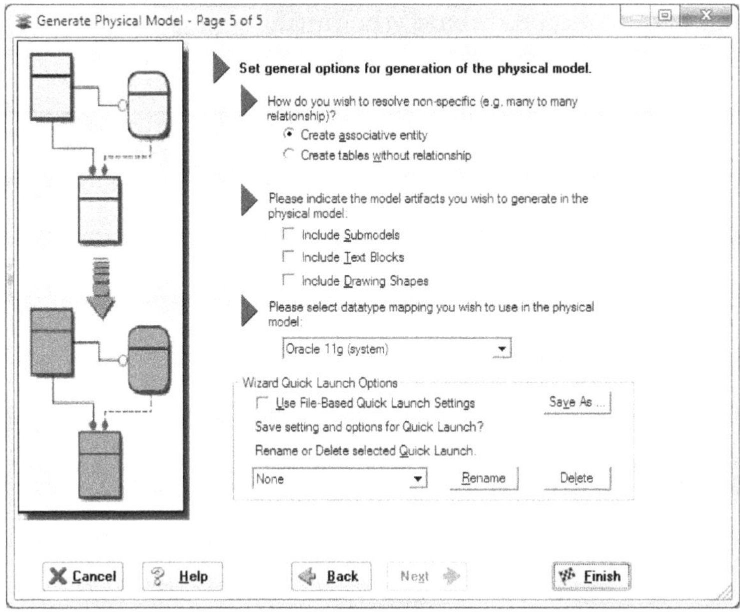

Figure 10.7 Generate Physical Model Page 5 of 5

Click <Finish> to exit the wizard and generate the physical data model.

GENERATING A PHYSICAL DATA MODEL FROM A DATABASE (REVERSE ENGINEERING)

ER/Studio allows you to create a new physical data model by reverse-engineering a live database or importing a SQL file. First open the `Options` screen.

Menu	Toolbar	Explorer	Shortcut Key	Shortcut Menu
`Tools > Options`	n/a	n/a	<ALT + T>, then <P>	n/a

Using the *Application* tab under *Options*, you can specify whether reverse engineering always produces both logical and physical data models or produces logical data models only. You can also specify the column sequence for new models that you reverse engineer. Once applied, this customization will apply to all of your reverse-engineering projects. Click <OK> to exit *Options* and have your settings saved.

To reverse engineer from a database, the initial steps are the same as creating any new data model.

Menu	Toolbar	Explorer	Shortcut Key	Shortcut Menu
`File > New`	Application toolbar:	n/a	<CTRL + N> or <ALT + F>, then <N>	n/a

The screen in Figure 10.8 appears.

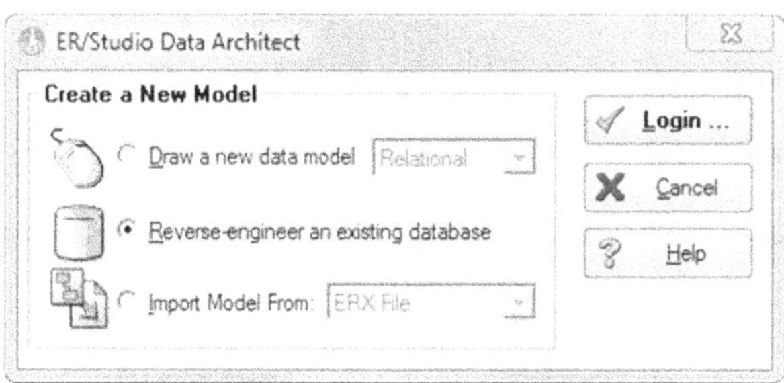

Figure 10.8 New model screen

Reverse-engineer means taking an actual database structure and importing it into ER/Studio to create a picture of what the database looks like. Reverse-engineering is a great first step in understanding how an existing application works (especially when that existing application may not have been properly data modeled to begin with!). The third option on this submenu is to import a data model from different formats such as CA ERwin® Data Modeler® or SQL files. We will discuss how to import from CA ERwin® Data Modeler® in Chapter 13 and how to import from SQL in this chapter as importing from SQL is also reverse engineering.

Choose `Reverse-engineering an existing database` and click <Login...>.

We will reverse engineer a Microsoft Access® database, a MongoDB database, and a Hive database. We will keep the default settings through each of the Wizards. For learning more about specific settings when reverse engineering, refer to the User Guide or hit <F1> on this screen.

Reverse Engineering from Microsoft Access®

On this first screen, titled *Reverse Engineer Wizard – Page 1 of 5*, click <Setup...> and choose `MS Access Database` from the *User DSN* tab. Under the *Datasource:* drop-down, choose `MS Access Database`. Click <Next> and the *Select Database* screen appears. I use an Access database to handle data modeling class registration, so I selected this Access file on this screen, entered the user name and password, and clicked <Next> to advance to Page 2 of the Wizard. (Note that in order to reverse engineer a database, you must have both CONNECT and RESOURCE roles assigned to your user ID for the database you want to access.)

I kept all of the default settings on Page 2. However, if you would like to also bring in System Tables, make sure this is checked as well. Click <Next> and Page 3 gives you the option to choose which tables to reverse engineer. Once you are done selecting the tables, click <Next> to go to Page 4 of the Wizard, shown in Figure 10.9.

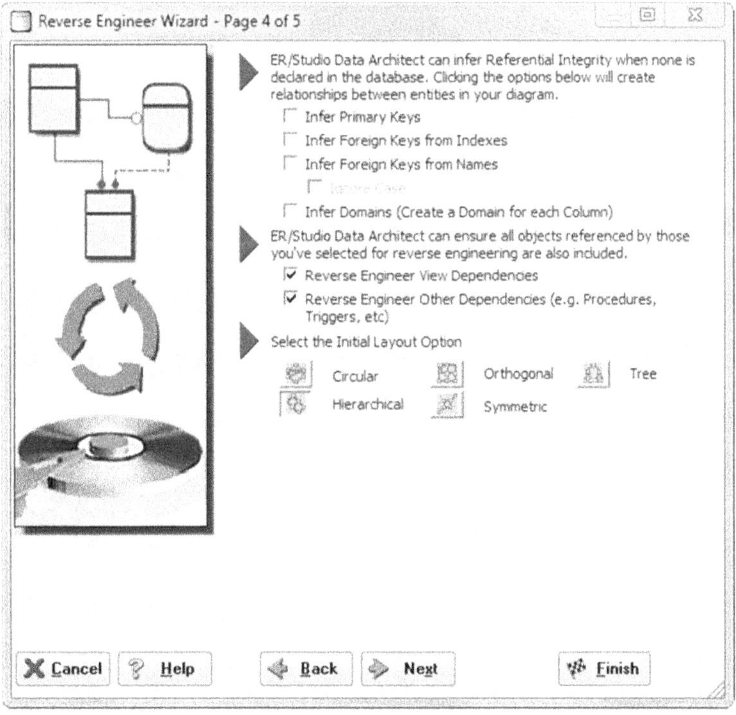

Figure 10.9 Page 4 of the Reverse Engineer Wizard

On this screen there are three sections, each distinguished by a blue arrow. The first section contains checkboxes you can select if you would like ER/Studio to take a guess at what the primary and foreign keys and indexes should be if they are not defined in the database. Definitely check these boxes if you believe the database does not have keys or indexes defined and it is your job to build a better model. These checkboxes can give you a great head start on improving the model. In inferring primary keys, ER/Studio examines the unique indexes on a table. In inferring foreign keys, you can choose whether to have ER/Studio look for indexes whose columns match the names, datatype properties, and column sequences of a primary key or choose to have ER/Studio just infer foreign keys from names. If you choose `Infer Domains`, ER/Studio creates a domain for each unique combination of a column name and its associated datatype properties. The second section on this screen allows you to also bring in other structures such as views and triggers. The third section allows you to decide how to arrange the model once it is brought into the tool. I kept `Circular` checked and clicked <Next> to go to Page 5 of the Wizard, shown in Figure 10.10.

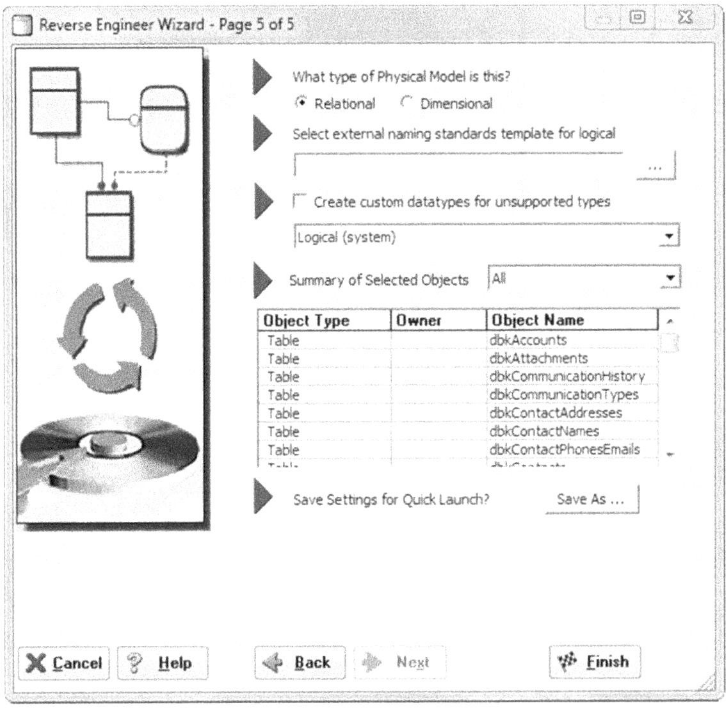

Figure 10.10 Page 5 of the Reverse Engineer Wizard

On this screen you can decide whether the model should be reverse engineered using relational or dimensional structures and optionally apply a naming standard template to the logical names. (More on naming standards in Chapter 14.) You can also save the settings you have chosen during this Wizard as a *Quick Launch*, meaning just by loading the *Quick Launch* file you can automatically apply the settings you chose during the Wizard to save time in future reverse engineering efforts and also improve consistency. You can load your saved *Quick Launch* file on Page 1 of this Wizard. *Quick Launch* was discussed earlier in this chapter. Click <Finish> and the database will be imported.

Reverse Engineering from MongoDB®

On this first screen, titled *Reverse Engineer Wizard – Page 1 of 5*, click the *Connection Type:* `Native/Direct Connection` and choose `MongoDB` from the drop-down. Enter the *Datasource*, which in the case of MongoDB is the host name of the MongoDB server. Alternately, users may specify a MongoDB connection URI in standard format. If you are unsure of the MongoDB host name, run *getHostName()* at the command prompt. Click <Advanced Options...>. The screen in Figure 10.11 appears.

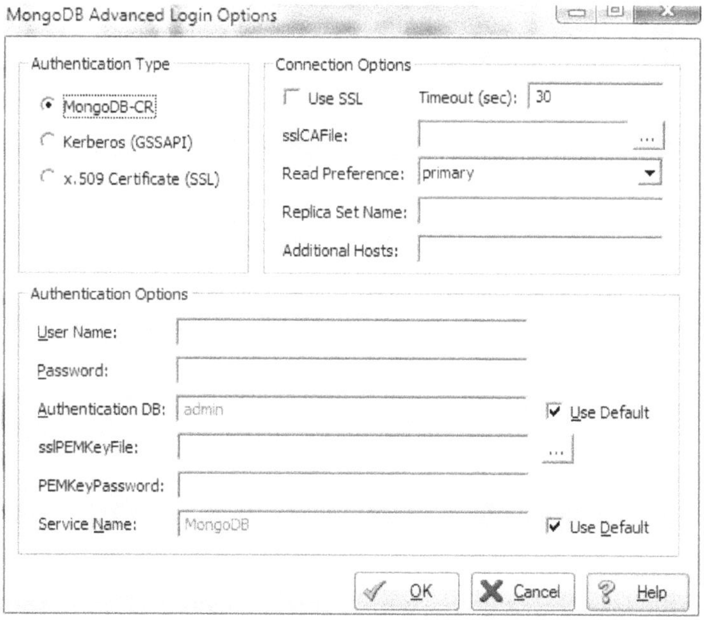

Figure 10.11 MongoDB Advanced Login Options

Choose the *Authentication Type*. MongoDB-CR is the default setting and admin is the default authentication database (which can be changed by unclicking Use Default). Users may choose to encrypt the connection to MongoDB with SSL by checking the Use SSL option.

Click <OK> and the screen in Figure 10.12 appears.

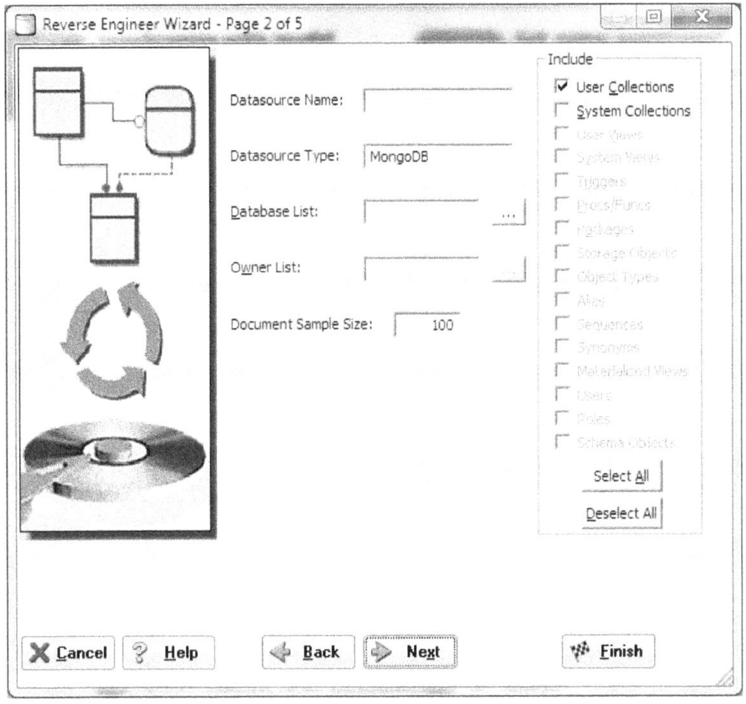

Figure 10.12 Page 2 of the Reverse Engineer Wizard

Choose the objects you would like to include, and the number of MongoDB documents that should be analyzed in order to include all potential document fields and embedded documents. Then click <Finish>. Then you can select the database you would like to reverse engineer and click <Ok>.

Reverse Engineering from Hive®

On this first screen, titled *Reverse Engineer Wizard – Page 1 of 5*, click the *Connection Type:* Native/Direct Connection and choose Hive from the drop-down. Enter the *Datasource*, which in the case of Hive is the host name of the Hive server.

As you go through the wizard, you will see many similarities with the MongoDB reverse engineer process including the option to choose which columns to skew and cluster (bucketing).

GENERATING A PHYSICAL DATA MODEL FROM A SQL FILE

Follow the same steps as in the previous section for creating a new model.

Menu	Toolbar	Explorer	Shortcut Key	Shortcut Menu
`File > New`	Application toolbar:	n/a	<CTRL + N> or <ALT + F>, then <N>	n/a

You will see the screen in Figure 10.13. This time, choose the `Import Model From:` radio button and select `SQL File` from the drop-down list.

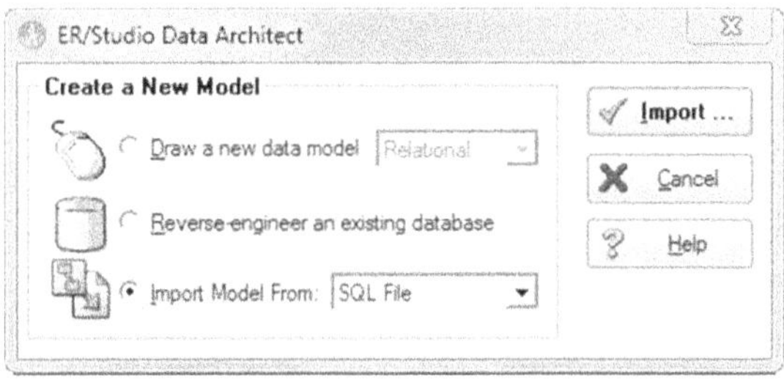

Figure 10.13 New Model Screen

Click <Import> and the screen in Figure 10.14 appears, which has most of the same settings that were discussed when reverse engineering an Access database.

On this screen, there are seven sections, each distinguished by a blue arrow. The first section is where you select the SQL file you would like to import. The second section is where you select the target database platform, and the third section is where you can ask ER/Studio to take an educated guess regarding what the primary and foreign keys should be, along with domains. If you choose `Infer Domains`, ER/Studio creates a domain for each unique combination of a column name and its associated datatype properties.

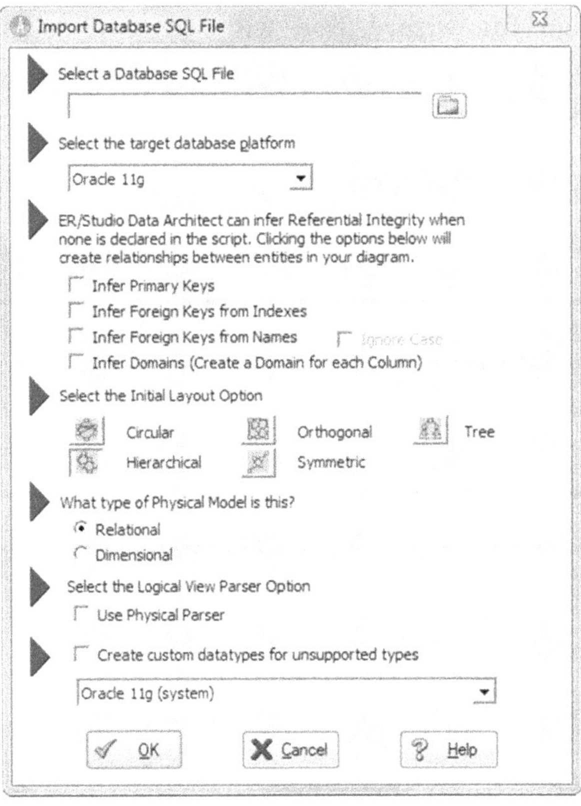

Figure 10.14 Import Database SQL File screen

The fourth section allows you to choose the layout in which the imported structures will be arranged, the fifth section whether relational or dimensional, and the sixth section on whether you want to use the `Physical Parser`, which if checked will apply a platform-specific syntax interpreter. The seventh section, when checked, will create custom datatypes for unsupported types. Click <OK> and the file will be imported.

Generating a Database Using ER/Studio

Once the physical data is created, we can have ER/Studio generate the database. In Explorer, click on the physical data model.

Menu	Toolbar	Explorer	Shortcut Key	Shortcut Menu
`Database > Generate Database…`		Right-click on physical data model, `Generate Database…`	<ALT + B>, then <G>	Right-click on model white space, `Generate Database…`

I would like to generate MongoDB JSON code. Page 1 of 3 appears of the wizard as shown in Figure 10.15.

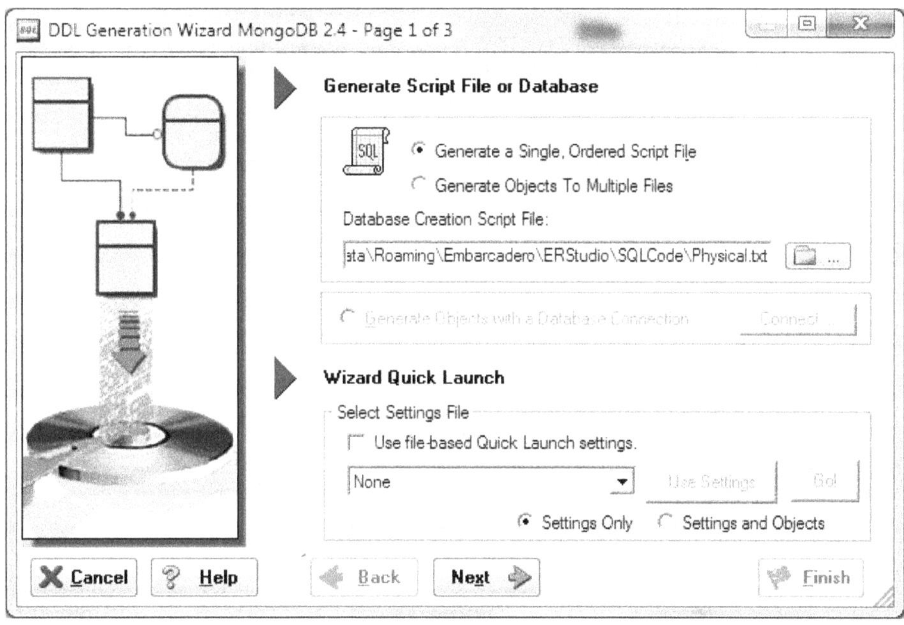

Figure 10.15 Page 1 of the DDL Generation Wizard

The file path for the Database Creation Script File is where the JSON code will be stored. On Page 2 of 3 you can decide which collections to generate. On Page 3 of 3 you can finalize the settings and then generate the JSON. The field names will appear in the JSON but not the field values because there is no data stored in ER/Studio. Figure 10.16 contains an example of the JSON that will appear.

order
_id (PK)
orderActualDeliveryDate
orderLine
orderNumber
orderScheduledDeliveryDate
orderShortDescription
orderStatusCode
orderStatusDescription
orderTotalAmount
orderTypeCode
orderTypeDescription
orderWeight
orderLine
orderLineQuantity
productID
//
// COLLECTION: order
//
{
_id : new ObjectId(),
orderActualDeliveryDate : "",
orderLine : [
{
orderLineQuantity : 0,
productID : ""
}],
orderNumber : "",
orderScheduledDeliveryDate : "",
orderShortDescription : "",
orderStatusCode : "",
orderStatusDescription : "",
orderTotalAmount : "",
orderTypeCode : 0,
orderTypeDescription : "",
orderWeight : 0
}

Figure 10.16 Sample JSON code

EDITING TABLES

The steps for editing an entity are similar for editing a table:

Menu	Toolbar	Explorer	Shortcut Key	Shortcut Menu
`Click on table, Edit > Edit Table...`	n/a	Right-click on table, `Edit Table...`	Click on table, <ALT + E>, then <E>	Right-click on entity, `Edit Table...`

The *Table Editor* appears as shown in Figure 10.17. Many of the settings here are similar to what appeared under the *Entity Editor*. This screen can be resized by clicking and dragging the lower right corner. This screen can also be maximized by clicking the square symbol in the upper right corner (to the left of the "x," which closes the window) and then returned back to its original size by clicking the two square symbols in the upper right corner.

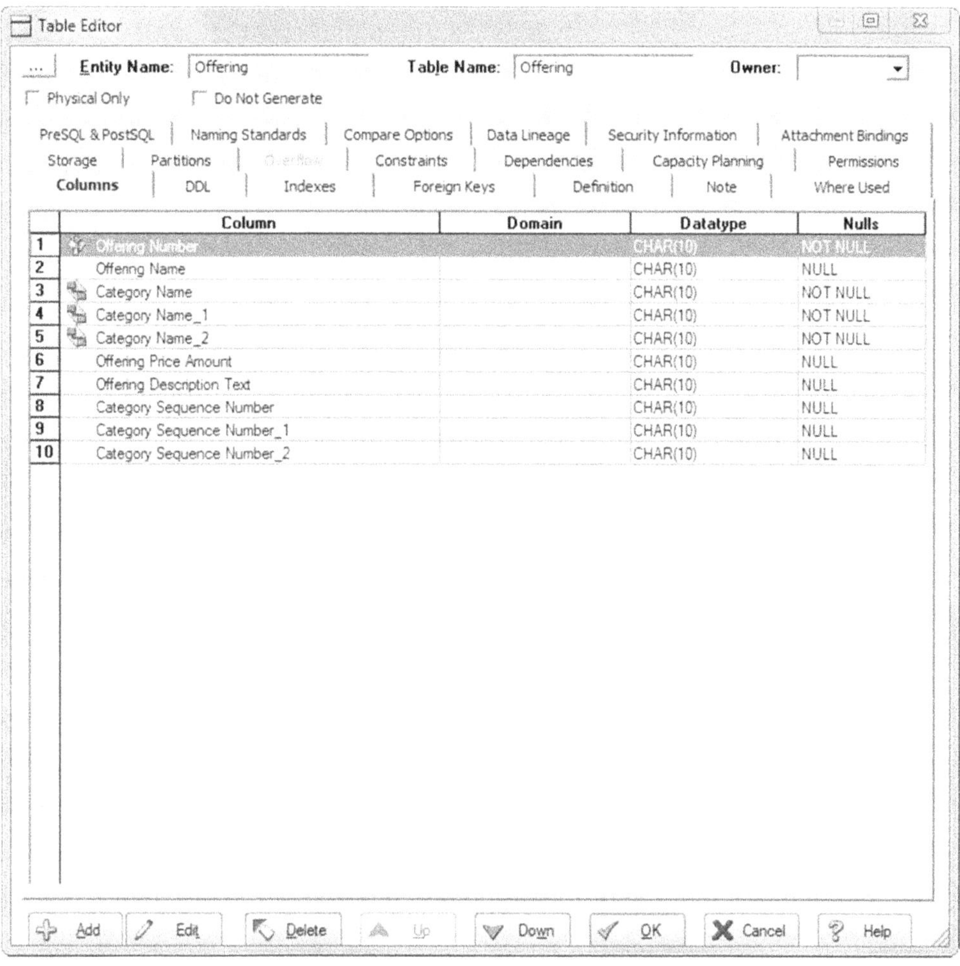

Figure 10.17 Table Editor

There are 17 standard tabs on this screen, each described in the following spreadsheet. There are also additional tabs displayed depending on the particular database you have chosen (e.g., Oracle will have several different tabs than Teradata).

Tab	Here's what you need to know:
Columns	Create, edit, and arrange columns.
DDL	View and edit the Data Definition Language (DDL). DDL is the language that is used to build the database from the PDM.

Tab	Here's what you need to know:
Indexes	View the keys that were created on the corresponding table in the logical data model and also add new indexes that will be physical only (such as those added to improve retrieval performance).
Foreign Keys	View and edit the relationships that were created on the corresponding table in the logical data model.
Definition	This is where the full definition for the table is stored. If the target database supports it, ER/Studio adds this definition as a table comment when generating SQL code. The macro **Definition Editor** allows for easily entering definitions for multiple objects. More on macros in Chapter 16.
Note	Use this for any other text outside the definition such as questions to ask business experts, known issues, or action items. HTML tags used in *Notes* will be applied as formatting in the HTML reports. The macro **Notes Editor** allows for easily entering notes for multiple objects. More on macros in Chapter 16.
Where Used	See which logical and physical data models and submodels contain the table. From this tab you can edit mappings and user-defined mappings.
Storage	Define table-specific parameters, such as extents and table compression, that will be used when this table is created in the database.
Constraints	A constraint is a rule that is checked before data is allowed in the database. For a table instance (also called a record), these are rules that can be created and edited to determine what can be added to the database table. These constraints become part of the SQL used to build the table.
Dependencies	Displays the views and other database-specific objects that depend upon this table.
Capacity Planning	Set the volumetrics information such as the number of initial rows the table will contain and table rate of growth.
Permissions	Select detailed permissions (e.g., insert, select, update, and delete) for users and roles for this table. This is a tab that would be used in the physical data model and not the logical data model.

Tab	Here's what you need to know:
Naming Standards	Allows you to apply different naming standards to different objects when portions of a model require different versions of a standard. For example, some objects already exist in the database and you may not want to apply a newer naming standard to them. The `Freeze Names` option, when selected, prevents any naming standards applied to the model from changing the name of the attribute selected. We'll talk more about this tab in Chapter 14, Naming Standards.
Compare Options	Select which, if any, properties (e.g., table name, definition, notes) of the table to ignore when comparing this table to another using the *Compare and Merge Utility*, which will be discussed in Chapter 15.
Data Lineage	Map the rules from source to target tables in the model. We'll cover this tab in Chapter 12, Data Lineage.
Security Information	You can assign security settings that are defined in the Data Dictionary to this table. The Data Dictionary will be discussed in Chapter 11.
Attachment Bindings	Bind an external piece of information, such as a Microsoft Word document or PDF file, to the table. Very useful for requirements documents, user stories, etc. Attachments are created in the Attachments folder of the Data Dictionary (discussed in Chapter 11) and must be added to the model before they will display on this tab.

Customizing Datatype Mapping

When you generate the physical data model from the logical data model, the logical formats and lengths are converted into database-specific formats and lengths. For example, a logical attribute defined as integer may be converted into the number format in Oracle. When you set the physical database option (such as to Oracle or Teradata), a default mapping converts all of the logical formats and lengths to physical.

You can, however, change this default mapping by using the *Datatype Mapping Editor*.

Menu	Toolbar	Explorer	Shortcut Key	Shortcut Menu
`Tools > Datatype Mapping Editor`	n/a	n/a	<ALT + T>, then choose `Datatype Mapping Editor`	n/a

Become an ER/Studio Hotshot:

- The mapping changes you make will only be effective for new physical data models you generate, and not existing ones.

The screen in Figure 10.18 appears where you edit the data-type.

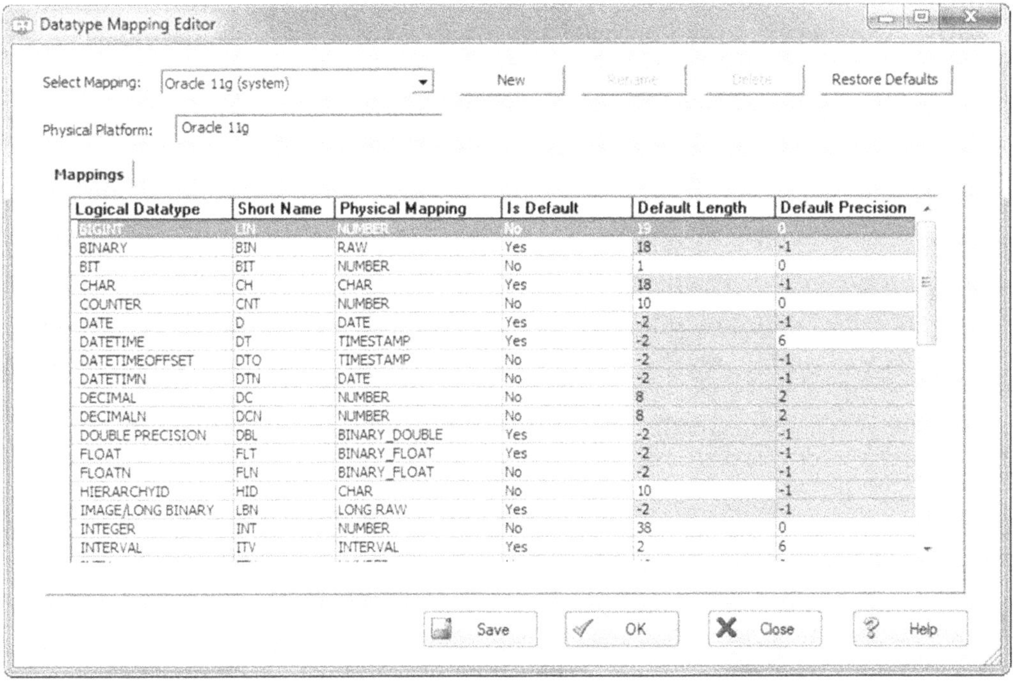

Figure 10.18 Datatype Mapping Editor

DENORMALIZATION

Denormalization is the process of selectively violating normalization rules and reintroducing redundancy into the model (and, therefore, the database). This extra redundancy can reduce data retrieval time, which is the primary reason for denormalizing. We can also denormalize to create a more user-friendly model. For example, we might decide to denormalize company information into an entity containing employee information because usually when employee information is retrieved, company information is also retrieved.

There are a number of different ways to denormalize. In this section, we'll discuss the two most common, Rolldown and Rollup. We will apply these two techniques to an **Offering/Category** subset of our publisher logical data model. See Figure 10.19 for the starting point logical for **Offering** and **Category** and their physical counterparts using each of these two techniques.

Our Normalized Starting Point:

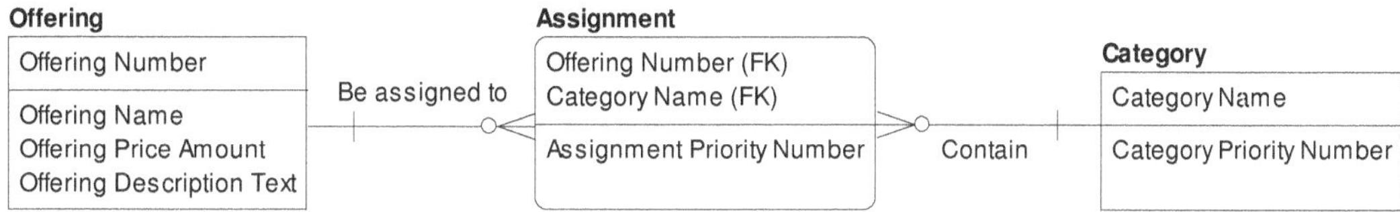

Rolldown Denormalization:

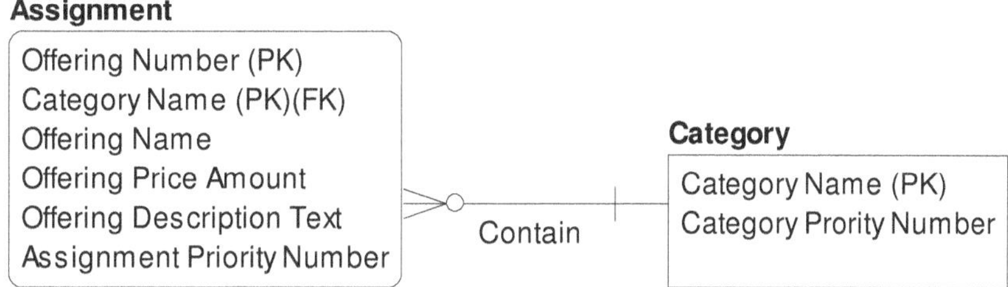

Rollup Denormalization:

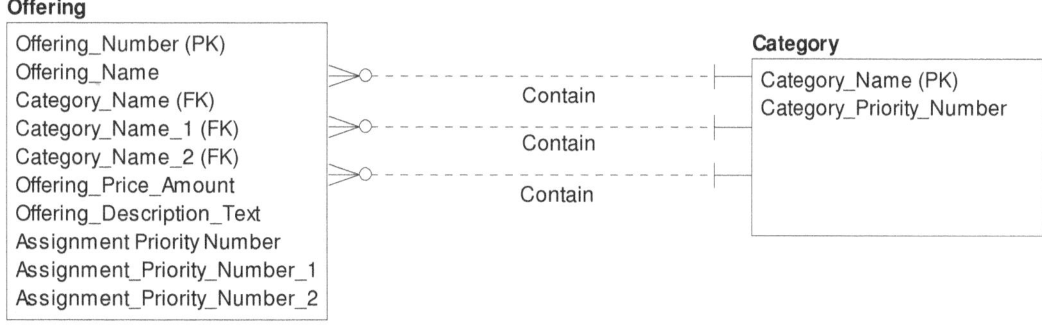

Figure 10.19 Offering and Category logical with two different physical designs

ROLLDOWN DENORMALIZATION

Rolldown is the most common of the denormalization techniques. The parent entity in the relationship disappears, and all of the parent's columns and relationships are moved down to the child entity. You'll recall that the child entity is on the many side of the relationship and contains a foreign key back to the parent entity, which appears on the one side of the relationship.

In addition to choosing denormalization because of the need for faster retrieval time or for more user friendly structures, rolldown can be chosen in the following situations:

- **When you need to maintain the flexibility of the normalized model.** Folding the columns and relationships together using rolldown still allows one-to-one and one-to-many relationships to be stored (but not enforced in the database). In Figure 10.19, for example, we did not lose the flexibility that an **Offering** can belong to many **Categories**.

- **When you want to reduce development time and complexity.** Often there is a direct relationship between the number of tables and relationships on a model and the amount of effort it will take to develop the application. A developer will need to write code that jumps from one table to another to collect certain columns, and this can take time and add complexity. Denormalizing into fewer tables using rolldown means the columns and relationships from different entities now exist in the same entity. In Figure 10.19, for example, if the developer needs to retrieve both offering information and the category name, they can easily do so from the same entity, **Assignment**.

ROLLUP DENORMALIZATION

In rollup, the same column or group of columns is repeated two or more times in the same entity. Also known as an *array*, rollup requires making the number of times something can occur static. Recall that in 1NF we removed repeating groups; rollup means we are adding back in repeating groups. We had to decide in Figure 10.19, for example, that the maximum number of categories an offering can be assigned is three.

In addition to choosing denormalization because of the need for faster retrieval time or for more user friendly structures, repeating groups may be chosen in the following situations:

- **When it makes more sense to keep the parent entity instead of the child entity.** When the parent entity is going to be used more frequently than the child entity, or if there are rules and columns to preserve in the parent entity format, it makes more sense to keep the parent entity.
- **When an entity instance will never exceed the fixed number of columns added.** In Figure 10.19, we are only allowing up to three categories for an offering. If we had a fourth category for an offering, for example, how would we handle this?

STAR SCHEMA

Denormalization is a term that is applied exclusively to relational physical data models because you can't denormalize something unless it has already been normalized. However, denormalization techniques can be applied to dimensional models as well—you just can't use the term *denormalization*. So the relational term *rolldown*, for example, can still be applied to a dimensional model; we just need to use a different term like *flattening* or *collapsing*.

A star schema is the most common dimensional physical data model structure. The term *meter* from the dimensional logical data model is replaced with the term *fact table* on the dimensional physical data model. A star schema results when each set of tables that make up a dimension is flattened into a single table. The fact table is in the center of the model, and each of the dimensions relate to the fact table at the lowest level of detail. A star schema is relatively easy to create and implement, and it visually appears simplistic to both IT and the business.

Recall the dimensional logical data model example from Figure 10.2, repeated here in Figure 10.20.

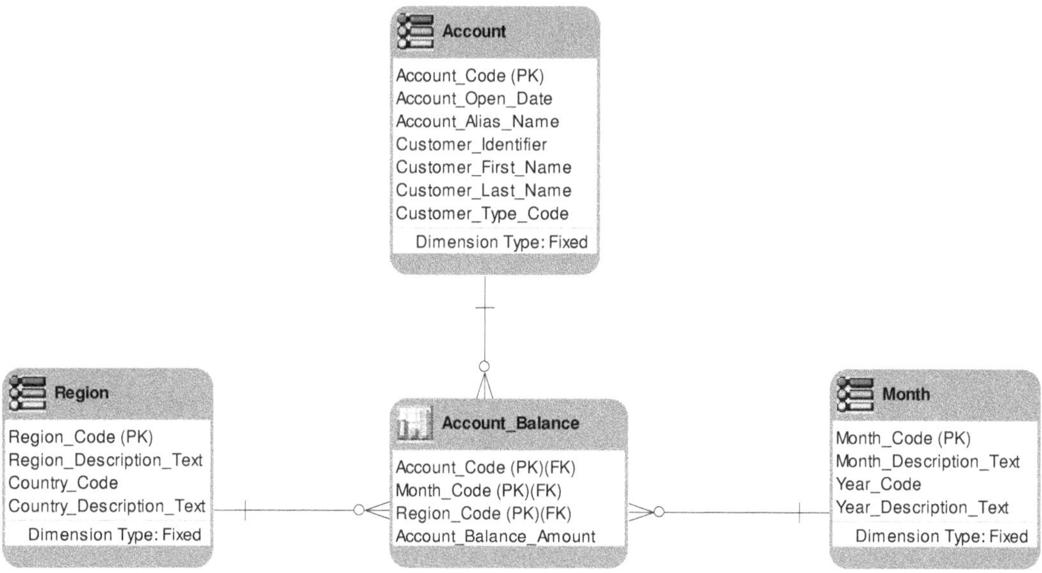

Figure 10.20 Financial dimensional PDM

A star schema is when each hierarchy is flattened into a single table. So on this star schema, **Customer** is flattened into **Account**, **Country** is flattened into **Region**, and **Year** is flattened into **Month**.

DENORMALIZING IN ER/STUDIO

ER/Studio comes equipped with denormalization wizards to help you optimize the physical design. The wizards automate the denormalization process and keep the ties between the physical tables and the logical entities. The denormalization wizards available depend on which tables are selected. For example, if two tables that are related to each other are selected, the valid operations would be rollups or rolldowns.

To bring up the denormalization wizard, highlight those entities you would like denormalized on the physical data model and decide whether you would like to rollup or rolldown.

Menu	Toolbar	Explorer	Shortcut Key	Shortcut Menu
`Model > Denormalization Mapping > Rollups or Rolldowns`	Modeling toolbar:	n/a	<ALT + M>, then <Z>, then either <R> for Rollups or <O> for Rolldowns	Right-click on one of highlighted entities, `Denormalization Mapping > Rollups or Rolldowns`

We saw examples of rolldown and rollup in the previous section where we combined entities that had a one-to-many relationship. We can also apply rolldown and rollup to a subtyping structure. The subtyping structure needs to be resolved on the physical data model as there is no subtyping relationship defined in a relational database. There are three ways of resolving the subtyping symbol on the physical data model: identity, rolldown, and rollup. All three types, along with the original subset from the publisher logical data model, are shown in Figure 10.21.

Identity is the starting point when we first generate the physical from the logical. Identity is the closest to subtyping itself because the subtyping symbol is replaced with a one-to-one relationship for each supertype/subtype combination. We did not denormalize yet, and identity may possibly be the final physical structure as we may not need to denormalize. The main advantage of identity is that all of the business rules at the supertype level and at the subtype level remain the same as in the logical data model. That is, we can continue to enforce relationships at the supertype or subtype levels as well as enforce that certain columns be required at the supertype or subtype levels. Identity allows us to still require the **Print Version Weight Amount** for print versions and the **eBook Download Size** for ebooks, for example. The main disadvantage of identity is that it can take more time to retrieve data as it requires navigating multiple tables to access both the supertype and subtype information.

Recall that rolldown means we are moving the attributes and relationships of the parent entity down to the child entity. In the case of subtyping, this means we are moving the supertype's attributes and relationships down into each of the subtypes. Rolling down can produce a more user-friendly structure than identity or rolling up, because subtypes are often more concrete concepts than supertypes, making it easier for the users of the data model to relate to the subtypes. However, we are repeating relationships and columns, which could reduce any user-friendliness gained from removing the supertype. In addition, the rolling down technique enforces only those rules present in the subtypes. This could also lead to a less flexible data model as we can no longer easily accommodate new subtypes without modifying the data model. If a new type of **Title** is required in addition to **Print Version** and **eBook**, this would require effort to accommodate.

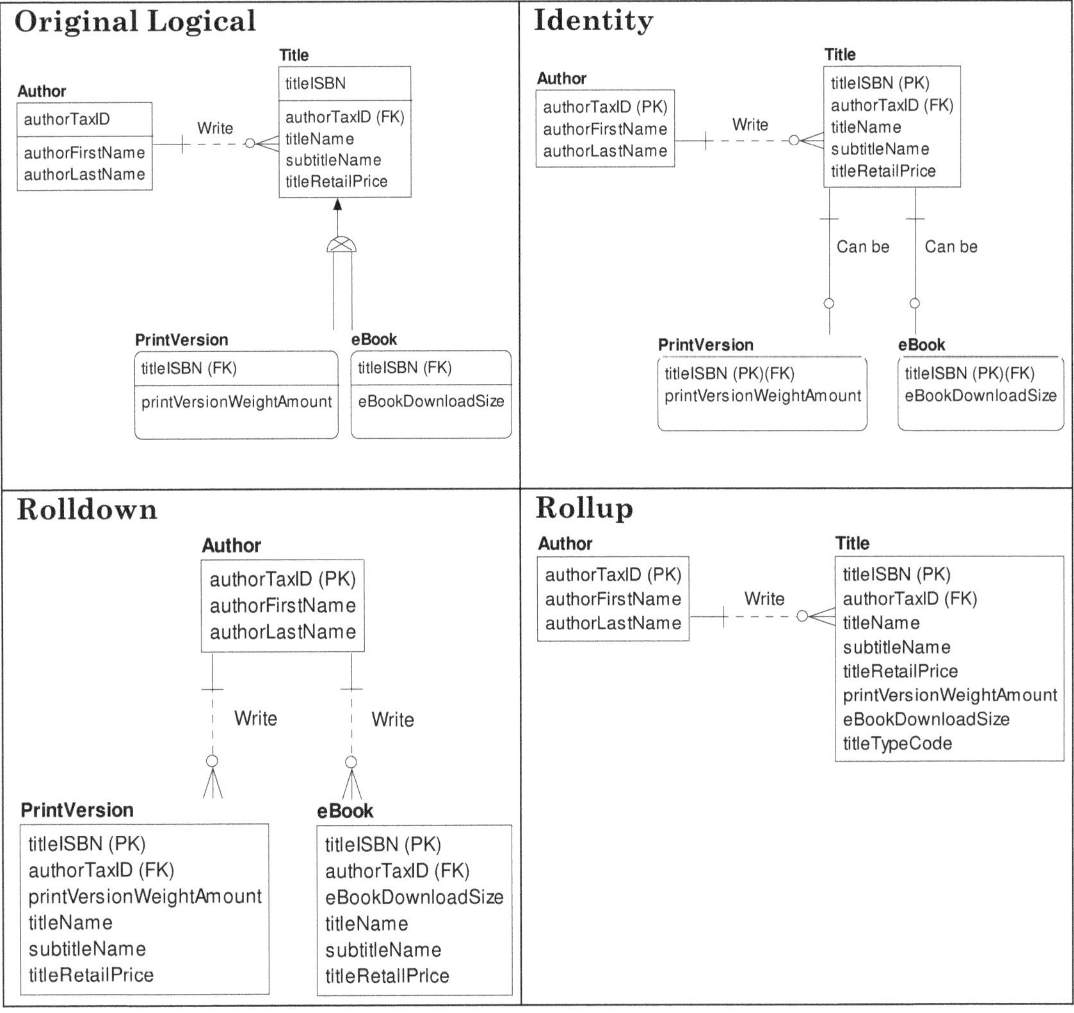

Figure 10.21 Original LDM subtyping structure plus three ways of resolving on the physical

Rollup means rolling up the child entity into the parent. With subtyping, this means moving the subtypes' attributes and relationships up into the supertype. The subtypes disappear, and all columns and relationships only exist at the supertype level. Rolling up adds flexibility to the data model because new types of the supertype can be added, often with no model changes. However, rolling up can also produce a more obscure model as the audience for the model may not relate to the supertype as well as they would to the subtypes. In addition, we can only enforce business rules at the supertype level, not the subtype level. For example, now **Print Version Weight Amount** and the **eBook Download Size** are optional instead of required. When we roll up, we often need a way to distinguish the original subtypes from each other, so we frequently add a type column such as **Title Type Code**.

EXERCISE 10.1: DENORMALIZING

For this exercise, create all four of the models from Figure 10.21. First create the logical and then generate three different physical data models: identity, roll down, and roll up.

VIEWS

A view is a virtual table. It is a dynamic "view" or window into one or more tables (or other views) where the actual data is stored. A view is defined by a SQL query that specifies how to collect data from its underlying tables. A SQL query is a request that a user (or reporting tool) makes of the database such as "Bring me back all **Customer IDs** where the **Customer** is 90 days or more behind in their bill payments." The difference between a query and a view, however, is that the instructions in a view are already prepared for the user (or reporting tool) and stored in the database as the definition of the view, whereas a query is not stored in the database and may need to be written each time a question is asked.

Figure 10.22 contains a view of **Assignment** and **Category** to create a simple way to display offerings along with their assigned categories.

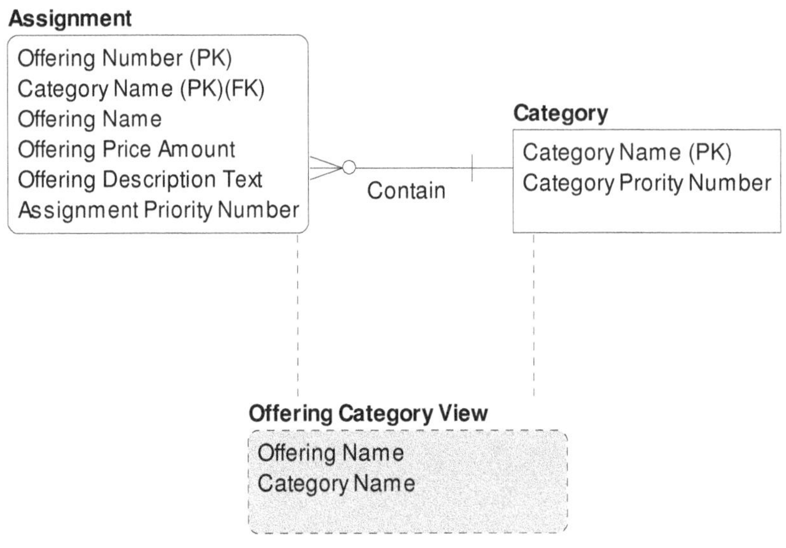

Figure 10.22 View creating a listing of offerings with their categories

Behind this view is the following SQL query needed to retrieve the authors and their titles:

```
CREATE VIEW "Offering Category View" AS
SELECT Assg."Offering Name", Ca."Category Name"
FROM Assignment Assg, Category Ca
WHERE Assg."Category Name" = Ca."Category Name"
ORDER BY Assg."Category Priority Number" DESC
```

Here is a sample of the results returned:

Offering Name	Category Name
The DAMA-DMBOK Print Edition	DAMA-DMBOK
The DAMA Dictionary of Data Management 2nd Edition, Print Format	DAMA-DMBOK
Portuguese Version of DAMA-DMBOK	DAMA-DMBOK
Data Modeling Master Class – Spring 2015	Public Seminars

VIEWS IN ER/STUDIO

To create a view, first create the view box and then relate this box to its underlying entities. To create a view box, choose one of these options:

Menu	Toolbar	Explorer	Shortcut Key	Shortcut Menu
`Insert > View`	Modeling toolbar:	Right-click on `Views, New View...`	<ALT + I>, then <V>	Right-click on white space, `Insert View`

Become an ER/Studio Hotshot:

- ER/Studio supports "sticky buttons," meaning you can create many occurrences of an object and then, when you are done, right-click on any white space to return the cursor to the default selector symbol.
- The status bar at the bottom of the screen shows the number of views in the model or submodel. You can hide or show this status bar using `View > Status Bar` or <ALT + V> then <S>.

To relate this view to its underlying entities, you will need to create a view relationship from each of the entities that are needed for the view, to the view box. Choose one of these options:

Menu	Toolbar	Explorer	Shortcut Key	Shortcut Menu
`Insert > Relationship > View Relationship`	Modeling toolbar:	n/a	<ALT + I>, then <R>, then <V>	Right-click on white space, `Insert Relationship > View Relationship`

Become an ER/Studio Hotshot:

- View relationships cannot be edited, but they can be deleted.
- You can create more than one relationship from the same table to the view. Doing so automatically creates an alias for the parent table that is replicated more than once in the view.
- Choose *View > Diagram And Object Display Options* or click on the icon and then experiment with the display level settings on the *View* tab.

We can bring up the *View Editor* to modify the view.

Menu	Toolbar	Explorer	Shortcut Key	Shortcut Menu
Click on view, `Edit > Edit Database View…`	n/a	Right-click on view, `Edit > Edit Database View…`	Click on view, <ALT + E>, then <E>	Right-click on view, `Edit Database View…`

After applying one of these commands, the *View Editor* appears (see Figure 10.23). This is the place to modify the SQL query that generates the view.

This screen can be resized by clicking and dragging the lower right corner. This screen can also become maximized by clicking the square symbol in the upper right corner (to the left of the "x," which closes the window) and then returned back to its original size by clicking the two square symbols in the upper right corner.

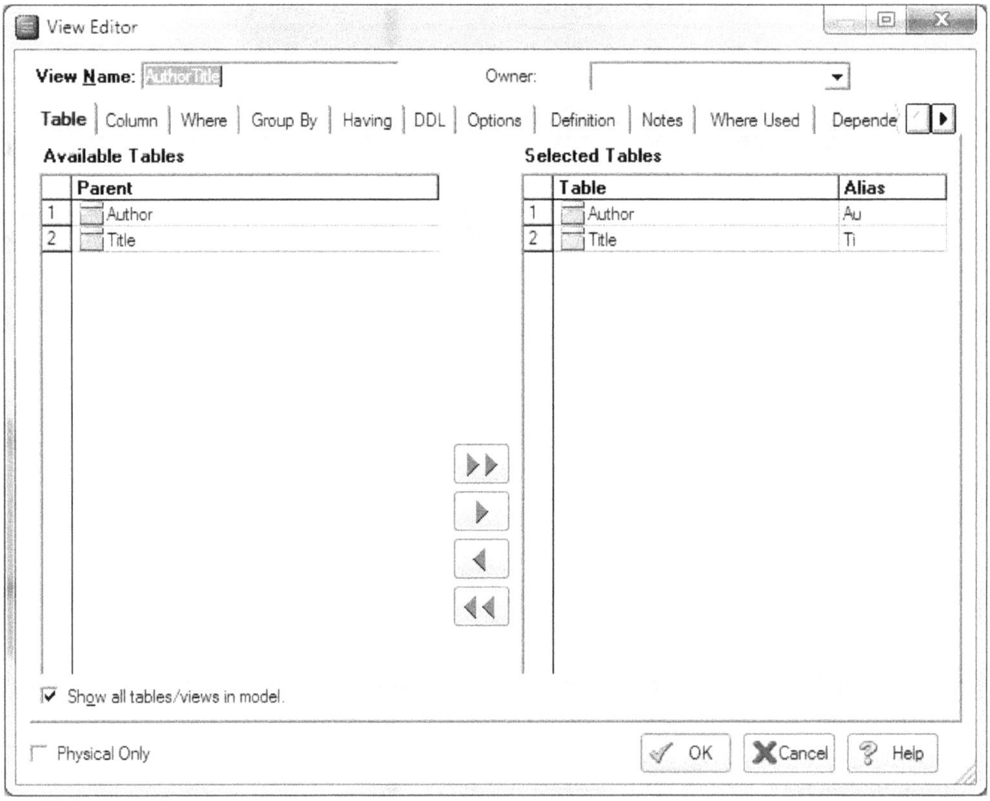

Figure 10.23 View Editor screen

There are 15 tabs on this screen:

Tab	Here's what you need to know:
Table	Decide which tables are needed for the view. There are four arrow buttons that allow you to select single tables or all tables and remove single tables or all tables.
Column	Decide which columns within the tables you selected you would like in the view. You also have the option to resequence the columns, give each column an alias (a different, usually simpler, name—very useful when the same column can appear multiple times in the view), and add column expressions for situations when the column did not exist in one of the source tables such as a derived column for sales amount. This tab defines the SELECT part of the SQL query.
Where	Optionally add conditions that must be met to bring back records in this query. This tab defines the WHERE part of the SQL query.
Group By	Optionally decide how you would like the records to be organized. This tab defines the GROUP BY part of the SQL query.
Having	If you did a GROUP BY, you can restrict the results returned in the GROUP BY condition by using a HAVING clause. This tab defines the HAVING part of the SQL query.
DDL	Defines the Data Definition Language (DDL) for the view SQL query. The DDL gives the database software (e.g., Oracle, Teradata, etc.), the instructions on how to build the database, and in this case how to build the view. You can display and edit the SQL query here.
Options	Sort the columns alphabetically.
Definition	This is where the full definition for the view is stored. If the target database supports it, ER/Studio adds this definition as a view comment when generating SQL code.
Notes	Use this for any other text outside the definition such as questions to ask business experts, known issues, or action items. HTML tags used in *Notes* will be applied as formatting in the HTML reports.
Where Used	See which physical data models and submodels contain the view. From this tab you can edit mappings and user-defined mappings.

Tab	Here's what you need to know:
Dependencies	Create, edit, or delete any scripted procedures that are bound to the view. If any procedures or functions are bound to the view, the folder is expandable.
PreSQL & PostSQL	Enter SQL to be applied before (PreSQL) or after (PostSQL) the CREATE OBJECT statement.
Permissions	Select detailed permissions (e.g., insert, select, update, and delete) for users and roles for this view.
Security Information	Assign security settings that are defined in the Data Dictionary to this view. The Data Dictionary will be discussed in Chapter 11.
Attachment Bindings	Bind an external piece of information, such as a Microsoft Word document or PDF file, to the view. Very useful for requirements documents, user stories, etc. Attachments are created in the Attachments folder of the Data Dictionary (discussed in Chapter 11) and must be added to the model before they will display on this tab.

EXERCISE 10.2: CREATING VIEWS

Create the view along with SQL statement from Figure 10.22.

INDEXING

An index is a value and a pointer to instances of that value in a table. In Chapter 6, Attributes and Domains, we talked about and created primary keys, alternate keys, and inversion entries. Primary keys, alternate keys, and inversion entries are converted into indexes on the physical data model. Primary and alternate keys are converted into unique indexes, and inversion entries are converted into non-unique indexes.

INDEXING IN ER/STUDIO

You can create additional indexes on the physical data model, both unique and non-unique.

Menu	Toolbar	Explorer	Shortcut Key	Shortcut Menu
Click on table, `Edit > Edit Table…`	n/a	Right-click on table, `Edit Table…`	Click on table, <ALT + E>, then <E>	Right-click on entity, `Edit Table…`

Go to the *Indexes* tab to view the indexes that migrated from the logical data model and also to add more indexes by clicking the <ADD> button. The screen in Figure 10.24 appears.

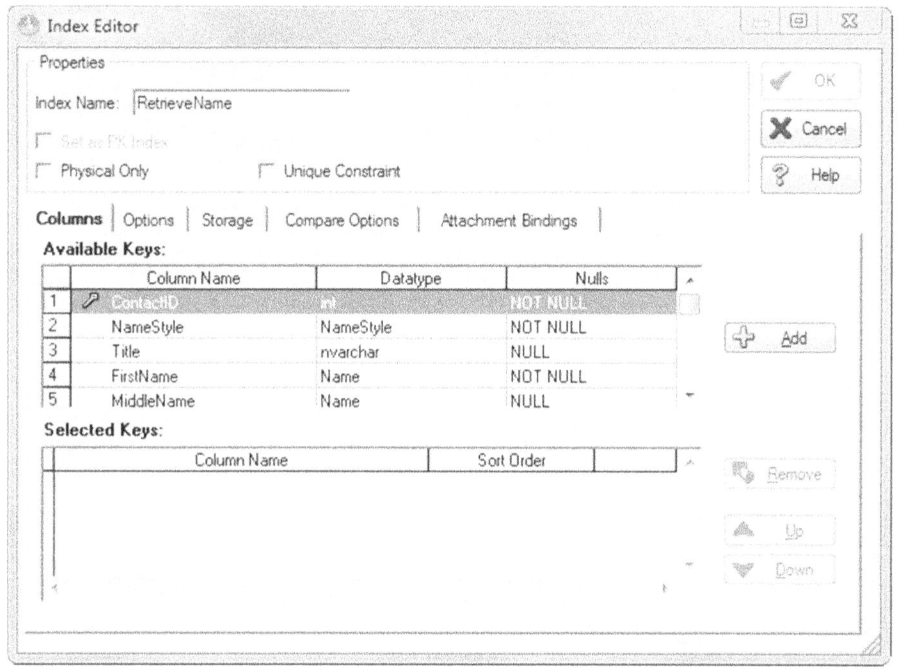

Figure 10.24 Index Editor

Name the index and optionally decide whether it should only exist on the physical data model (by checking `Physical Only`) and whether it is a unique index (by checking `Unique Constraint`). You can then highlight those columns you would like in the index and click the <ADD> button. If you have more than one column in an index (called a composite index), you can resequence the columns in the index using the <UP> and <DOWN> arrow keys. It is important to arrange the columns in a sequence that they will be accessed by most often. For example, if we add an index on first name and last name columns, it would be important to know how these columns are accessed most frequently—either by first name first or last name first. This is how we should sequence the columns.

EXERCISE 10.3: INDEXING

In Figure 10.25 you can see that we added a non-unique index (inversion entry) on **Offering Name** and **Offering Price Amount**. Create this index on your model.

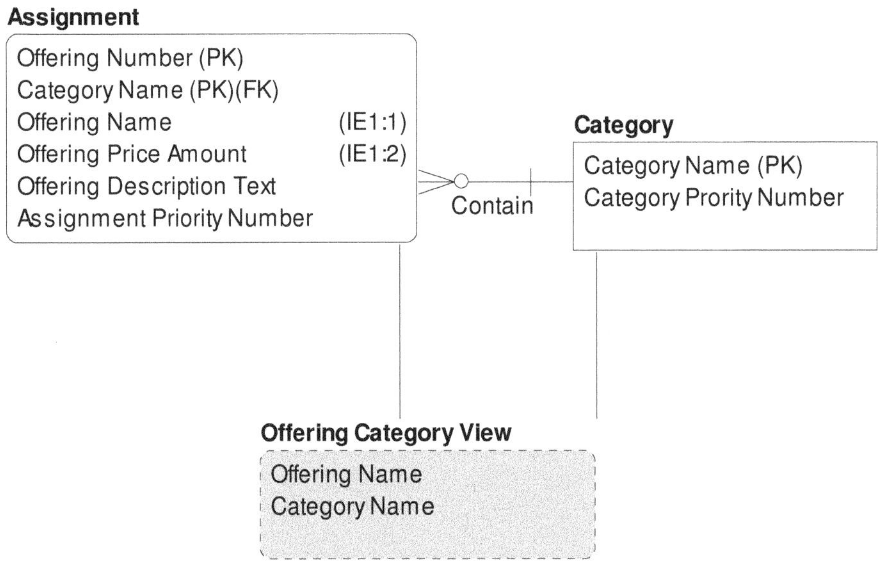

Figure 10.25 Non-unique added to model

Note that if the index is not displaying on the model, make sure the `Inversion Entry` checkbox is checked under *Diagram and Object Display Options* (choose `View > Diagram And Object Display Options` or click on the icon), and in the *Table* tab, click on `Inversion Entry`.

PARTITIONING

Partitioning is when a table is split up into two or more tables. Vertical partitioning is when columns are split up, and horizontal is when rows are split up. It is common for both horizontal and vertical to be used together. That is, when splitting rows apart we in many cases learn that certain columns only belong with one set of rows.

Both vertical and horizontal partitioning are common techniques when building analytics systems. A table might contain a large number of columns and perhaps only a subset are volatile and change often, so this subset can be vertically partitioned into a separate table. Or we might have ten years of orders in a table, and to improve query performance we horizontally partition by year so that when queries are run within a given year the performance will be much faster.

Partitioning can be used as a reactive technique, meaning that even after an application goes live, the designer might choose to add partitioning after monitoring performance and space and determine that an improvement is needed.

PARTITIONING IN ER/STUDIO

To create a horizontal partition, highlight the entity and choose one of these options:

Menu	Toolbar	Explorer	Shortcut Key	Shortcut Menu
Model > Denormalization Mapping > Horizontal Splits…	Modeling toolbar:	Right-click on table, Denormalization Mapping > Horizontal Splits…	<ALT + M>, then <Z>, then <H>	Right-click on entity, Denormalization Mapping > Horizontal Splits…

I would like to create a horizontal partition on **Assignment** from Figure 10.25, where we put offerings less than $10 in one partition and offerings $10 or higher in a second partition.

After starting the wizard, the screen in Figure 10.26 appears, and I select two splits (one for offerings less than $10 and the other for offerings $10 or greater).

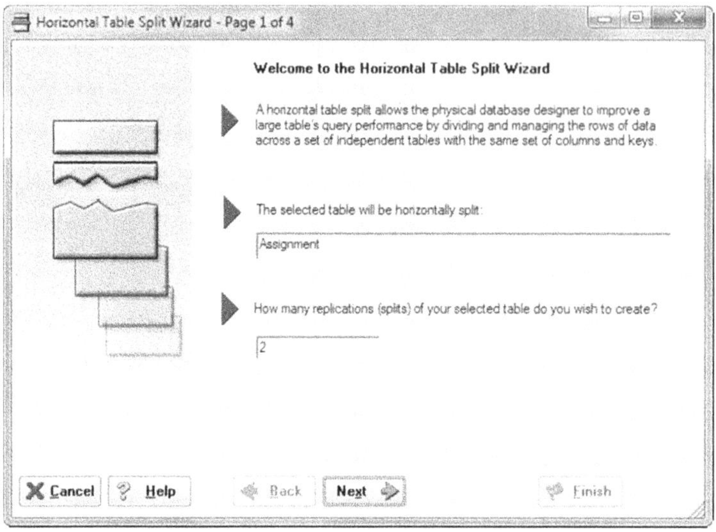

Figure 10.26 Page 1 of 4 of the Horizontal Split Wizard

I click <Next>, and I'm then given the option of changing the table names on Page 2 of the Wizard. I chose **LessThan10** and **10orMore** as the two table names. See Figure 10.27.

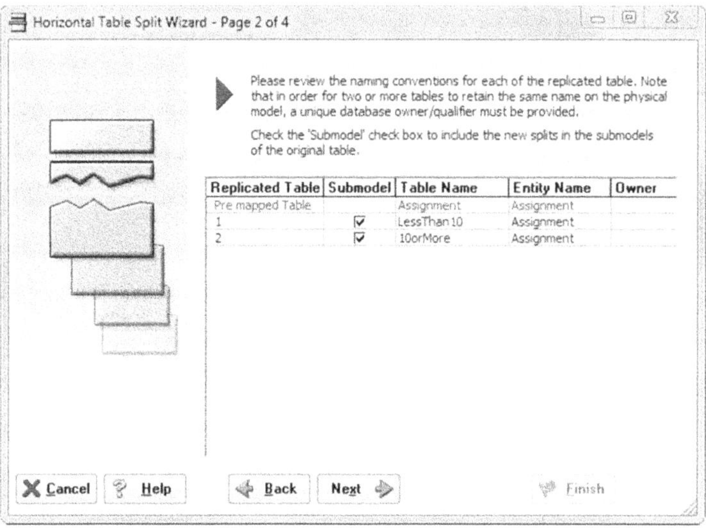

Figure 10.27 Page 2 of 4 of the Horizontal Split Wizard

I click <Next>, and in Page 3 I'm given the option to remove certain relationships from certain partitions. I will keep all of the relationships intact. See Figure 10.28.

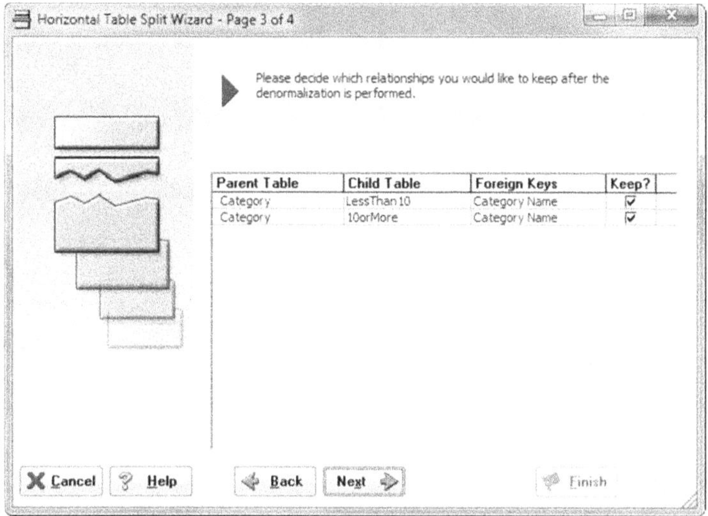

Figure 10.28 Page 3 of 4 of the Horizontal Split Wizard

I click <Next>, and in Page 4 I'm given the option to name this Horizontal split. I call it **SplitBasedOnPrice**. See Figure 10.29.

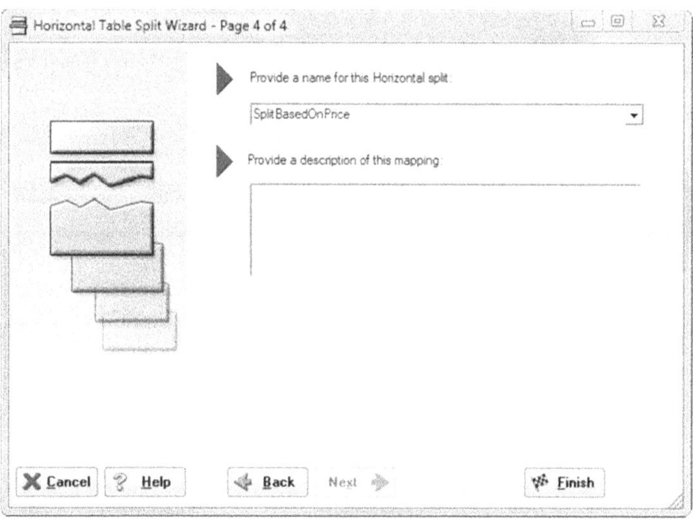

Figure 10.29 Page 4 of 4 of the Horizontal Split Wizard

I click <Finish> to exit the wizard. A note appears that I need to fix the SQL for the view created because the view is now referencing the pre-split table. This is an easy fix in the view editor. The model in Figure 10.30 appears.

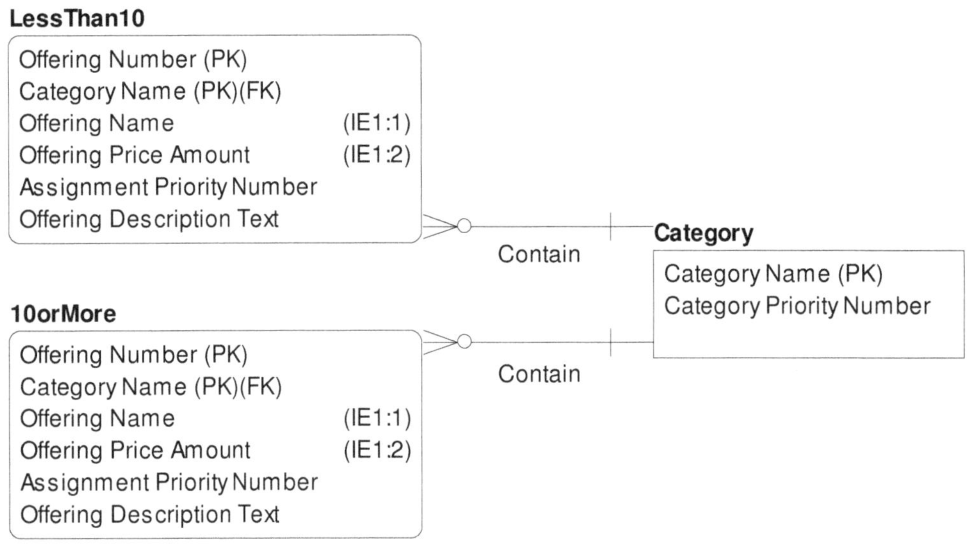

Figure 10.30 Horizontal Split based on price

To create a vertical partition, choose one of these actions:

Menu	Toolbar	Explorer	Shortcut Key	Shortcut Menu
Click on table, `Model > Denormalization Mapping > Vertical Splits…`	Modeling toolbar:	Right-click on table, `Denormalization Mapping > Vertical Splits…`	Click on table, <ALT + M>, then <Z>, then <V>	Right-click on entity, `Denormalization Mapping > Vertical Splits…`

The **Vertical Split Wizard** is identical to the **Horizontal Split Wizard**, with the exception of Page 2 of the wizard, where you can click and drag columns to the tables for assignment.

EXERCISE 10.4: PARTITIONING

Create the horizontal split as shown in Figure 10.30. If you are feeling adventurous, play with vertical partitioning as well.

EXERCISE 10.5: TRACING FROM PHYSICAL BACK TO LOGICAL

One of the neat features in ER/Studio is the ability to easily perform impact analysis by tracing tables back to other tables and also back to their logical data model entity through the *Where Used* tab in the *Table Editor*. For this exercise, play with this feature, and while you do, think of all of the possible uses for table lineage. What an awesome feature!

Key Points

- The physical data model (PDM) is the logical data model compromised for specific software or hardware.
- In ER/Studio, the physical data model must be based on an existing logical data model or reverse engineered from an existing database (such as the actual database or a data definition language such as SQL).
- Denormalization is the process of selectively violating normalization rules and reintroducing redundancy into the model (and, therefore, the database).
- A star schema is when each set of tables that make up a dimension is flattened into a single table.
- A view is a virtual table. It is a dynamic "view" or window into one or more tables (or other views) where the actual data is stored.
- An index is a value and a pointer to instances of that value in a table.
- Partitioning is when a table is split up into two or more tables. Vertical partitioning is when columns are split up, and horizontal is when rows are split up.
- ER/Studio supports forward and reverse engineering of both relational (e.g., Oracle, Teradata) and NoSQL databases (e.g., MongoDB, Hive).

SECTION IV
Additional ER/Studio Features

Section IV discusses additional features of ER/Studio. Chapter 11 covers the data dictionary; Chapter 12, data lineage; Chapter 13, import, export, printing, and reporting; Chapter 14, naming standards; Chapter 15, the compare and merge functionality; and Chapter 16, several features for agile teams and continuous improvement. Please refer to the ER/Studio User Guide for other features available in ER/Studio as well as for more details on each of the additional features discussed in this section.

CHAPTER 11
Data Dictionary

Important to share,
Enterprise consistency,
Save time and effort

The Data Dictionary is a feature of ER/Studio that allows the sharing of many objects including domains, defaults, rules, and attachments. If you are using the Repository, you can share the data dictionary across your organization. Objects in the data dictionary can be imported into your data model, saving time and leading to greater enterprise consistency. If you are not using the Repository, you can still import data dictionary objects from another ER/Studio file into your data model.

In this chapter, we assume you are not using the Repository and therefore will explain how to import a data dictionary into ER/Studio. I will provide an overview to several types of objects that can be imported from a data dictionary including domains, user datatypes, reference values, and attachments. Additional types of objects can be imported as well but are outside the scope of this chapter.

Importing a Data Dictionary

If you are not using the Repository, you can still import data dictionary objects from another ER/Studio file into your current ER/Studio file. Any changes you make to your local data dictionary objects, however, will not be propagated back into a central data dictionary, which is only possible when using the Repository.

When you import a data dictionary, the new objects are merged with the existing data dictionary in your data model. You can import the data dictionary of another data model diagram (.dm1 file), which can save you modeling time and increase consistency across the enterprise.

Menu	Toolbar	Explorer	Shortcut Key	Shortcut Menu
`File > Import Data Dictionary`	n/a	n/a	<ALT + F>, then <Y>	n/a

Become an ER/Studio Hotshot:

- The Northwind data model that ships with ER/Studio has a fantastic data dictionary. You can open any data model and import the Northwind data dictionary, which is in the Sample Data Models folder.
- You can copy data dictionary objects such as domains from one dictionary to another. Just right-click on the object you would like to copy, select *Copy Dictionary Objects*, locate the target data dictionary, and then right-click on any node and select *Paste Data Dictionary Objects*.

Upon executing one of these commands, the screen in Figure 11.1 appears.

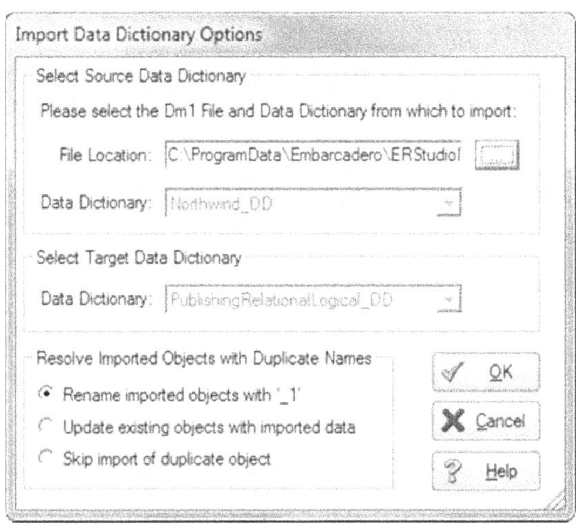

Figure 11.1 Import data dictionary options

To the right of the *File Location* text box, select the button with the three dots and choose the ER/Studio file whose data dictionary you would like to import. You can select the Northwind data model from the Sample Data Models folder. If there are multiple data dictionaries associated with the data model you selected, choose the one you would like to import from the *Data Dictionary* drop-down. In the case of the Northwind data model, there is only one data dictionary, so it is already selected and grayed out to indicate it will be imported.

In the *Resolve Imported Objects with Duplicate Names* section on this screen, choose how you want to handle name duplications by selecting one of the options listed. For example, if you currently have the domain **City** in your existing model, and the imported data dictionary contains a **City** domain as well, choosing `Rename imported objects with '_1'` will rename the imported **City** domain **City_1**, choosing `Update existing objects with imported data` will update the **City** domain in your model with the imported **City** domain, and choosing `Skip import of duplicate object` will not bring in the **City** domain from the imported data dictionary. After choosing one of these three options, click <OK>. Click on the *Data Dictionary* tab on the bottom of the Explorer pane (as shown in Figure 11.2) and you will see what was imported.

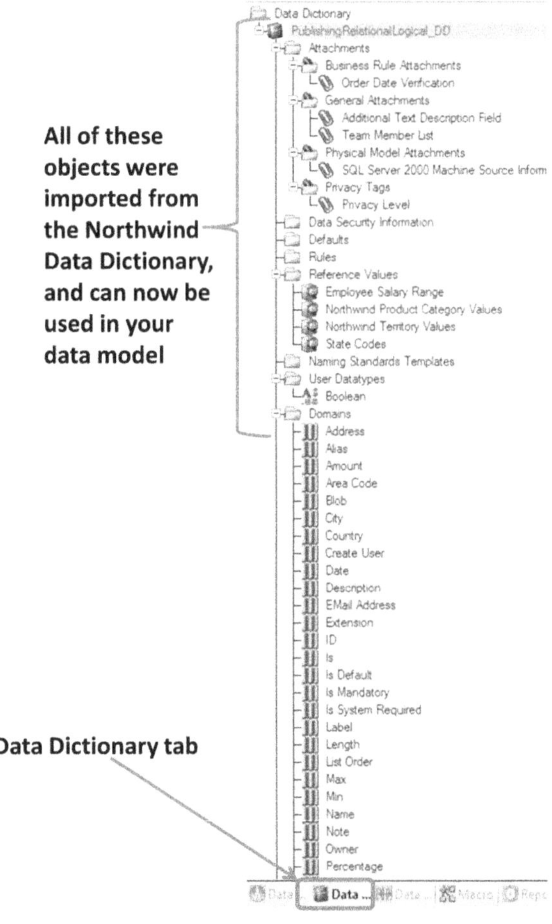

Figure 11.2 Imported data dictionary from Northwind data model

Types of Objects Imported from a Data Dictionary

There are several types of objects that are imported into your data model when importing a data dictionary including domains, user-defined datatypes, reference values, and attachments.

DOMAINS

Recall our definition of a domain from Chapter 6: *A domain is a set of validation criteria that can be applied to more than one attribute; it provides a means of standardizing the characteristics of the attributes.*

Creating a domain allows you to define the object once and then use it repeatedly by applying the domain to attributes. You construct domains as you would attributes, specifying a name, datatype properties, null status, default values, and validation rules. By defining a domain, you also gain the power of propagating changes to the underlying domain definition to all attributes that reference it. For example, if you make any changes to the domain **City**, then all attributes that use this domain will now reflect the updated **City** domain.

ER/Studio allows you to organize your domains using domain folders. You can classify domains in unique groups by creating different domain folders such as domains for measures, names, IDs, etc. When you delete a domain folder, all domains and subfolders within that folder are also deleted. Domain integrity refers to the rules governing what values an attribute can be assigned. By restricting and validating an attribute's values, you can implement important business rules such as ensuring that a checking account maintains a positive balance or preventing the entry of invalid phone numbers.

DOMAINS IN ER/STUDIO

Domains are created and managed in the data dictionary. You can define domains to create "templates" or reusable attributes. For example, a domain **BusinessDate** can be created for attributes that are constrained by a business date such as **Order Entry Date** or **Employee Hire Date**. Reference values, defaults, and rules can be implemented directly on a domain. For example, we can set the default value of `Monday` to **BusinessDate**.

Domains appear under the *Data Dictionary* tab in Explorer as was seen in Figure 11.2. To create a new domain, use the following command:

Menu	Toolbar	Explorer	Shortcut Key	Shortcut Menu
n/a	n/a	Right-click on `Domains` (or on a domain folder) then choose `New Domain`	n/a	n/a

Become an ER/Studio Hotshot:

- To create a new folder for domains, right-click on `Domains` or any domain folder, and choose `New Folder`.
- Domains can be dragged and dropped into an entity to create a new attribute with this assigned domain.
- To edit a domain, double-click on its name in Explorer to launch the editor.

The *Add Domain* screen appears as in Figure 11.3.

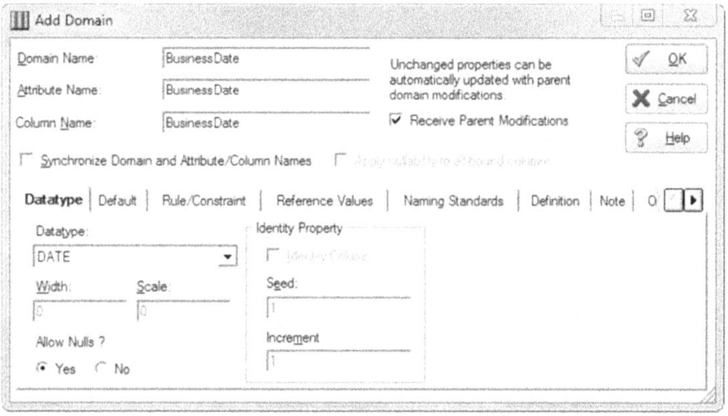

Figure 11.3 Add Domain screen

Enter a domain name in the *Domain Name* text box. I chose **BusinessDate**. You will also need to give the domain an attribute and column name. The attribute name will be the name chosen whenever this domain is used to create a new attribute in the logical model. The column name will be applied similarly in the physical model. The name may be the same as the domain name, if you wish.

Clicking on `Receive Parent Modifications` means that if there is a parent domain to the domain we are creating, changes to this parent domain will also be applied to the new child domain.

Clicking on `Synchronize Domain and Attribute/Column Names` means that the domain, attribute, and column names will all be the same. Therefore, if you entered different names in the Domain, Attribute, and Column fields on this screen, clicking this synchronize checkbox will make all of the names the same.

The `Apply nullability to all bound columns` checkbox becomes available when you select a datatype that can have nulls; you can choose to disallow nulls by clicking `No` for `Allow Nulls`. There are ten tabs on this screen:

Tab	Here's what you need to know:
Datatype	Define the format and whether the domain is required (allow nulls equals `No`) or not required (allow nulls equals `Yes`). If you select a data type that can be used as a surrogate key, such as TINYINT, you can click on `Identity Column` and choose the starting value (`Seed`) and the increment value (`Increment`).
Default	Enter a default value for `Declarative Default` or choose another default from the `Default Binding` list. You will see a default in the drop-down when a default value has been bound to the domain (*Data Dictionary* > *Defaults* > *Edit Default Definition* > *Binding Information*). The defaults you choose will appear in the SQL produced when you select `Generate Database` from the physical data model.
Rule/Constraint	Similar to the *Default* tab, you can add a check constraint or choose a value from the drop-down if one has already been defined in the data dictionary. This is a tab that would be used for columns, not for attributes.
Reference Values	Bind reference values to the domain. Reference values are attributes that define allowed data values. We'll talk about reference values shortly. You can choose a reference value from the drop-down list if you would like the domain constrained by specific values such as postal codes or currencies.

Tab	Here's what you need to know:
Naming Standards	When a *Naming Standards Template* is bound to a domain, that template overrides the *Naming Standards Template* selected in the *Naming Standards Utility* or the *Generate Physical* data model utility. This allows you to apply different naming standards to different objects when portions of a model require different versions of a standard. For example, if some objects already exist in the database and you do not want to apply a newer naming standard to them.
Definition	Define the domain.
Note	Capture any other text outside the definition such as questions to ask business experts, known issues, or action items. Using HTML tags in *Notes* will get applied as formatting in the HTML reports.
Override Controls	Controls what can or cannot be overridden on attributes bound to this domain. The *General Overrides* area contains allow/disallow options for datatypes, defaults, etc. *Name Synchronization* completely detaches the domain name from the bound attributes. By detaching the domain name, you can change the domain name without impacting the names of the attributes assigned to this domain. *Attachment Synchronization* keeps attachments in the domain in sync with the bound attribute. Any attachments added to a domain will propagate to the attributes. You can still add other attachments directly to the attributes.
Attachment Bindings	Bind an external piece of information, such as a Microsoft Word document or PDF file, to the domain. Very useful for requirements documents, user stories, etc. Attachments are created in the Attachments folder of the data dictionary and must be added to the model before they will display on this tab.
Binding Information	Select the object classes and/or specific objects to which you want to bind this attachment. You can override this setting by using the attribute tab of the entity.

Click <OK> to save your changes and exit the editor.

EXERCISE 11.1: CREATING DOMAINS

Create a name domain and assign it to all attributes in our publishing data model that are names: **Offering Name**, **Category Name**, **Speaker First Name**, **Speaker Last Name**, and **Conference Hotel Name.**

USER-DEFINED DATATYPES

A user-defined datatype is a combination of format and length that you can define once and use many times. Depending on the type of database, these user-defined types can also be forward engineered into the database. User-defined datatypes are a powerful mechanism for ensuring the consistent definition of domain properties throughout a data model. You can build a user-defined datatype from base datatypes, specifying width, precision, and scale, as applicable. In addition, you can bind rules and defaults to the user-defined datatype to enforce domain integrity. After creating a user-defined datatype, you can use it in attributes and domains without needing to define its underlying definition each time. User-defined datatypes are particularly useful with commonly referenced attributes in a database such as **Phone Number**, **Postal Code**, or **Part Number**.

Creating a user-defined datatype and using it many times eliminates the tedium and potential for errors users can encounter when manually editing each attribute. For example, you can define a surrogate key in the **Part** table, **PartNo**, as an integer for efficiency. You can define a user datatype, **PartNumber**, to represent every use of **PartNo** throughout the database design. Subsequently, you learn that the data to be converted from a legacy system contains some part numbers in character format. To accommodate the change, you only need to edit the definition of **PartNumber** from an integer to a character-based user datatype. ER/Studio automatically converts all columns using **PartNumber** to the new definition.

Although only a few database platforms currently support user-defined datatypes, ER/Studio extends their utility to all database platforms in the physical data model. ER/Studio automatically converts user-defined datatypes to their base definitions when generating SQL code for any database platforms that do not provide native support.

USER-DEFINED DATATYPES IN ER/STUDIO

To create a new user-defined datatype, click on the *Data Dictionary* tab, and then choose the following command:

Menu	Toolbar	Explorer	Shortcut Key	Shortcut Menu
n/a	n/a	Right-click the `User Datatypes` node and then select `New User Datatype...`	n/a	n/a

The *Edit User-Defined Datatype* screen appears as shown in Figure 11.4.

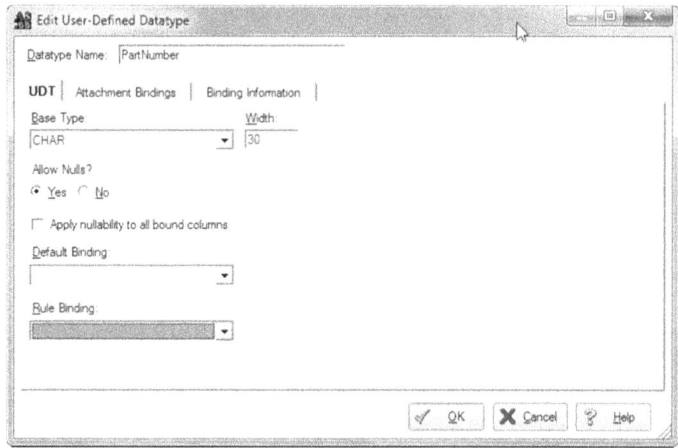

Figure 11.4 Edit User-Defined Datatype screen

You can enter the name of the new data type after *Datatype Name*. There are three tabs on this screen:

Tab	Here's what you need to know:
UDT	Define the format and width of the new data type and whether the user-defined datatype is required (allow nulls equals `No`) or not required (allow nulls equals `Yes`). The `Apply nullability to all bound columns` checkbox becomes available when you select a datatype that can have nulls, but you can choose to disallow nulls by clicking `No` in `Allow Nulls`. If you would like to bind the new datatype to a default value or rule, choose the desired one from the drop-down menus.

Attachment Bindings	Bind an external piece of information, such as a Microsoft Word document or PDF file, to the user-defined datatype. Very useful for requirements documents, user stories, etc. Attachments are created in the Attachments folder of the data dictionary and must be added to the model before they will display on this tab.
Binding Information	Select the object classes and/or specific objects to which you want to bind this attachment. You can override this setting using the attribute tab of the entity.

Click <OK> to save your changes and exit the editor.

EXERCISE 11.2: CREATING USER-DEFINED DATATYPES

Create a user-defined datatype called **StandardName** and assign it to the name domain you created in the last exercise. Did changing this name domain automatically propagate the change to all of the attributes you tied to this domain in the last exercise?

REFERENCE VALUES

Reference Values are ranges of values or itemized lists that define allowed data. They can be assigned to attributes or domains.

REFERENCE VALUES IN ER/STUDIO

To create a new reference value, click on the *Data Dictionary* tab and then choose the following command:

Menu	Toolbar	Explorer	Shortcut Key	Shortcut Menu
`n/a`	n/a	Right-click the `Reference Values` node and then select `New Reference Value…`	n/a	n/a

Become an ER/Studio Hotshot:
You can import or export multiple reference values from Excel using a macro. On the *Macro* tab of the *Data Model Explorer*, choose `Sample Macros > Meta Data Management Macros` to see the import and export reference value macros that are available.

The *Reference Value Editor* appears as shown in Figure 11.5.

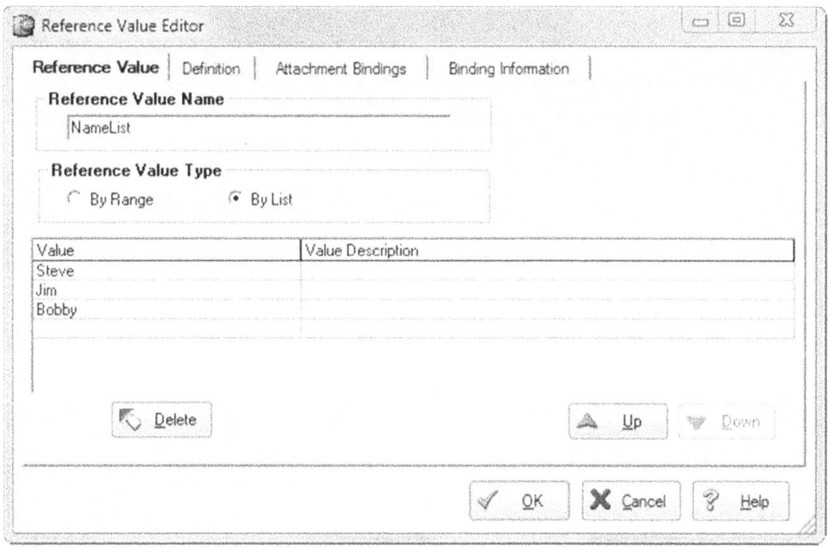

Figure 11.5 Reference Value Editor

There are four tabs on this screen:

Tab	Here's what you need to know:
Reference Value	Enter a name for the reference value and click the radio button for either defining a range or a list. If you click `By Range`, enter a minimum and maximum value. If you click `By List`, you can enter a list of values and description for each value. (Double-click in the *Value* column to enter a value.)
Definition	Define the reference value.
Attachment Bindings	Bind an external piece of information, such as a Microsoft Word document or PDF file, to the reference value. Very useful for requirements documents, user stories, etc. Attachments are created in the Attachments folder of the data dictionary and must be added to the model before they will display on this tab.
Binding Information	Select the object classes and/or specific objects to which you want to bind this attachment. You can override this setting using the attribute tab of the entity.

Click <OK> to save your changes and exit the editor.

EXERCISE 11.3: CREATING REFERENCE VALUES

Create a reference value called **NameList** and enter about ten different names (your choice). Then assign **NameList** to your name domain.

ATTACHMENTS

An attachment is a document that you can associate with an ER/Studio object such as a data model, entity, or attribute. Attachments and attachment types offer a structured method for you to associate an external piece of information to your data model. You can extend your metadata this way and include supporting documentation such as meeting notes, risk analysis, and spreadsheets. You can bind attachments to virtually any file or application on your system.

Attachments are organized into two key objects:

- **Attachment Types**. An organizational system where you can group together similar attachments and specify which objects can have this type of attachment bound to them. Attachment types define the scope of the attachments created underneath them. Use attachment types to organize attachments by the object types to which they are applied (e.g., entities, relationships, attributes), by the business subject area (e.g., customer, product, account), or by function (e.g., issues, questions, requirement documents). Once you create an attachment, you can bind it to any data model objects associated with the attachment type.

- **Attachment**. Information that you can associate with the diagram objects types selected for the Attachment Type. Attachments can take many different forms such as an external file, a date, or a list.

ATTACHMENTS IN ER/STUDIO

Let's first create a new attachment type and then a new attachment. To create a new attachment type, click on the *Data Dictionary* tab, and then choose the following command:

Menu	Toolbar	Explorer	Shortcut Key	Shortcut Menu
n/a	n/a	Right-click the Attachments folder and then select New Attachment Type…	n/a	n/a

The *Attachment Type Editor* screen appears as in Figure 11.6.

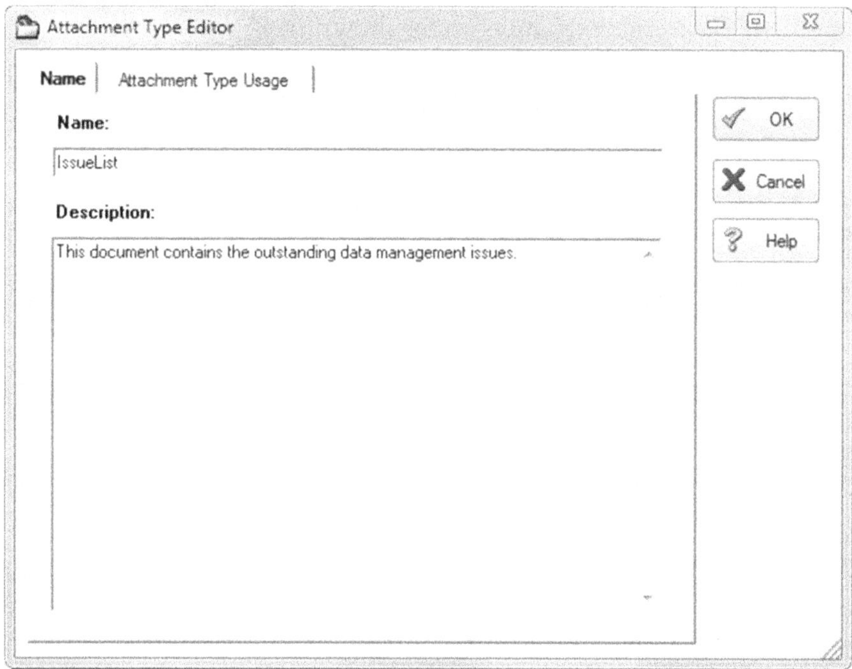

Figure 11.6 Attachment Type Editor screen

There are two tabs on this screen:

Tab	Here's what you need to know:
Name	Enter a name for the attachment type and, optionally, a description.
Attachment Type Usage	Any object classes you select here will be bound to this attachment type and will be displayed subsequently on the *Binding Information* tab of the *Attachment Editor*.

To create a new attachment, click on the *Data Dictionary* tab and then choose the following command:

Menu	Toolbar	Explorer	Shortcut Key	Shortcut Menu
n/a	n/a	Right-click on the attachment type and select `New Attachment…`	n/a	n/a

The *Attachment Editor* screen appears as shown in Figure 11.7.

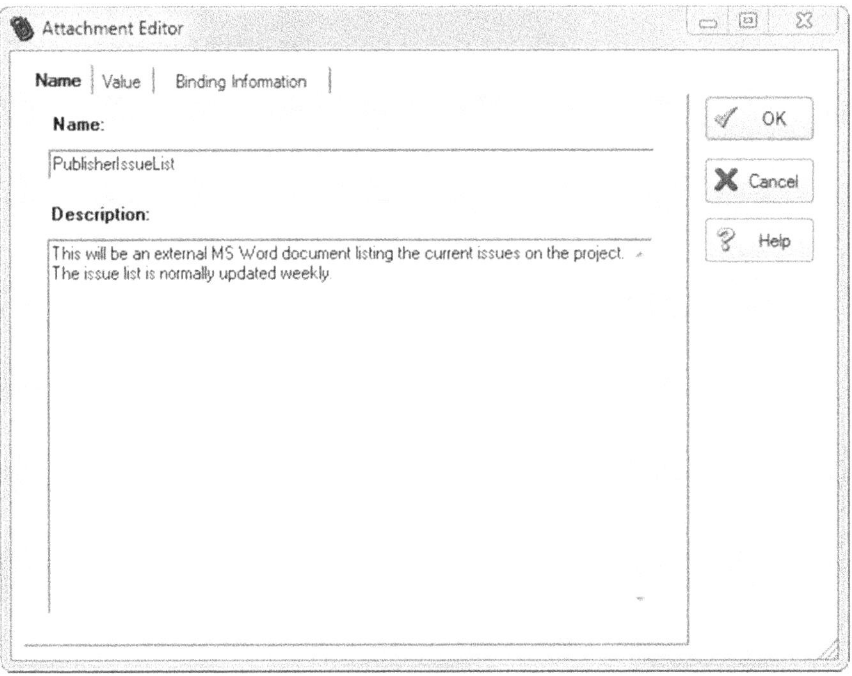

Figure 11.7 Attachment Type Editor screen

There are three tabs on this screen:

Tab	Here's what you need to know:
Name	Enter a name for the attachment and, optionally, a description.

Tab	Here's what you need to know:
Value	Select what kind of data this attachment contains. For *Text List* datatypes, you can list possible data values and then set the default value. For *External File Path*, for example, you can browse for a specific file such as a Microsoft Word file.
Binding Information	Select the object classes and/or specific objects to which you want to bind this attachment. You can override this setting using the attribute tab of the entity.

EXERCISE 11.4: CREATING ATTACHMENTS

Create a new attachment type for issues and then a new attachment that is a list of issues specific to our publisher example. Create a test Microsoft Word document and bind this Word document to this attachment.

Key Points

- The data dictionary is a feature of ER/Studio that enables reuse of many objects across data models including domains, defaults, and attachments.
- Creating a domain allows you to define the object once and then use it repeatedly by applying the domain to the entity attributes and table columns. Domains are reusable attribute templates that promote consistent attribute definitions.
- A user-defined datatype is a combination of format and length that you can define once and use many times.
- Reference values are ranges of values or itemized lists that define permitted data. They can be assigned to attributes or domains.
- An attachment is a document that you can associate with an ER/Studio object such as a data model, entity, or attribute. Attachments and attachment types offer a structured method for you to associate an external piece of information with your data model.

CHAPTER 12
Data Lineage

Need to know the source?
Data Lineage is how,
Let's connect the dots

The Data Lineage feature of ER/Studio enables you to document the movement of data from point A to point B (and any intermediate steps in between). Points A and B can be anything from flat files such as XML, data models, databases such as MongoDB, Access, Teradata, Oracle and DB2, and Excel worksheets. This movement is sometimes referred to as Extraction, Transformation, and Load (ETL) or source to target mapping. In addition to functionality within ER/Studio for documenting and view mappings, you can also use ER/Studio Data Lineage, which is a separate tool in the ER/Studio family, to explore existing or proposed ETL mappings to quickly and accurately perform impact analysis.

Figure 12.1 contains a common data movement process for data warehousing.

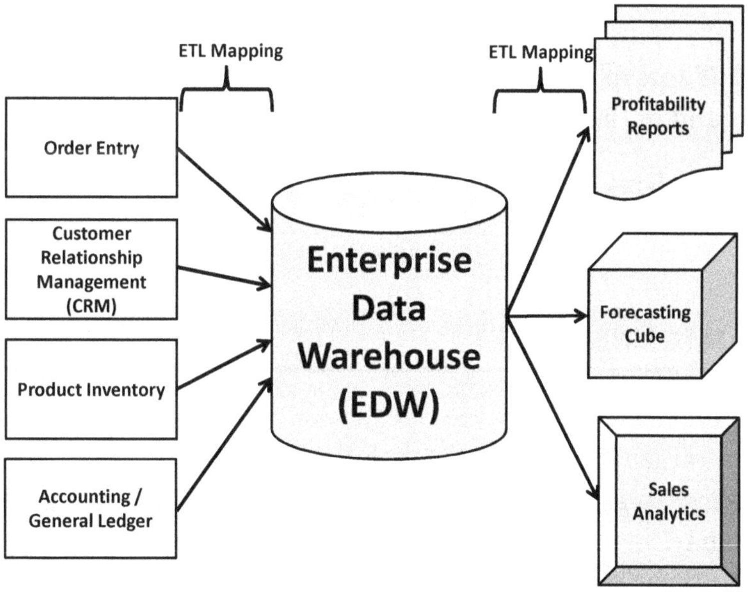

Figure 12.1 Data warehouse data movement process

In this illustration, the data is sourced from various systems on the left and fed to a data warehouse that stores the data in a format that is more conducive to reporting. This reduces the amount of overhead on the source systems so resources are not used for reporting directly on them. The data also must be cleansed to ensure the quality of the data used for reporting, multi-dimensional cubes, data mining applications, etc., which are targeted for specific audiences and purposes. An organization using ER/Studio would hopefully have a model of each source application such as Order Entry, the enterprise data warehouse, and the different reporting applications.

There needs to be a data mapping (also known as "data lineage") that "connects the dots" from each source system to the enterprise data warehouse and then from the enterprise data warehouse to each reporting application. This mapping document is provided to the ETL developer as their requirements document so they can develop the code necessary to implement the mapping.

In ER/Studio, you can document and view data lineage using the *Data Lineage* tab in *Model Explorer*. You can create a visualization of the data movement and transformation so you can see the relationships between the source and target, how the data flows from one table to another, and how the data is transformed. You can further expand the data lineage documentation in the *Table Editor* and in the *Table Column Editor*.

We'll first talk about using the *Data Lineage* tab and then cover the *Table Editor* and the *Table Column Editor*.

USING THE DATA LINEAGE TAB

You can document everything that is needed to take data from a source and load it into a target. There are three main components required to document lineage: sources, rules, and data flows. Sources are the starting points for the lineage and may be other ER/Studio data models, a SQL file, or a database. Rules are the types of changes (also known as "transformations") that can be applied to the source structures prior to loading the target structures. The data flow is one complete mapping, which includes specific sources, rules, and targets. Targets are the structures on the current model that we are loading.

For example, in Figure 12.2, we have **Author** from one of the models from Chapter 10 (Recall Figure 10.17) as the target model, and we have **Person** from the data model that is going to send us author data as the source.

Our goal is to document how to populate the **Author** columns. The model we are working in contains **Author,** and this is our target. We define the source **Person** and one of the rules for populating **Author**, which is a create rule for when to add new authors. Whenever we come across a social security number in the source that does not match any of the tax identifiers in the target, we create a new **Author** record. Data from the **Person FName** column will load into the **Author First Name** column, and data from the **Person Lname** column will load into the **Author Last Name** column.

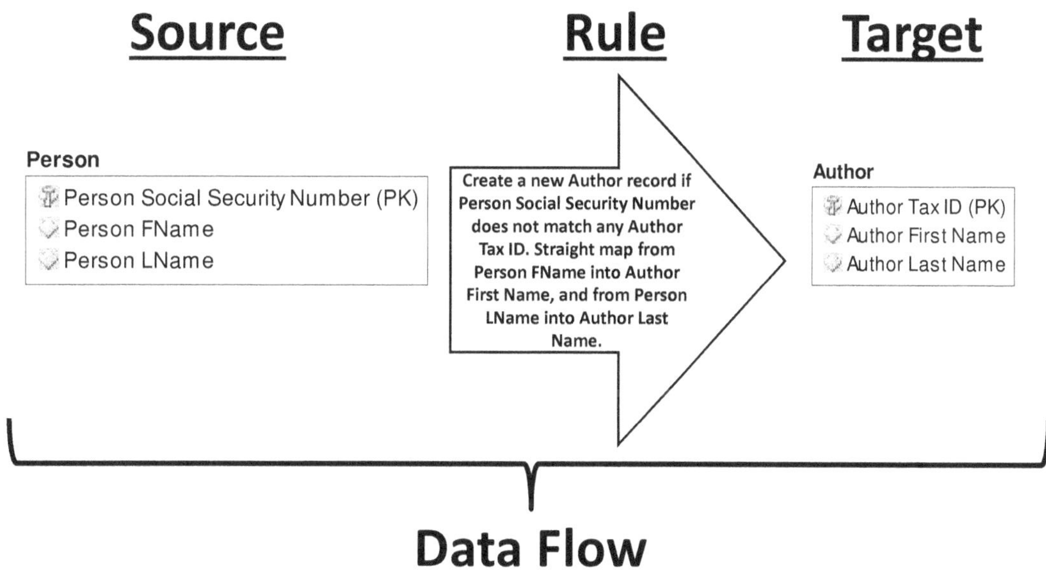
Source
Rule
Target
Person
Person Social Security Number (PK)
Person FName
Person LName
Create a new Author record if Person Social Security Number does not match any Author Tax ID. Straight map from Person FName into Author First Name, and from Person LName into Author Last Name.
Author
Author Tax ID (PK)
Author First Name
Author Last Name
Data Flow

Figure 12.2 Example of lineage from Person to Author

So using the data from Table 12.1 as an example, this particular rule would only load Henry Winkler and Eddie Murphy, as these are the only two authors that do not currently exist. Robin Williams already exists, so this record would not be loaded. This data flow example is just one of the many rules we would need to create. This is a create data flow (and a simple one!), yet there could be many other data flows to handle updating data, deleting data, archiving data, etc.

Person				Author		
Social Security Number	FName	LName	Create Rule	Tax ID	First Name	Last Name
123-45-6789	Robin	Williams	Don't load, already exists	123-45-6789	Robin	Williams
343-53-4421	Henry	Winkler	New record—load this!			
333-54-4911	Eddie	Murphy	New record—load this!			

Table 12.1 Sample data needing to be loaded from Person to Author

The target is already defined for us as this is our open model. Let's go through how to define sources, rules, and then the complete data flow.

Defining Source Systems in ER/Studio

Data sources can originate from the model you are working in, from external sources imported into the active diagram, or from data sources created on the Data Lineage tab. The source can be imported from other ER/Studio files, databases, or SQL files. If you are using the Repository, to add a new source, click on the *Data Lineage* tab and then choose the following command:

Menu	Toolbar	Explorer	Shortcut Key	Shortcut Menu
`n/a`	n/a	Right-click on `Other Sources` and then select `New Source...`	n/a	n/a

You may receive the pop up window in Figure 12.3, which warns you that the list of changes you made up to this point will be erased from the undo history, meaning once you proceed, you will not be able to undo any changes you made previously. You can click <Yes> and also suppress this message from appearing in the future by clicking `Do not display this dialog again`.

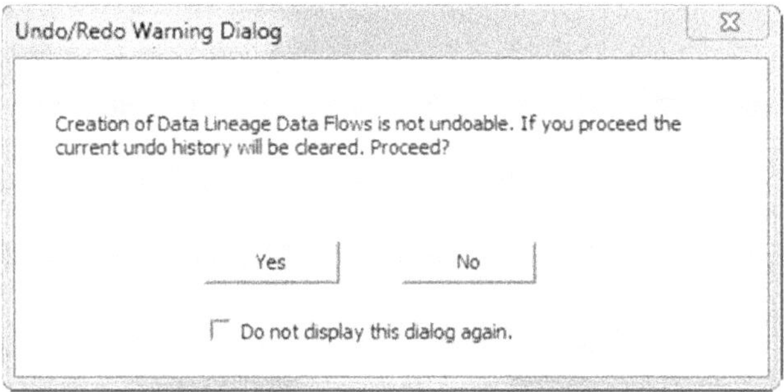

Figure 12.3 Undo/Redo Warning pop up

The *Data Source Properties* editor appears as in Figure 12.4.

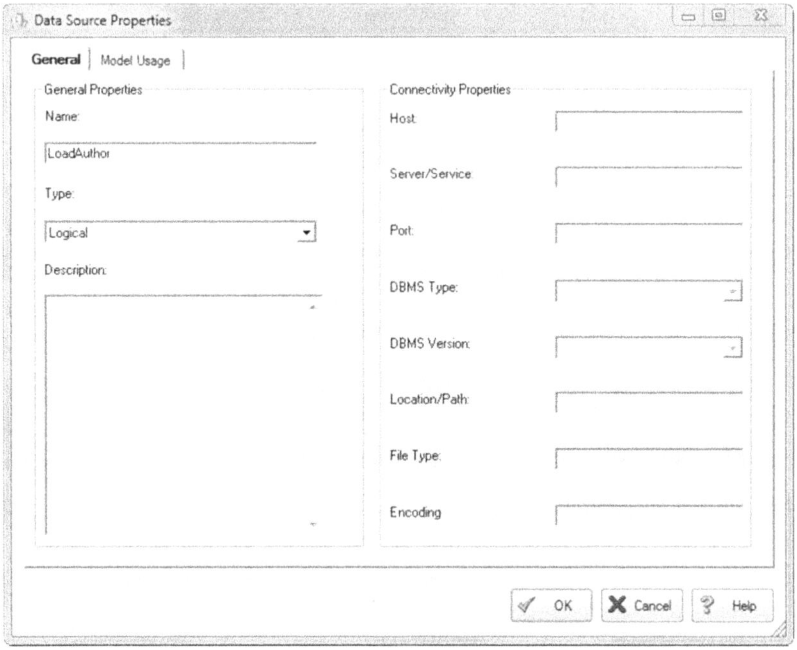

Figure 12.4 Data Source Properties editor

There are two tabs on this screen:

Tab	Here's what you need to know:
General	The name you provide here will be displayed as a data source in the *Other Sources* node within the *Data Lineage* tab. Select from the drop-down the type of source it is (whether `Logical`, `Physical`, `Flat File`, or `Other`). You can also add a definition for the source on this tab. *Connectivity Properties* are useful to enter when connecting to a database. You can leave this section on the screen empty for ER/Studio files that you are sourcing from.
Model Usage	This is a read-only display of the source defined on the *General* tab. Ensure that it matches your intentions.

If you are not using the Repository, to add a new source, click on the *Data Lineage* tab and then choose the following command:

Menu	Toolbar	Explorer	Shortcut Key	Shortcut Menu
n/a	n/a	Right-click on `Other Sources` and then select `Import New Source…`	n/a	n/a

The first of a five-page wizard appears. See Figure 12.5 for Page 1 of 5.

I created a data model just containing the **Person** entity from Figure 12.2, and I selected this model by clicking on the yellow folder to the right of *From a model in another DM1 file*. As with other wizards, you are given the option to load settings from a prior import source operation. Click <Next> to go on to Page 2 of the wizard as shown in Figure 12.6.

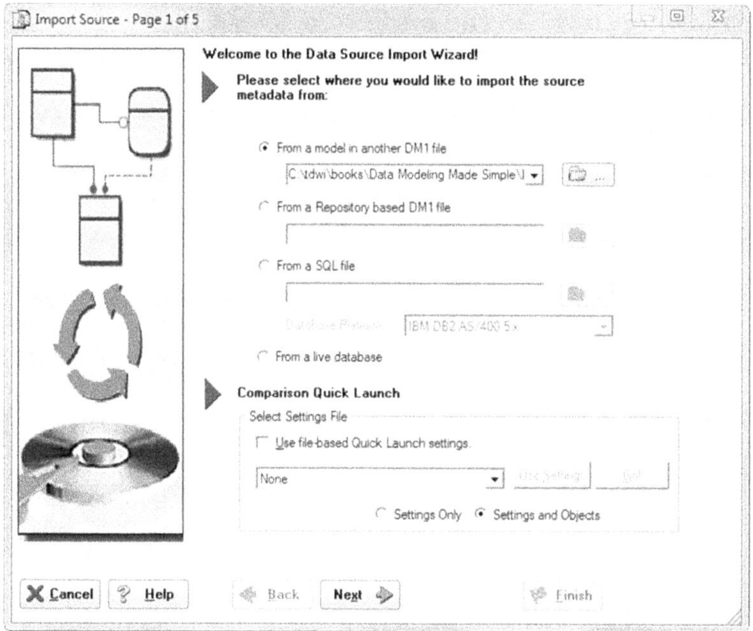

Figure 12.5 Import Source – Page 1 of 5

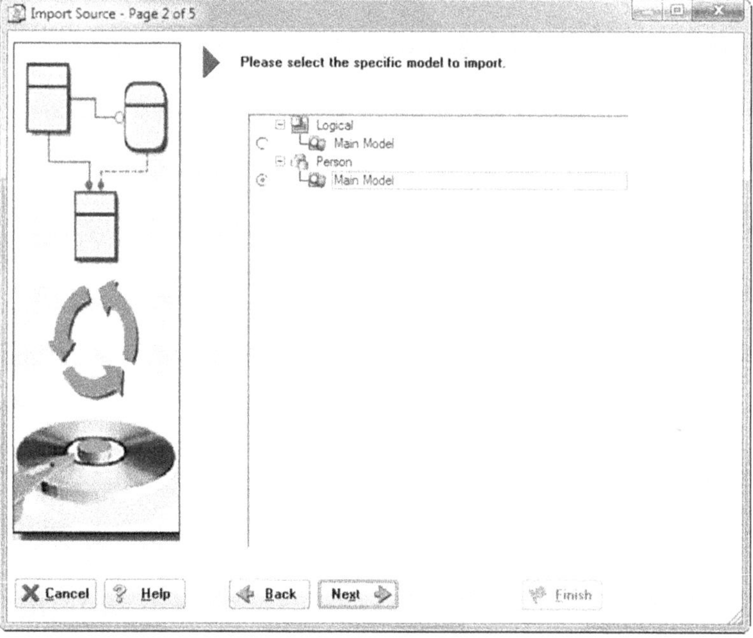

Figure 12.6 Import Source – Page 2 of 5

On this screen, you can select the model you would like to import. I chose the Person physical data model. Click <Next> to go on to Page 3 of the wizard as shown in Figure 12.7.

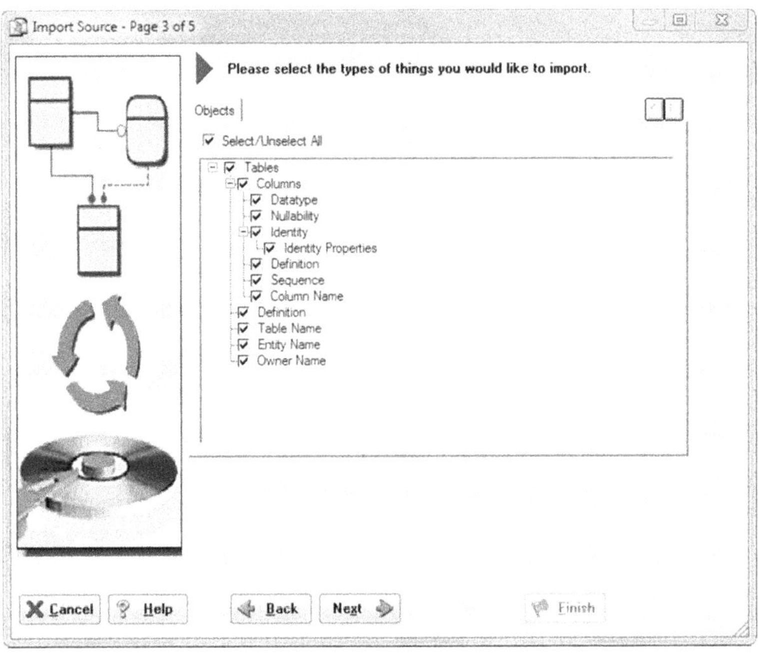

Figure 12.7 Import Source – Page 3 of 5

On this screen, select the types of metadata you would like imported. The default is to bring in everything. Click <Next> to go on to Page 4 of the wizard as shown in Figure 12.8.

On this screen you can select the entities you would like to import. Because our model in this example has just the single entity **Person**, it is an easy screen to complete. You can also optionally save your settings so you can load them to save time the next time you import a source. Click <Next> to go on to Page 5 of the wizard as shown in Figure 12.9. On this screen, we can go through each source entity and decide what to do if an entity with that same name already exists in our model. In this case it is easy because the **Person** entity does not exist in our model. We can also run a report to review these results in HTML or RTF format. Click <Finish> to complete the wizard. You will notice the new source appearing in the *Other Sources* folder.

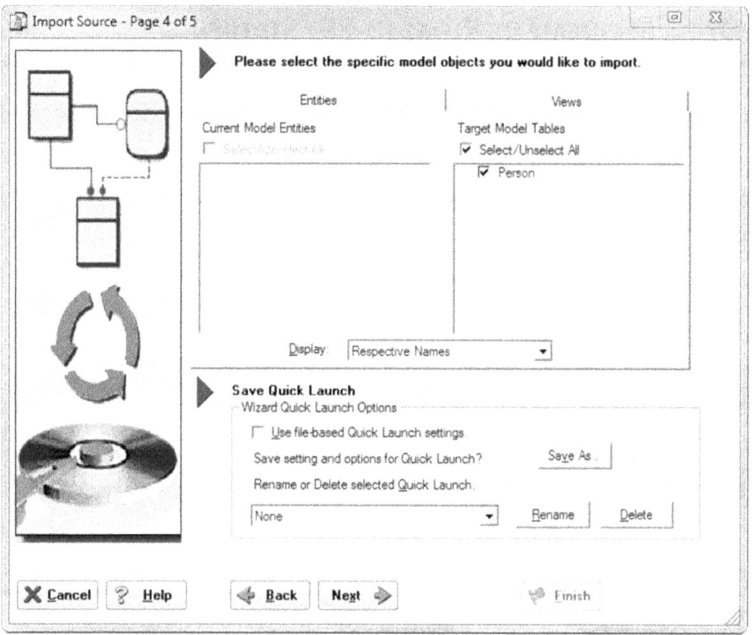

Figure 12.8 Import Source – Page 4 of 5

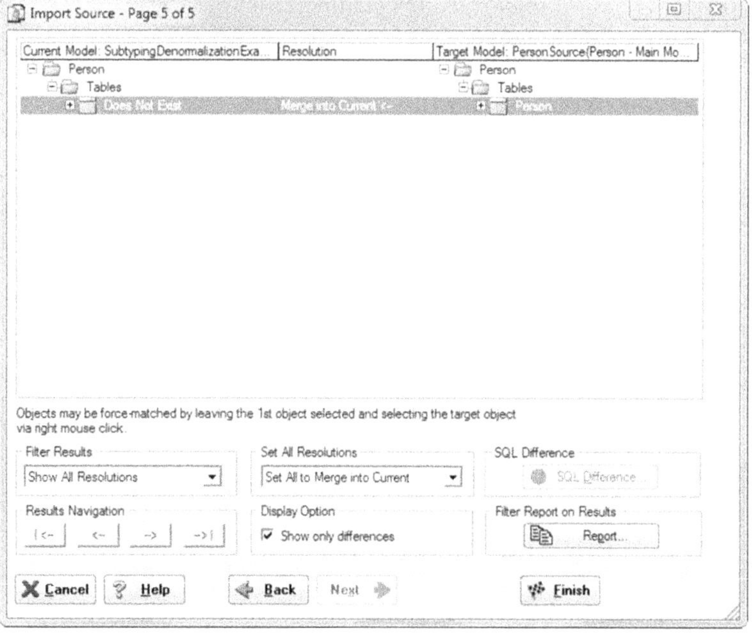

Figure 12.9 Import Source – Page 5 of 5

CREATING DATA MOVEMENT RULES IN ER/STUDIO

Data Movement rules describe the different ways in which source and target tables can be related. Types can include create, update, archive, backup, etc. You can relate source data to one or more tables and entities in the same model, the active diagram, or to tables imported from external systems. To add a data movement rule, click on the *Data Lineage* tab and then choose the following command:

Menu	Toolbar	Explorer	Shortcut Key	Shortcut Menu
`n/a`	n/a	Right-click the `Data Movement Rules` node and then `New Data Movement Rule`	n/a	n/a

The *Data Movement Rule* editor appears as in Figure 12.10.

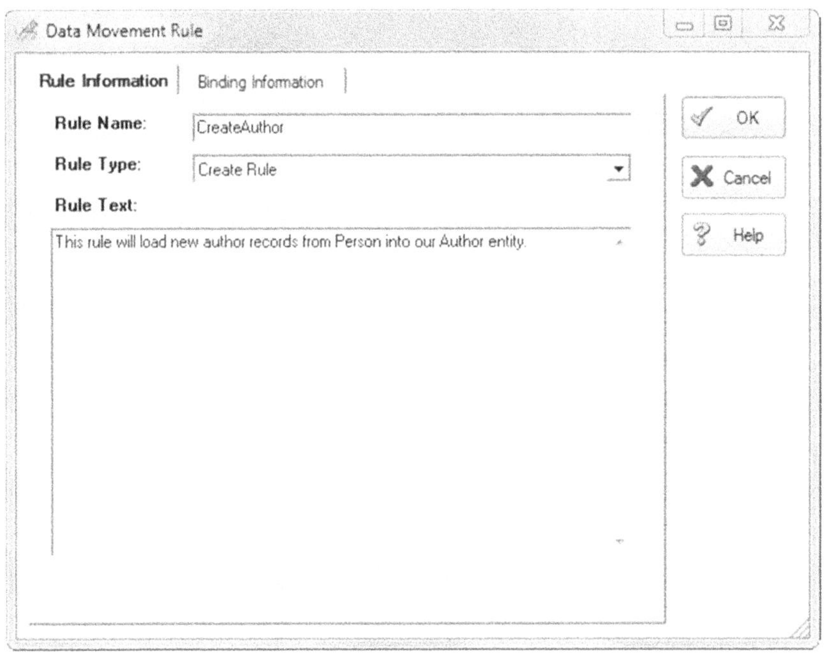

Figure 12.10 Data Movement Rule editor

There are two tabs on this screen:

Tab	Here's what you need to know:
Rule Information	Enter a name that indicates the operation and objects acted on, depending on the specifics of your binding definition. Under the `Rule Type` drop-down, select the generic rule type that best describes the data movement such as a create rule or archive rule. Under `Rule Text`, document your data movement plan, perhaps adding instructions or contingency plans.
Binding Information	Select the object classes and/or specific objects to which you want to bind this attachment. You can override this setting using the *Data Lineage* tab of the entity.

After clicking <OK> you will notice the new rule appearing in the *Data Movement Rules* folder.

Creating a Data Flow in ER/Studio

Now let's put the pieces together by creating a Data Flow. The data flow organizes and encapsulates one data transformation and the source tables and columns used in the transformation to produce the target data. To create a data flow, click on the *Data Lineage* tab on the bottom of the Explorer pane (as shown in Figure 12.11).

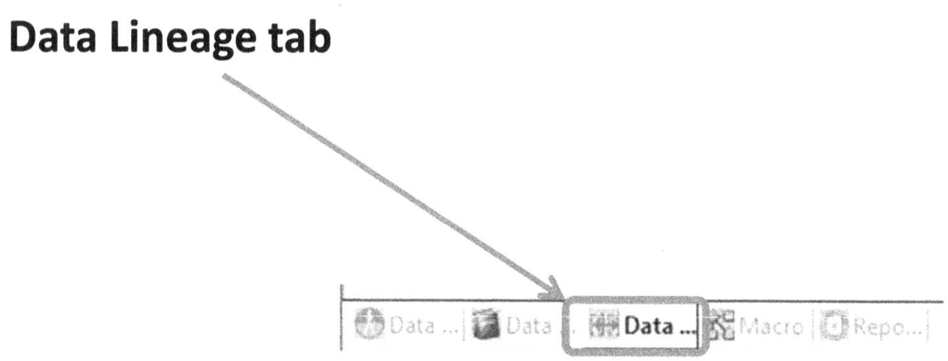

Figure 12.11 Data Lineage tab from Explorer pane

If there are not yet any data lineages defined, the pop-up in Figure 12.12 will appear.

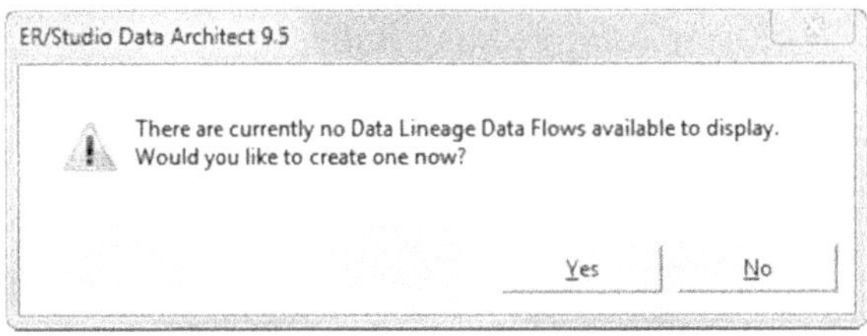

Figure 12.12 Data Lineage pop-up

You are then prompted to enter the name of the new data lineage. See Figure 12.13. I entered **AuthorPopulation**. Click <OK>.

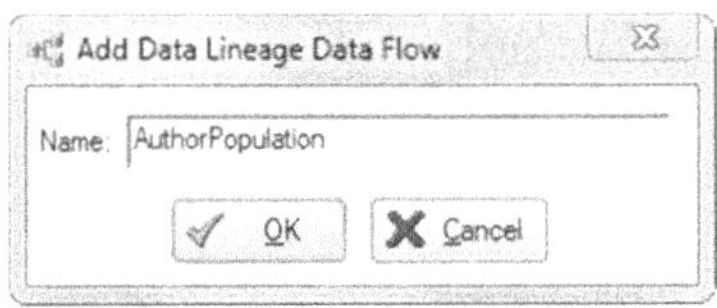

Figure 12.13 Enter data lineage flow name

You will notice the new data flow now appears in the *Data Flows* folder.

To add a data lineage after one is already added, click on the *Data Lineage* tab and then choose the following command:

Menu	Toolbar	Explorer	Shortcut Key	Shortcut Menu
`n/a`	n/a	Right-click the `Data Flows` node and then select `Create Data Flow`	n/a	n/a

Now that we created a data flow, we can create a complete mapping in ER/Studio including transformations. Click on the **AuthorPopulation** data flow. The data flow view appears in the *Data Model Window*.

Let's start by clicking and dragging the **Person** entity from the *Other Sources* folder on the Lineage tab to the *Data Model Window*.

ER/Studio contains our target entities in the Local Models subfolder on the Lineage tab. Find **Author** and click and drag **Author** to the *Data Model Window,* which is our target entity.

Then create a transformation object.

Menu	Toolbar	Explorer	Shortcut Key	Shortcut Menu
`Insert > Transformation`	Modeling toolbar:	Right-click on data flow, `Create Transformation`	<ALT + I>, then <T>	Click on white space, `Insert Transformation`

Click anywhere in the *Data Model Window* to create the transformation object.

Now let's "connect the dots." That is, create a line (called a "data stream") from the source entity to the transformation and then from the transformation to the target entity. To create a data stream, choose one of these commands:

Menu	Toolbar	Explorer	Shortcut Key	Shortcut Menu
`Insert > Data Stream`	Modeling toolbar:	n/a	<ALT + I>, then <D>	Click on white space, `Insert Data Stream`

Click on the source entity, **Person**, and then click on the transformation entity. This creates a data stream into the transformation. Next click on the transformation entity and then click on **Author**. This creates a second data stream from the transformation to the target entity.

Next, double-click on the transformation object to bring up the *Transformation Editor*. See Figure 12.14.

Enter a name for the transformation (I chose **PersonToAuthorCreate**) and select a type of transformation from the Type: drop-down list. The type is the high-level function of the transformation such as a direct map or lookup. If you are unsure of the type, you can leave it unspecified.

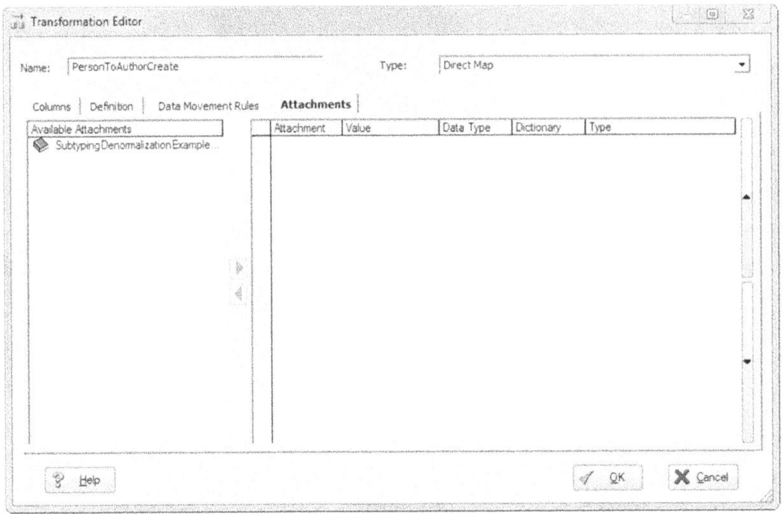

Figure 12.14 Transformation Editor

There are four tabs on this screen:

Tab	Here's what you need to know:
Columns	Define the input and output columns. Click the rectangle with the three dots for both input and output to add the columns.
Definition	Describe the transformation. There is also a text file to capture the actual transformation code.
Data Movement Rules	Choose one of the data movement rules that were previously defined. You can use the arrow key to move the rule to the right pane and then customize the rule, if needed, by entering actual values. (Double-click in the values cell and a window will appear where you can enter the values.)
Attachments	Bind an external piece of information, such as a Microsoft Word document or PDF file, to the transformation. Very useful for requirements documents, user stories, etc.

Click <OK> to exit the editor, and now you have completed your first data flow!

USING THE TABLE EDITOR TO FURTHER DOCUMENT LINEAGE

You can double-click any entity to enter the *Entity Editor* and choose the *Data Lineage* tab to expand the documentation on the data flow such as how often is the data sourced and when it was last sourced. You can also assign additional rules to the entity on this tab.

Using the Column Editor to Further Document Lineage

At the column/attribute level, you can document additional transformation logic for source/target attribute mapping. Simply bring up the *Entity Editor*, choose the *Attributes* tab and select the attribute you would like to document ETL for, and click <Edit>. Click on the *Data Lineage* for the attribute tab. Click the Edit button to enter transformation information.

Exercise 12.1: Creating a Data Lineage

Walk through the example in this chapter and practice mapping **Person** to **Author**. If you are feeling adventurous, add more advanced transformation logic to the mapping.

A Less Formal Way to Connect Things: User-Defined Mappings

A User-Defined Mapping (UDM) is a relationship you can build between any objects within the same ER/Studio file. For example, if you have built a logical data model and would like to see how it maps to a legacy database to gauge overlap and gaps, you can import the legacy database physical data model and user UDMs to connect it to the logical data model.

UDMs are created purely for communication purposes and do not ever get forward engineered into code. To create a UDM, right-click on the entity either on the data model diagram or in Explorer and select *Where Used...* The screen in Figure 12.15 appears. Double-click on the model name or the pencil symbol, and then you can choose the entities you would like the entity to have a connection with.

When a logical data model is forward engineered into a physical data model, the *Where Used* tab will contain the mappings between logical and physical. A user-defined mapping is created between logical and physical entities.

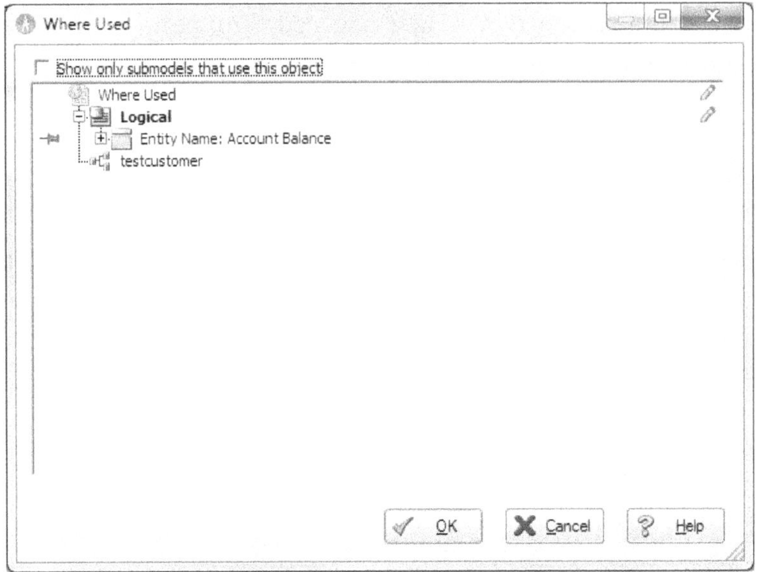

Figure 12.15 Where Used

Key Points

- The Data Lineage feature of ER/Studio enables you to document the movement of data from point A to point B (and any intermediate steps in between). Points A and B can be anything from flat files such as XML, data models, databases such as MongoDB, Access, Teradata, Oracle and DB2, and Excel worksheets.

- There are three main components required to document lineage: sources, rules, and data flows.

- Sources are the starting points for the lineage and may be either other ER/Studio data models, a SQL file, or a database.

- Rules are the types of changes (also known as "transformations") that can be applied to the source structures prior to loading the target structures.

- The data flow is one complete mapping, which includes specific sources, rules, and targets.

- Targets are the structures on our current model that we are loading.

CHAPTER 13
Importing, Exporting, Printing, and Reporting

Import and Export
Wow, many different formats
Print and report too

ER/Studio contains a number of features for getting model information in and out of the tool. There is the ability to import and export in multiple formats as well as printing and reporting, which will all be discussed in this chapter.

Importing into ER/Studio

In addition to all of the databases that you can reverse engineer into ER/Studio, there are over 100 different formats that can be imported into the tool. You can even import from other data modeling tools such as CA ERwin Data Modeler® and SAP Sybase PowerDesigner®.

To import, choose one of the following commands:

Menu	Toolbar	Explorer	Shortcut Key	Shortcut Menu
`File > New...`, then `Import Model From` or `File > Import File`	Application toolbar:	n/a	<ALT + F>, then <N> or <ALT + F>, then <M>	n/a

Importing from External Metadata

If you selected `From External Metadata...`, the first of three screens appears as shown in Figure 13.1.

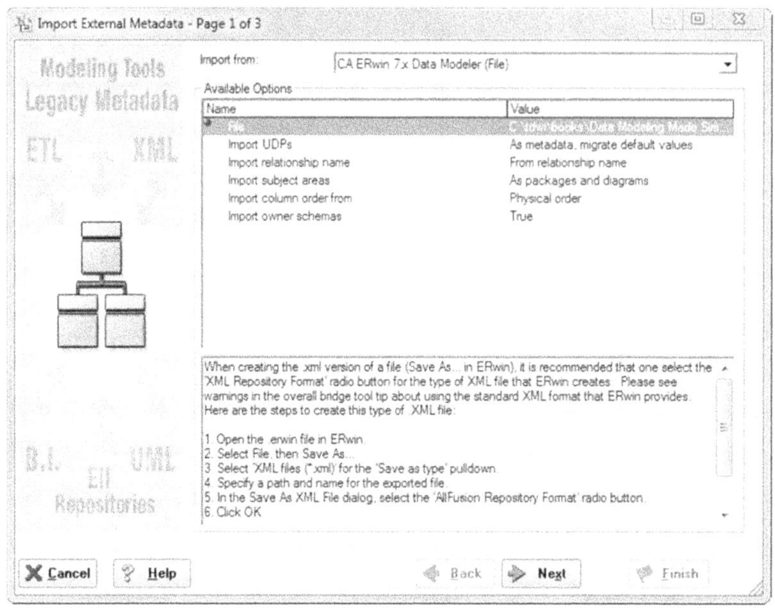

Figure 13.1 Import External Metadata Page 1 of 3

Choose the type of input source from the drop-down list. I chose to import a data model from CA ERwin Data Modeler version 7.x. After making a selection, click on the rectangle with the three dots to select the file you would like to import. On this screen, you are also provided with tips for importing from the format you selected. In this case, it is recommended to first convert the ERwin model to an XML format. I opened a data model in ERwin Data Modeler, saved it in XML Repository format, and then selected this file. See Figure 13.2 for the data model in native ERwin format.

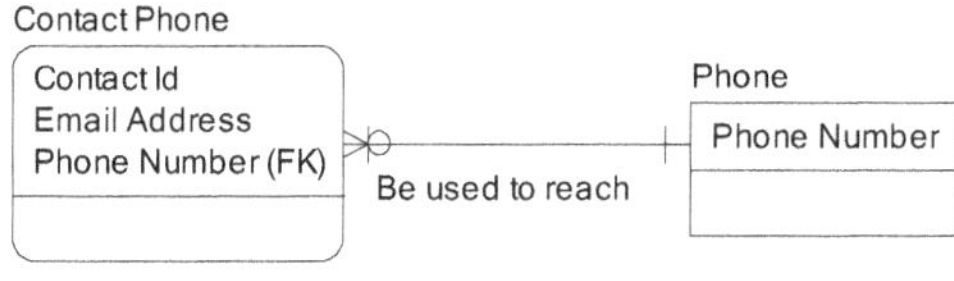

Figure 13.2 ERwin data model to be imported into ER/Studio

You can click on any of the values, such as `As metadata, migrate default values`, and a drop-down appears allowing you to select a different value. Tips appear for each selected row. On this screen, let's keep all of the other defaults and click <Next> so that the screen in Figure 13.3 appears. More settings that you can change appear with tips as in the prior screen.

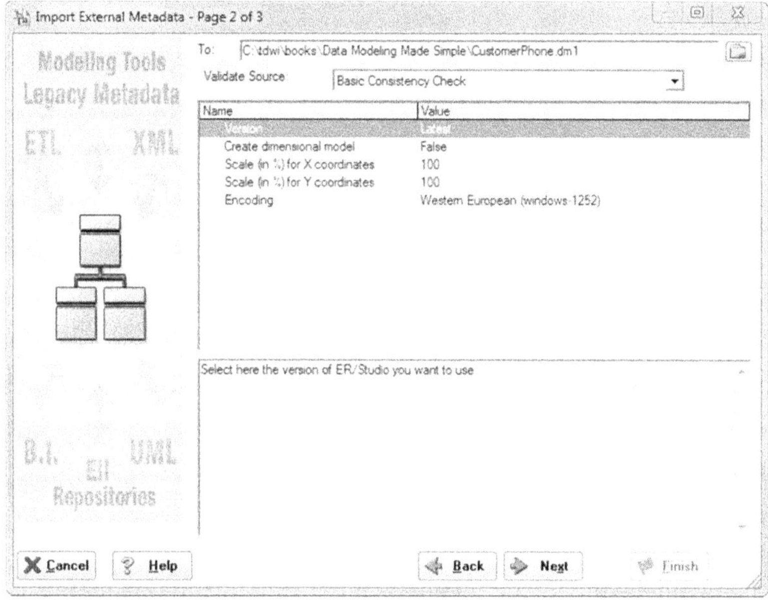

Figure 13.3 Import External Metadata Page 2 of 3

Click <Next> to arrive at the final screen, shown in Figure 13.4.

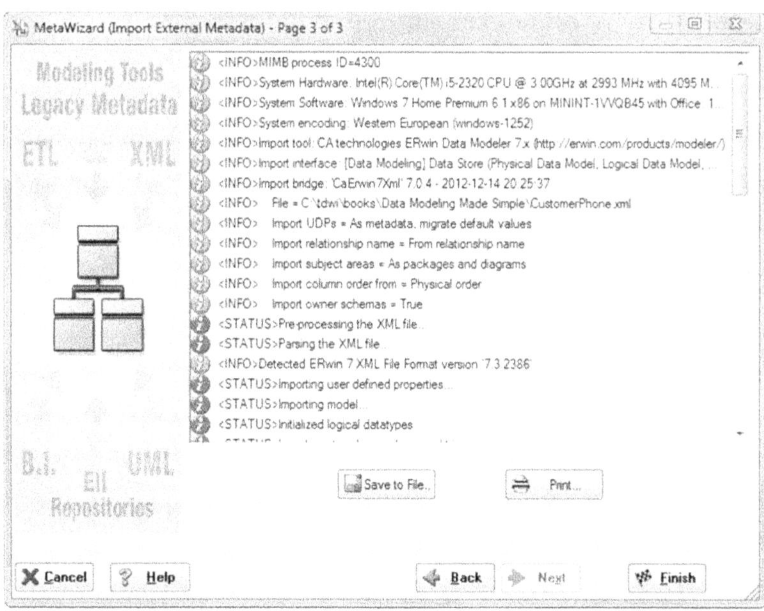

Figure 13.4 Import External Metadata Page 3 of 3

There are different status and error codes provided during import. Any statements prefaced by green or blue circles represent status or information, and anything in red, such as orange and red triangles or red circles, are warnings or error messages that will need to be addressed before importing. If you want to return to these messages, you can save them to a file by clicking <Save to File...> or print them by clicking <Print...>. Click <Finish> to complete the import process and view your model in ER/Studio as shown in Figure 13.5.

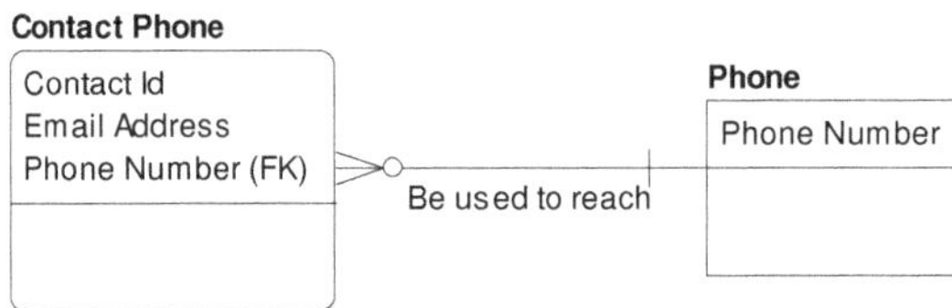

Figure 13.5 ER/Studio model of ERwin imported model from Figure 13.2

Importing from an ERX File

An ERX file was originally an ERwin file created in CA ERwin Data Modeler version 3.x; other tools such as Silwood Technology's Safyr® also export metadata to this format. Select the appropriate file and follow the instructions. Similar to importing from external metadata, you will have the option to save or print the log file. When done, click <Close> and save the new model. Note that CA ERwin Data Modeler version 3.x is a very old version of ERwin, but since other tools use this format, you may come across it. Remember to use the *Import External Metadata* wizard discussed in the previous section when importing data models created in a more recent version of CA ERwin Data Modeler.

Importing from a SQL File

This was covered in the reverse engineering discussion in Chapter 10.

EXPORTING OUT OF ER/STUDIO

In addition to all of the databases that you can forward engineer out of ER/Studio, there are over 100 different formats that can be exported from the tool. To export, choose one of the following commands:

Menu	Toolbar	Explorer	Shortcut Key	Shortcut Menu
`File > Export File`	n/a	n/a	<ALT + F>, then <F>	n/a

Become an ER/Studio Hotshot:

- Macros can be used to export portions of the model into Excel. Macros will be discussed in Chapter 16.

EXPORTING TO EXTERNAL METADATA

If you selected `External Metadata...`, the first of three screens appears as shown in Figure 13.6.

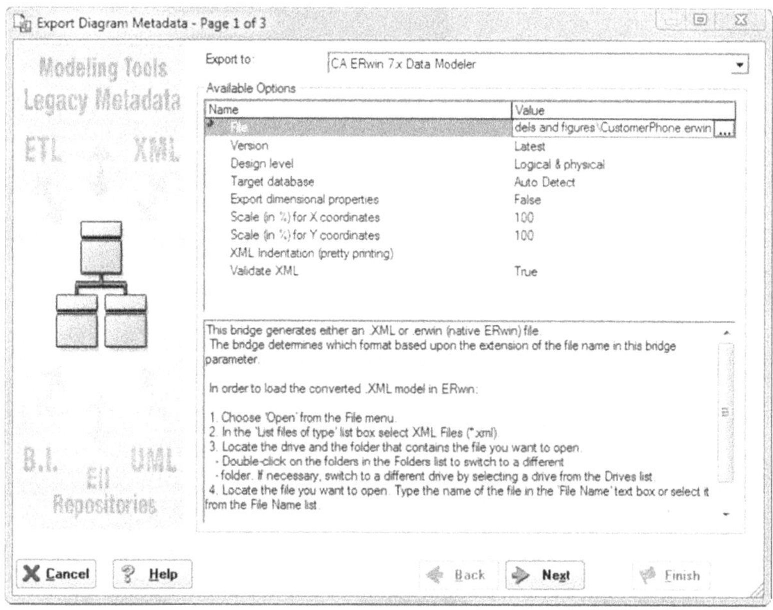

Figure 13.6 Export External Metadata Page 1 of 3

I am going to take the data model we imported from CA ERwin Data Modeler and send it back to CA ERwin Data Modeler. I created a new file on this screen and left the other values on the screen unchanged. Click <Next> and the second screen appears as in Figure 13.7.

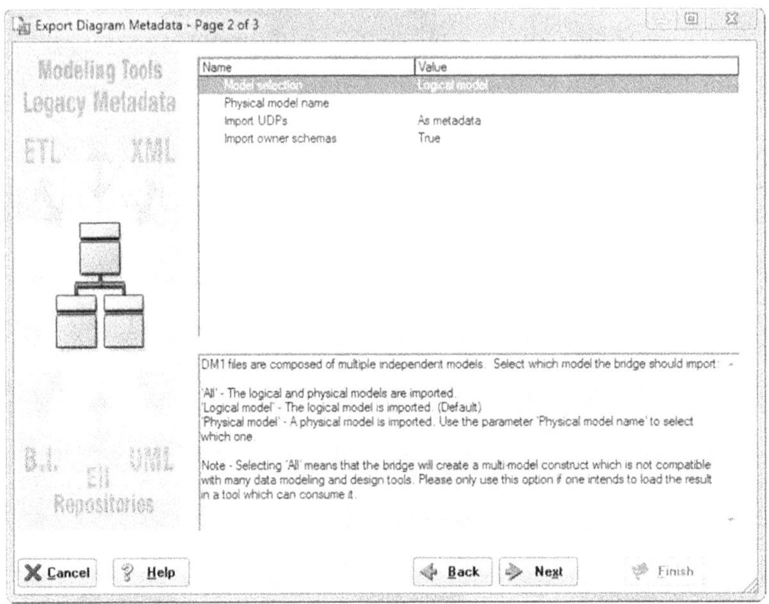

Figure 13.7 Export External Metadata Page 2 of 3

I left these defaults alone. Click <Next> and the third screen appears as in Figure 13.8.

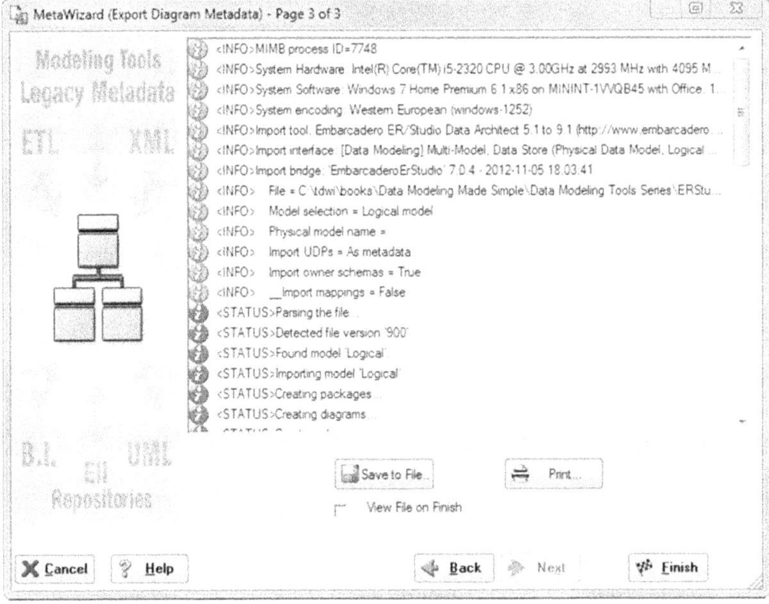

Figure 13.8 Export External Metadata Page 3 of 3

Note that it might take some time for this third screen to appear. Click <Finish> and the CA ERwin Data Modeler version of the model has now been created. I opened it in CA ERwin Data Modeler to test it, and it was accurately created and looked identical to Figure 13.2.

EXPORTING TO XML

The eXtensible Markup Language (XML) is a document format that is a standard for data representation and exchange on the Internet. XML is also now supported by many applications and platforms, allowing data modelers and application developers to collaborate on service-oriented architecture (SOA) initiatives. For example, the data modeler models the data and the relationships that describe how applications exchange data and exports the model to XML, which the application developer can then use to ensure that the applications interface correctly.

If you selected `XML File` as your export choice, you will need to choose one of three options:

- **Schema Definition (XSD).** The XSD formally describes the elements in an XML document. It is an abstract representation of an object's characteristics and how the object relates to other objects. The XSD is used to verify that each element in an XML document conforms to the element rules described in the XSD. Schemas are most often used in e-commerce, data control, and database-style applications where character data content must be validated, strict data control is needed, or where strong data typing is required. For example, many applications use an XSD to validate parameters in configuration files.
- **Document Type Definition (DTD).** The DTD is another XML schema language used in traditional text document publishing applications. The DTD is a description in XML declaration syntax of a particular type or class of documents. It defines what names are used for certain element types, where they may occur and how the elements fit together and also ensures that all documents conforming to the DTD are constructed and named in a consistent manner. Validators in applications, such as editors, search engines, browsers, and databases

can read the DTD before reading the XML file in order to prepare to display or otherwise work with the XML document.

- **XML Schema Generation**. The *XML Schema Generation Wizard* creates schemas that can be based on a logical or physical data model, a submodel, or even specific objects of a model or submodel. This wizard allows you to customize the XML schema structure by clicking the desired options and dragging the available objects from the database design into a tree representing the XML schema. This wizard provides advanced options to transform relational entities and attributes into complex types, elements and attributes, defines naming standards and datatype mapping, and incorporates the Quick Launch system used in other wizards to save previous settings and streamline repetitive operations.

Become an ER/Studio Hotshot:

- There are also quite a few XML export options available through the External Metadata function including XML Metadata Interchange (XMI). The XMI file format was designed primarily to allow the exchange of data between data modeling applications.
- You can use XML editing applications, such as Microsoft XML Notepad, Eclipse, Visual Studio, and Altova XML Spy, to view and edit the schema after export.

Exporting to XSD or DTD are the same process—simply create a file name under which to save the file and you are done. For *XML Schema Generation*, however, there is a five-page wizard, the first page appearing in Figure 13.9.

Create a file name for the target XML schema by clicking on the yellow envelope and creating a new file name. Similar to other wizards, you are given the option to load previous settings that you saved at a prior time. You will have an option on Page 5 to save your settings from this time to use for future exports. Click <Next> to go to Page 2 of 5, shown in Figure 13.10.

You can add a namespace (a grouping of identifiers or symbols used in modular code design) and other information and then click <Next> to go to Page 3 of 5, shown in Figure 13.11.

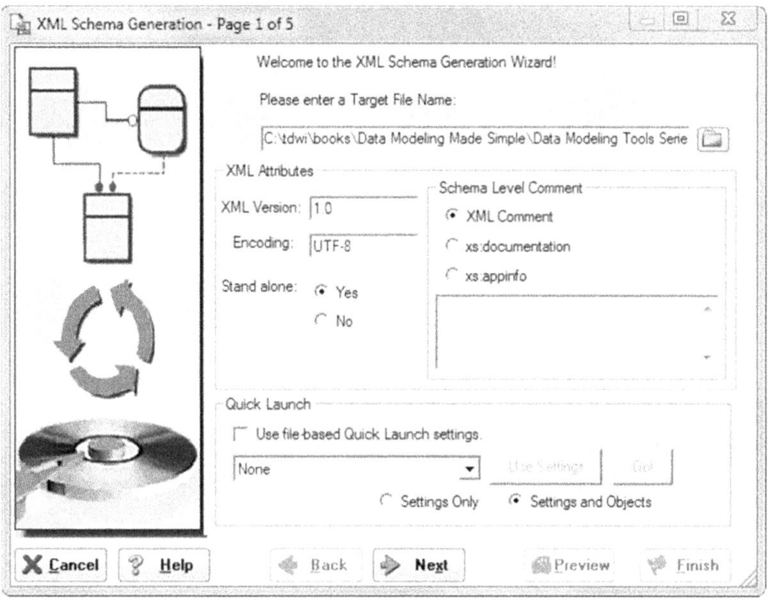

Figure 13.9 XML Schema Generation Page 1 of 5

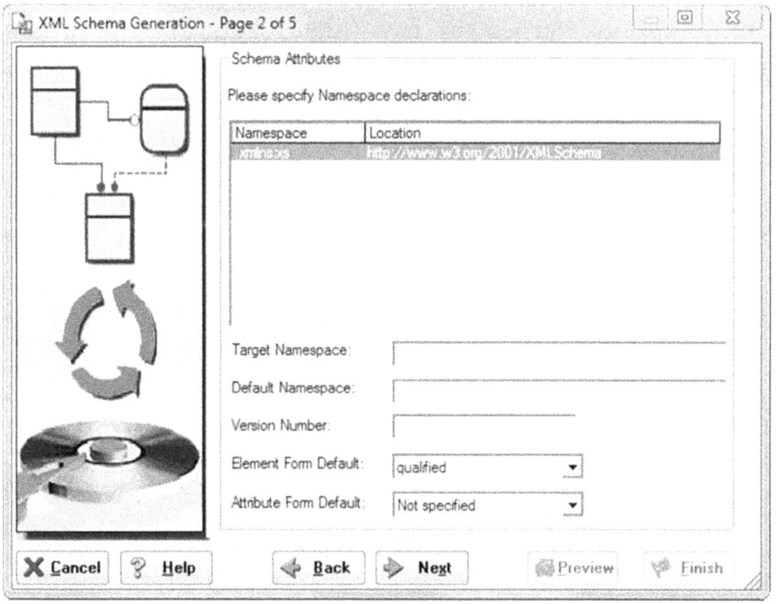

Figure 13.10 XML Schema Generation Page 2 of 5

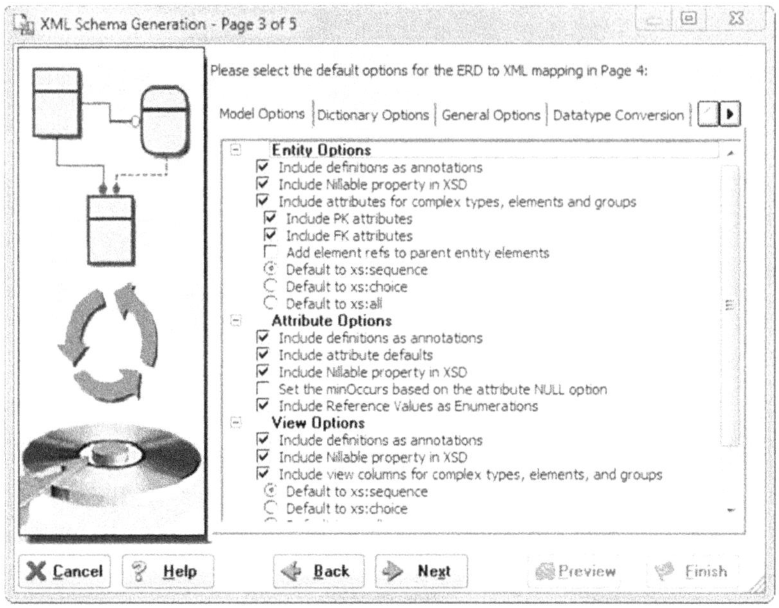

Figure 13.11 XML Schema Generation Page 3 of 5

There are many options across the five tabs. I kept the defaults and clicked <Next> to go to page 4 of 5, shown in Figure 13.12.

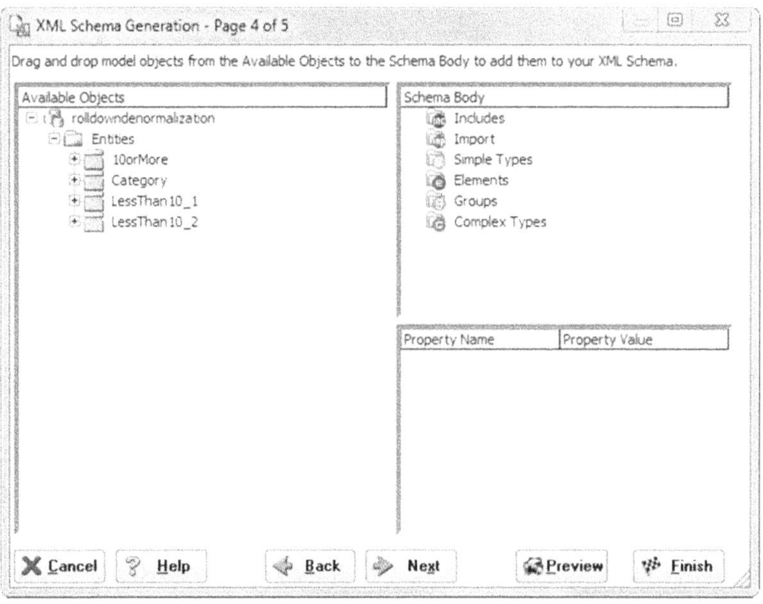

Figure 13.12 XML Schema Generation Page 4 of 5

On this screen, you can select which objects should be exported and how they should appear in the XML file. Click <Next> to go to Page 5 of 5, shown in Figure 13.13.

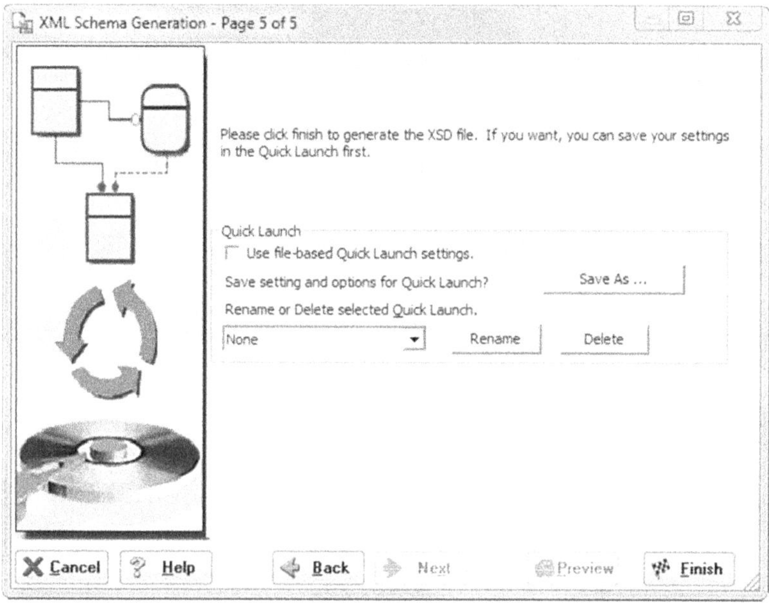

Figure 13.13 XML Schema Generation Page 5 of 5

Similar to other wizards, you are given the option to save your settings for *Quick Launch* later. Click <Finish> and you are given the option to view the XML schema.

EXPORTING TO A SQL FILE

This was covered in Chapter 10.

EXPORTING AN IMAGE

From ER/Studio, you can create a screenshot image of your data model to distribute to your reviewers. This feature is very handy if your audience does not have a copy of ER/Studio and they need to see only the visual (and not the metadata behind the model such as definitions). Alternatively, you could always email them a screenshot plus an Excel spreadsheet that you generated via one of the supplied macros. For the screenshot, you can choose from several different image formats including EMF, JPEG, GIF, BMP, and PNG. Use one of these commands:

Menu	Toolbar	Explorer	Shortcut Key	Shortcut Menu
`File > Export Image`	n/a	n/a	<ALT + F>, then <E>	n/a

You will see the screen in Figure 13.14.

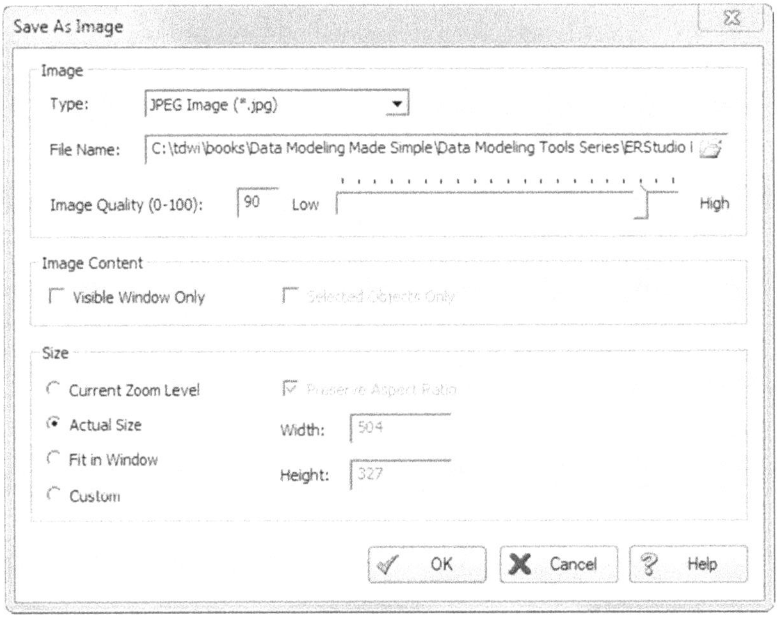

Figure 13.14 Save As Image screen

Choose the image format (such as JPEG) from the drop-down and create a new file name using the yellow folder. You are also given the option of selecting the quality of the image, where the higher the quality of the image, the larger the image size. Click <OK> to save your model in the format you specified.

Printing in ER/Studio

To print the model, first make sure the right settings are selected under *Options*.

Menu	Toolbar	Explorer	Shortcut Key	Shortcut Menu
`Tools > Options`	n/a	n/a	<ALT + T>, then <P>	n/a

Then choose the *Display* tab. Select `Page Boundaries` to display the diagram lines that show how the model will be printed. Then to print, choose one of the following commands:

Menu	Toolbar	Explorer	Shortcut Key	Shortcut Menu
`File > Print…`	Application toolbar:	Right-click on model or submodel folder, `Print Model…`	<ALT + F>, then <T> or <CTRL + P>	Right-click on white space, `Print Model…`

Become an ER/Studio Hotshot:
Before printing your model, display the page boundaries so you can optimally place your objects for better viewing and printing. Choose `Tools > Options > Display > Page Boundaries.`

The screen in Figure 13.15 appears.

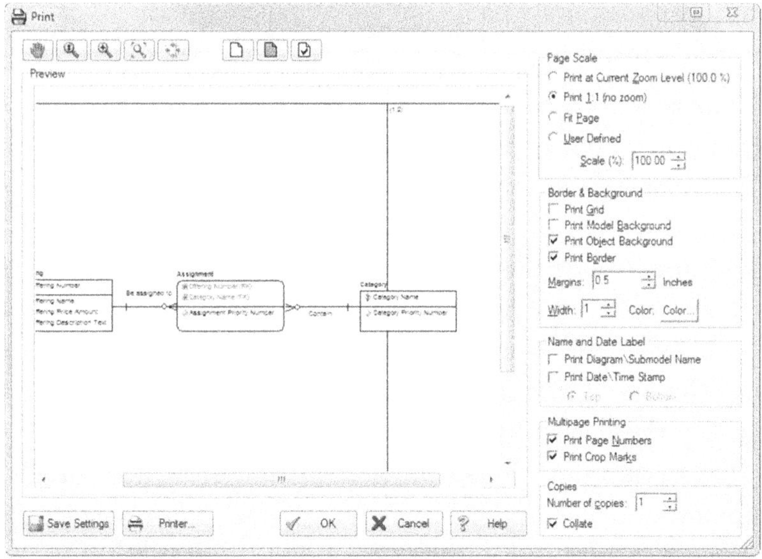

Figure 13.15 Print screen

There are a lot of really neat options you can select for printing. You also have the option of saving your settings for future use by clicking <Save Settings>. Under *Page Scale* you can decide the scaling of the model. For small models `Fit Page` is a good choice. Under *Border & Background*, you can decide whether the model gets printed in color or grayscale and whether you would like the grid and border to be printed as well. Under the *Name and Date Label* you can add auditing information to the model. Under *Multipage Printing*, you can print page numbers and crop marks to make it easy to tape the pages together for large models.

Choose the desired settings and click <OK> to print the model.

REPORTING IN ER/STUDIO

To generate a report, choose one of the following commands:

Menu	Toolbar	Explorer	Shortcut Key	Shortcut Menu
`Tools > Generate Reports…`	Application toolbar:	Right-click on model, `Generate Reports…`	<ALT + T>, then <R>	Right-click on white space, `Generate Reports…`

The first of four screens appears as shown in Figure 13.16. On this screen, first select whether you would like to produce a report in HTML format or in RTF format. HTML reports are great for sharing on the Internet or Intranet. RTF stands for *Rich Text Format*, and this is the format to choose if you would like to view and optionally edit the report in a tool like Microsoft Word. Next, select the directory for the report by clicking on the rectangle with the three dots. Optionally, you can load your settings from a prior go through the *Report Wizard* using the *Quick Launch* option. Note on the final page of the wizard you will be given the option to save your settings as a future *Quick Launch*. If you select `Use enhanced version`, the HTML file will be much smaller in size and therefore quicker to open and navigate in a browser. Click <Next> to move on to Page 2 as seen in Figure 13.17.

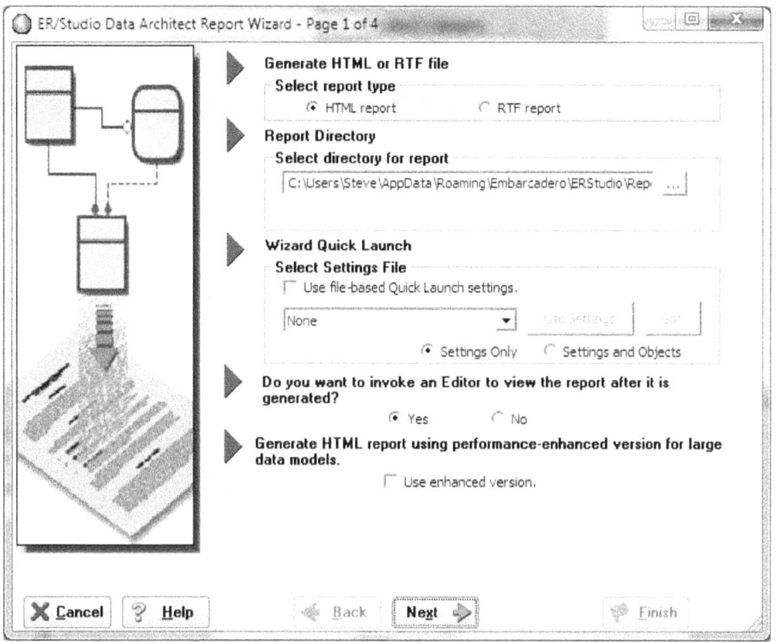

Figure 13.16 Report Wizard Page 1 of 4

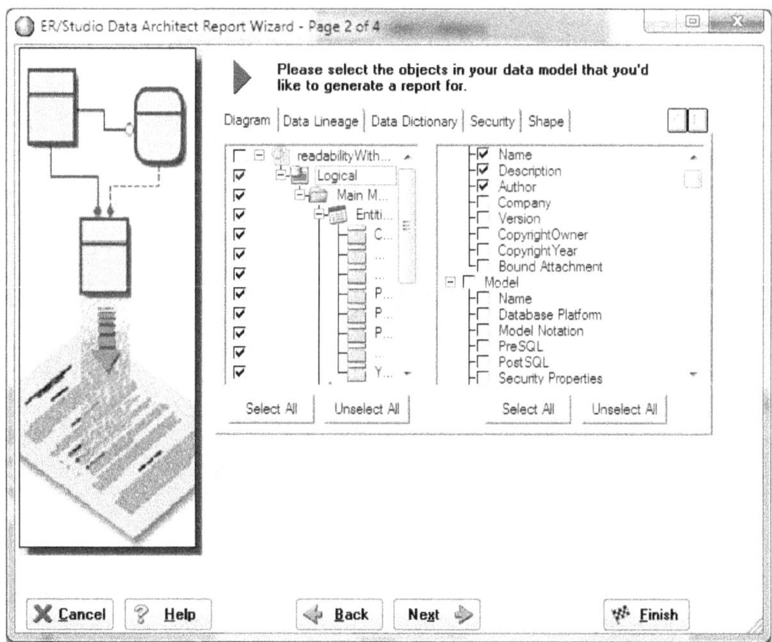

Figure 13.17 Report Wizard Page 2 of 4

On this screen, you can select the models you would like to generate a report from in the left pane and the objects you would like to report on in the right pane. When done, click <Next> and move on to Page 3 as seen in Figure 13.18.

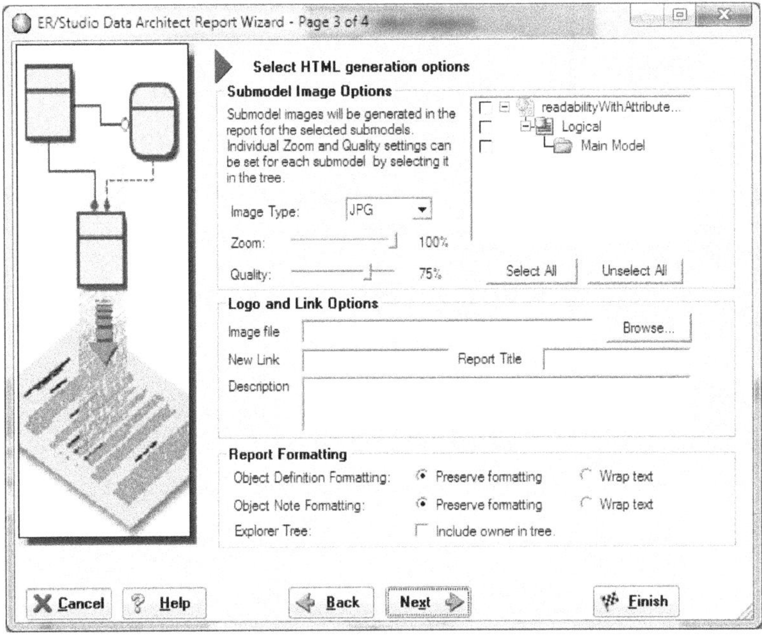

Figure 13.18 Report Wizard Page 3 of 4

This screen contains quite a few formatting choices including the option to upload your own logo to the report. Click <Next> to go to the final screen as seen in Figure 13.19. If you chose RTF reports instead of HTML reports, Page 3 is the only screen that would look different. There would be formatting options around displaying in a tool such as Microsoft Word including the ability to add a table of contents and page breaks. Here you can capture author and copyright information and optionally save your settings for a future time through the *Report Wizard*. Click <Finish> to complete the wizard and create the report.

EXERCISE 13.1: IMPORTING, EXPORTING, PRINTING, AND REPORTING

Import a data model from another data modeling tool or reverse engineer from an existing database. Then experiment with the printing and reporting features in ER/Studio. When you are comfortable with the features available for printing and reporting, export your data model to an XML file.

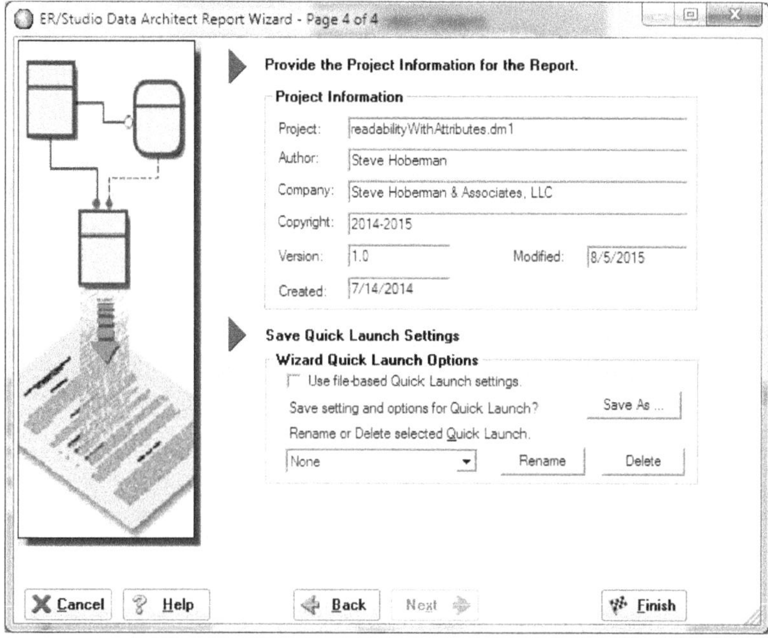

Figure 13.19 Report Wizard Page 4 of 4

Key Points

- In addition to all of the databases that you can reverse engineer into ER/Studio, there are over 100 different formats that can be imported into the tool. You can even import from other data modeling tools such as CA ERwin Data Modeler® and SAP Sybase PowerDesigner®.
- There is a similar variety in the formats to which you can export out.
- There are a lot of really neat options you can select for printing. You can create both HTML and RTF formats, and just like for printing, there are lots of options you can choose to give the reports your customized touch!

CHAPTER 14
Naming Standards

What should I call it?
A rose by any other
name is still a rose

ER/Studio provides support for naming standards through the *Naming Standards Template* and *Naming Standards Utility*. The *Naming Standards Template* allows you to define many standards across your organization, including an abbreviation list used to automatically convert logical to physical names and vice versa, and case, name length, and prefix standards. The *Naming Standards Utility* is used to apply the naming standards templates to a model or objects within a model.

This chapter will explain how to use the *Naming Standards Template* and *Naming Standards Utility* as well as how to assign naming standards to objects.

CREATING A NAMING STANDARDS TEMPLATE

Before creating the *Naming Standards Template*, view the default naming standard options. You can specify naming rules, such as maximum length, case, and synchronization level between entities and tables, under *Options*.

Menu	Toolbar	Explorer	Shortcut Key	Shortcut Menu
`Tools > Options`	n/a	n/a	<ALT + T>, then <P>	n/a

The first decision to make is whether you would like the *Naming Standard Template* to be bound just to the current data model (internal) or whether you would like the template to be used by multiple data models (external). If it will just be used internally in the current model, the template becomes part of the model's data dictionary. If it's part of an organization standard to be used by multiple models, the template is saved as an XML file and can be imported and applied as needed.

So the internal template is saved in the model's data dictionary, and the external is saved as an XML file in the Model directory with a file extension of .nst. Another difference between the two is that the *Attachment Bindings* and *Binding Information* tabs are only available for the internal template.

To create a naming standard template (either internal or external), click on the *Data Dictionary* tab in *Explorer* and choose one of these commands:

Menu	Toolbar	Explorer	Shortcut Key	Shortcut Menu
`Tools > Naming Standards Template Editor…`	n/a	Right-click on `Naming Standards Template`, then `New Naming Standards Template…`	n/a	n/a

Become an ER/Studio Hotshot:

- You can have multiple naming standards templates in the same data model.
- You can edit a naming standard template by double-clicking on it.
- You can delete a naming standard template by selecting the template and clicking the <Delete> key.

There are six tabs for the internal template and four for the external (*Attachment Bindings* and *Binding Information* tabs are only available for the internal template).

Tab	Here's what you need to know:
Name	Create a name for the template and also enter a description. If you are creating an internal template, there are two additional settings available on this tab that are not available on the external template; you can import an external *Naming Standards Template*, or you can export one. If you decide to import, this would be the XML template file. If you decide to export, you will be creating an XML template file that other models can then use.

Tab	Here's what you need to know:
Logical	Set the maximum length for each logical object type, the case (e.g., upper or lower case), and optionally a prefix and/or suffix for each logical object type.
Physical	Set the maximum length for each physical object type, the case (e.g., upper or lower case), and optionally a prefix and/or suffix for each physical object type.
Mapping	Define rules on the terms that can be used in the model. There are three sub-tabs on this tab: *Abbreviations*, *Order*, and *General*. The *Abbreviations* tab is where you can enter (or import/export) abbreviations, both logical and physical. You can also construct the building blocks of each name, such as an attribute can be named with a Prime word (e.g., `Customer` or `Product`), Qualifiers (sometimes called Modifiers), and a Class (sometimes called a *Class word* or *Classword*). So, for example, in **Customer Last Name**, `Customer` is the Prime, `Last` is the Qualifier, and `Name` is the Class. You can also make certain abbreviations illegal. The *Priority* column is used to resolve duplicate physical abbreviations as names are transformed from physical to logical. The default value of the *Priority* field is `Primary`. The priority changes to `Secondary` when you define a mapping for a physical name that is already mapped to a logical name. You can change the priority by selecting the priority field, clicking the down arrow and selecting another priority. The *Order* tab allows you to decide the sequence of prime, qualifier, and class. For example, should it be **Customer Last Name** or **Customer Name Last**? The *General* tab contains settings for how the terms should be separated (e.g., by underscore or space) and how to handle characters that are not allowed to be used such as `$` or `#`.
Attachment Bindings	Bind an external piece of information, such as a Microsoft Word document or PDF file, to the template. Very useful for requirements documents, user stories, etc. Attachments are created in the Attachments folder of the data dictionary (discussed in Chapter 11) and must be added to the model before they will display on this tab.

Tab	Here's what you need to know:
Data Movement Rules	We can assign a data movement rule to this attribute that will be carried through to the data definition language to build the database. We can enter a data movement rule here or use a data movement rule as defined on the lineage tab, which was discussed in Chapter 12.

APPLYING THE NAMING STANDARDS UTILITY

We apply the naming standards template to a data model through the *Naming Standards Utility*.

Menu	Toolbar	Explorer	Shortcut Key	Shortcut Menu
`Model > Naming Standards Utility…`	Application toolbar: [NSU]	Right-click on model name, `Naming Standards Utility…`	<ALT + M>, then <T>	Right-click on white space, `Naming Standards Utility…`

There are two tabs that appear:

Tab	Here's what you need to know:
Options	Select which template you would like applied to the model as well as whether you would like any name conversions to be performed when going from logical to physical or vice-versa. You can also load settings from a prior run or create new *Quick Launch* settings.
Output	Select which objects you would like to apply the template to as well as which objects you would like to freeze. When selected, the `Freeze Names` option in these editors prevents any naming standards applied to the model from changing the name of the object selected.

Click <OK> when done.

ASSIGNING NAMING STANDARDS TO OBJECTS

The *Naming Standards Template* can also be applied to domains, attributes, and entities through the *Naming Standards* tab in the object editors.

AUTOMATIC NAMING TRANSLATION

Instead of applying naming standards at certain points during the modeling phase, you can opt to automatically name the entities and attributes. This is one of the newer features in ER/Studio.

To enable automatic naming, choose the *Naming Handling* tab under Options.

Menu	Toolbar	Explorer	Shortcut Key	Shortcut Menu
`Tools > Options`	n/a	n/a	<ALT + T>, then <P>	n/a

The screen in Figure 14.1 appears.

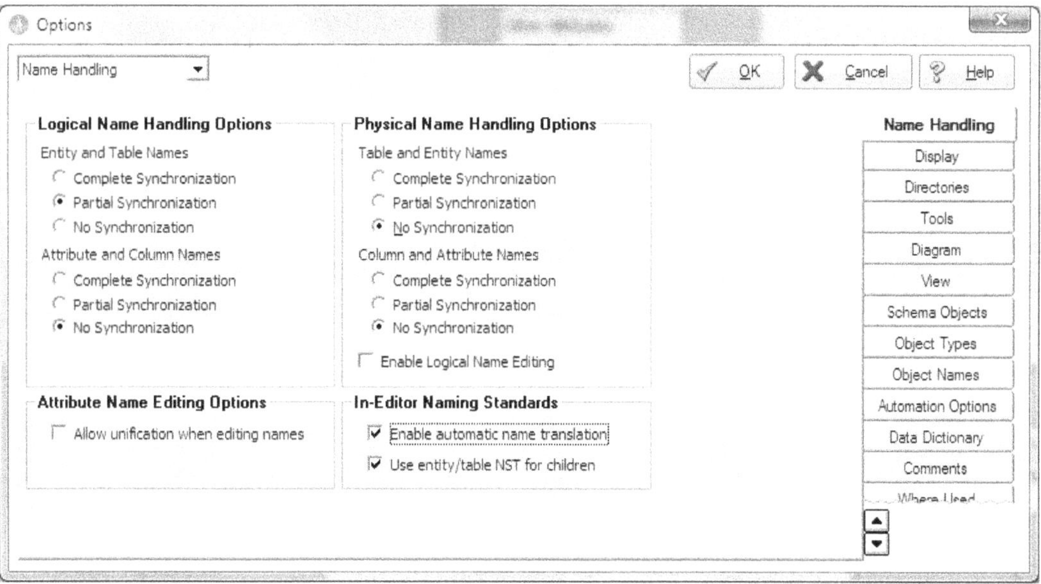

Figure 14.1 In-Editor Naming Standards screen

Checking the `Use entity/table NST for children` option allows the naming standards template tied to the parent entity (the one on the one side of the relationship) to be automatically applied to the child entities.

There are other interesting settings on this same tab. The logical and physical name handling options control what happens when you change the name of an object. For example, if we change the name of a logical attribute, `Complete Synchronization` under *Physical Name Handling Options* will update the corresponding physical column. Checking `Allow unification when editing names` allows you to change the role names of foreign attributes to the same names as other attributes in the same entity.

EXERCISE 14.1: CREATING A NAMING STANDARD TEMPLATE

Does your organization have a naming standard? If not, check out the international naming standard, ISO-11179. (There are good tips on writing definitions in this standard, too.) If you do have a naming standard, create an external *Naming Standard Template* for your standard. Then apply the *Naming Standards Utility* to one of your models based on the standard you defined in the template. Enterprise consistency does feel good, doesn't it?

Key Points

- The *Naming Standards Template* allows you to define many standards across your organization including an abbreviation list used to automatically convert logical to physical names and vice versa as well as case, name length, and prefix standards.
- The *Naming Standards Utility* is used to apply the naming standards templates to a model or objects within a model.
- The *Naming Standards Template* can also be applied to domains, attributes, and entities through the *Naming Standards* tab in the object editors.

CHAPTER 15
Compare/Merge Utility

The same they should be
Compare and Merge bring order
Life is back in check

The *Compare and Merge Utility* allows you to reconcile differences between models in the same file or between a model and a database. For example, imagine you have designed and created a model and then created a database based on that data model. A data modeler alters the model and adds the attribute **Employee Gender** to the **Employee** entity while independently, a database administrator alters the **Department** table in the database and adds a column **Department Name** to the table. The model and the database are no longer in synch. Applying the *Compare and Merge Utility* can identify differences such as these and merge the model and database so they are back in synch.

The *Compare and Merge Utility* compares, merges, and synchronizes models from a variety of comparison targets. It can perform different kinds of comparisons. You can use the information from these comparisons to perform merges or to create detailed reports. You can compare and merge a logical data model with:

- A physical data model in the same .dm1 file
- A logical data model of another ER/Studio data model
- A physical data model of another ER/Studio data model.

You can compare and merge a physical data model with:

- The logical data model of the same data model
- Another physical data model of the same data model that shares the same DBMS platform (and version)
- A logical data model of another ER/Studio data model
- A physical data model of another ER/Studio data model that shares the same DBMS platform (and version)

- A database (including a NoSQL database such as MongoDB) or SQL file.

You can compare and merge a submodel to a submodel within the same data model.

COMPARING MODELS AND SUBMODELS IN ER/STUDIO

Using the *Compare and Merge Utility*, you can compare two models, two submodels, or a model with a submodel and merge any differences found, if required. You can also report on the differences, and optionally synchronize your source model with another model or update the source or target models selectively. Open the first model (or submodel) to be synchronized. We can call this model the "source," although "source" and "target" names are arbitrary, and enter one of these commands:

Menu	Toolbar	Explorer	Shortcut Key	Shortcut Menu
`Model > Compare and Merge Utility…`	Application toolbar:	Right-click on source model (or submodel), `Compare and Merge Utility…`	<ALT + M>, then <M>	Right-click on white space, `Compare and Merge Utility…`

The first page of a five page wizard appears as shown in Figure 15.1.

On this screen, you can select what you would like to compare your data model to as well as load *Quick Launch* settings from a prior compare and merge operation. I decided to compare my model to another ER/Studio model, so I selected the second option and clicked on the yellow folder to bring up the browse window, which allows me to select the target model. Click <Next> to move on to the second page as shown in Figure 15.2. On this screen, we can pick the subset of the target file to compare with. There are one logical data model and two physical data models, and I chose the one logical data model. I could have also refined the comparison to a submodel in the target model. Click <Next> to move on to the third page as shown in Figure 15.3.

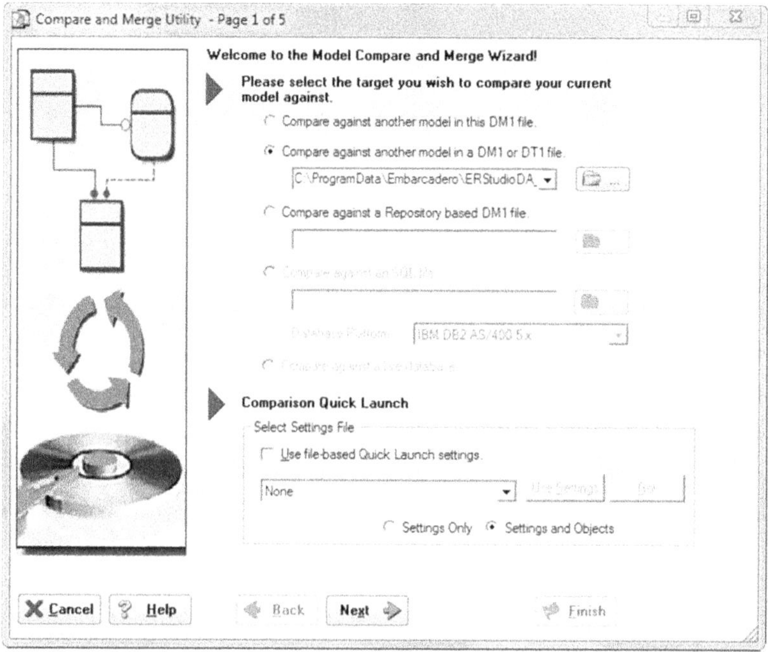

Figure 15.1 Compare and Merge Utility Page 1 of 5

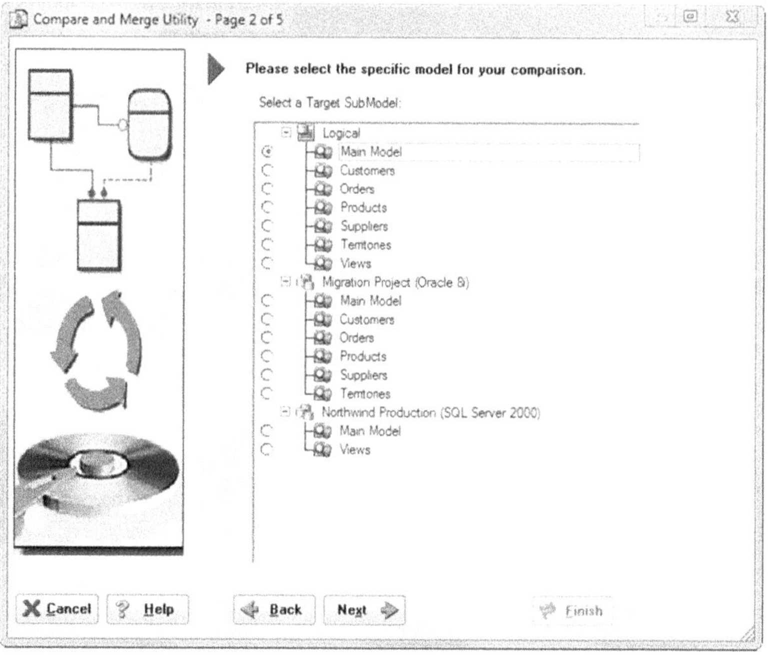

Figure 15.2 Compare and Merge Utility Page 2 of 5

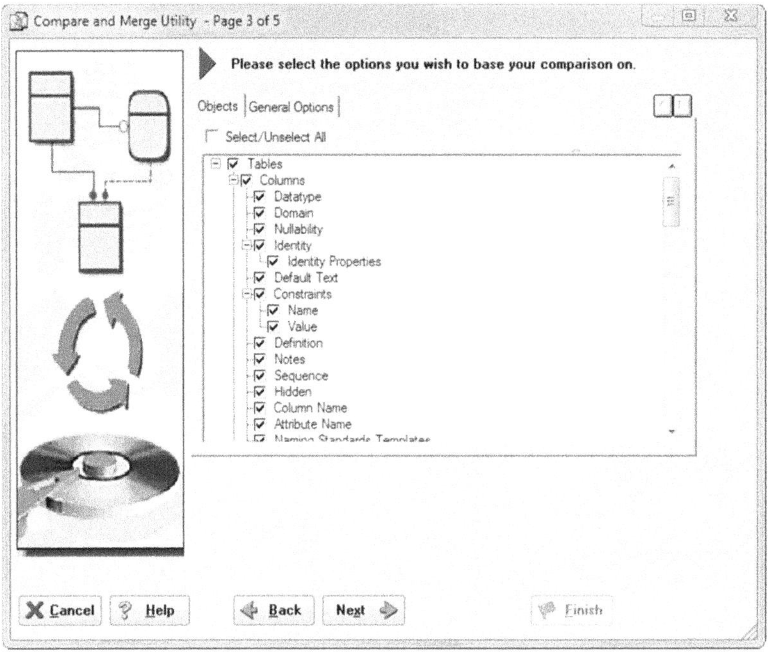

Figure 15.3 Compare and Merge Utility Page 3 of 5

On this screen, you can select the types of metadata to be compared between the two models. By default, everything is selected. The *General Options* tab contains more advanced settings such as whether to ignore case when comparing names and whether to exclude definitions from the comparison when dealing with new physical structures. Click <Next> to move on to the fourth page as shown in Figure 15.4.

On this screen, you can select the specific objects for comparison including entities, views, users, roles, and shapes. Optionally, you can also save your settings for a future compare and merge operation. Click <Next> to move on to the fifth page as shown in Figure 15.5. This screen contains the results of the compare and merge. Under the *Filter Results* drop-down, you can show a subset of the merge operation to make the exercise easier for comparison. If you click on one of the resolution values, such as `Ignore`, you will notice that a drop-down appears and provides you with several actions, including ignore the difference between the two models, delete from the current (also known as source) model, or merge into the target model. You are also given the option to produce a report in RTF or HTML format by clicking on <Report>.

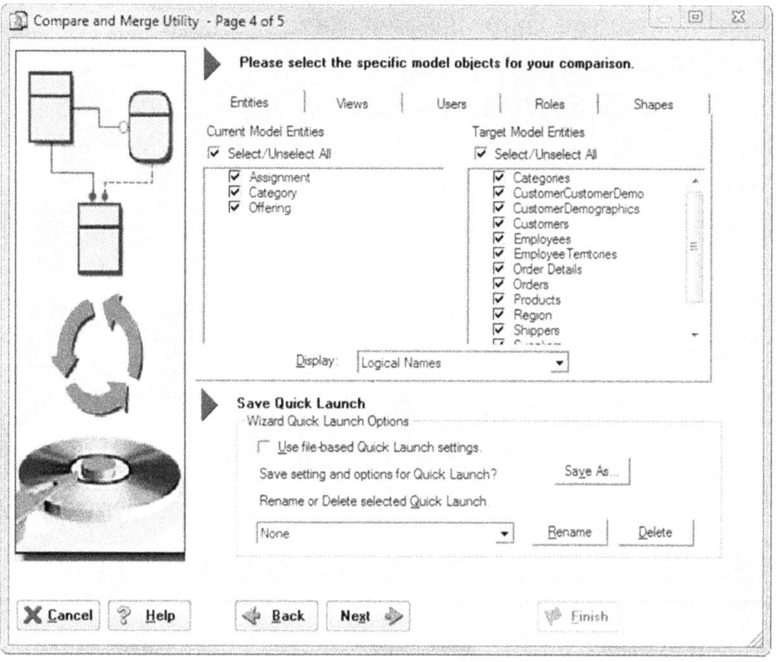

Figure 15.4 Compare and Merge Utility Page 4 of 5

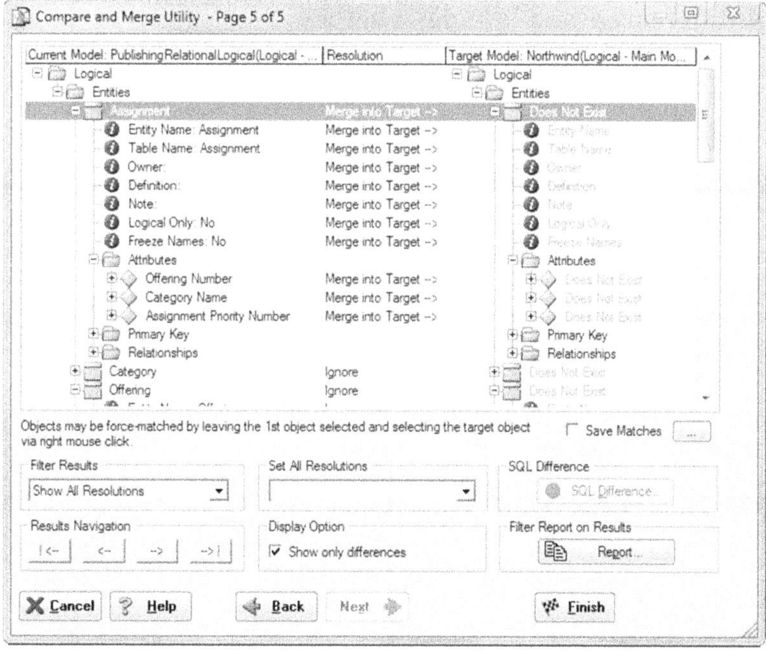

Figure 15.5 Compare and Merge Utility Page 5 of 5

If you click on <...> to the right of `Save Matches`, you can define a mapping between two models that will be saved so the next time the *Compare and Merge Utility* is run, ER/Studio will recognize that these two objects match and will not flag them as a difference. For example, if you define a mapping between **Customer** in Model A and **Client** in Model B, then **Customer** and **Client** will be considered a match and will not be flagged during the compare and merge process. If a mapping is made across ER/Studio files, this is called a Universal Mapping. If a mapping is made within an ER/Studio file, this is captured through a User-Defined Mapping.

When you are done with the *Compare and Merge Utility*, click <Finish> to exit the wizard. You will be prompted to save the models that have been changed.

EXERCISE 15.1: RUNNING THE COMPARE AND MERGE UTILITY

Compare a logical data model with its reverse-engineered database. Pick a database that you think could be different from the logical. Run the full compare and merge utility and produce a report to take to your colleagues to discuss the differences and decide whether the logical or physical should change.

Key Points

- The Compare and Merge utility allows you to reconcile differences between models in the same file or between a model and a database.
- This utility is a great way to catch changes made to a database that have not been consistently reflected in the logical.

CHAPTER 16
Features for Agile Teams and Continuous Improvement

Get the project done
Iterative dev – Ready?
Faster and faster

This chapter will discuss a number of features useful for iterative development practices including macros, reusable procedure logic, change management, and model validation.

MACROS

A macro is a function that is not part of the standard set of ER/Studio functionality but which automates or simplifies complex or repetitive tasks. For example, there is a macro in ER/Studio that allows you to convert all names to uppercase or lowercase. ER/Studio comes with over 70 macros, and you can also create your own. We will talk about running, creating, editing, deleting, and renaming macros in this section.

RUNNING MACROS

To create a macro, click on the *Macro* tab on the bottom of the Explorer pane (as shown in Figure 16.1).

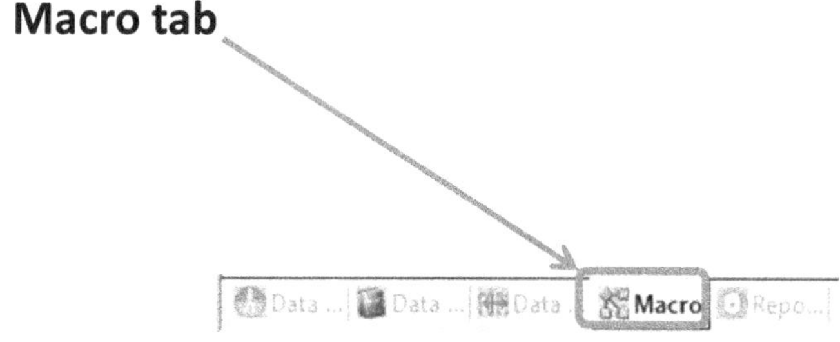

Figure 16.1 Macro tab from Explorer pane

You can run any of the macros that appear using one of these commands:

Menu	Toolbar	Explorer	Shortcut Key	Shortcut Menu
n/a	n/a	Right-click on macro, `Run Macro`	Right-click on macro, then <U>	n/a

Become an ER/Studio Hotshot:

- You can add any macro as a shortcut by right-clicking on the macro, choosing `Add/Remove to Shortcuts`, and then selecting where you would like to add it to (or remove it from). If you choose `Main Menu`, it will appear under the *Macro Shortcuts* menu.
- Some macros require highlighting the object that the macro is being applied to before running the macro. If you receive an error message running a particular macro, it could be due to not having the object selected prior to running.

TOP 5 FAVORITE MACROS

Here is a list of my Top 5 favorite macros (in no particular order):

1. **Export Meta Data to Excel**. Very quick and accurate way to display all of the model's metadata in a spreadsheet format.

2. **Definition Editor**. Makes it very easy to enter definitions for multiple entities and/or attributes.

3. **Notes Editor**. A very quick way to enter issues or other types of notes.

4. **Get Related Tables**. Great for highlighting portions of a complex diagram. Select one or more entities and run this macro to highlight in the diagram what the entities relate to. You can choose to highlight parents, children, or both.

5. **Convert Name Case.** Select one or more entities and run this macro to change the case. Much quicker and less error prone than doing this manually, which I have had to do in the past!

CREATING MACROS

In *Explorer*, click on the *Macros* tab on the bottom of the window. You can create a new macro using one of these commands:

Menu	Toolbar	Explorer	Shortcut Key	Shortcut Menu
`Tools > Basic Macro Editor`	n/a	Right-click on macro or macro folder, `Add Macro...`	Right-click on macro or macro folder, then <A> or <ALT + T>, then <B>	n/a

The screen in Figure 16.2 appears.

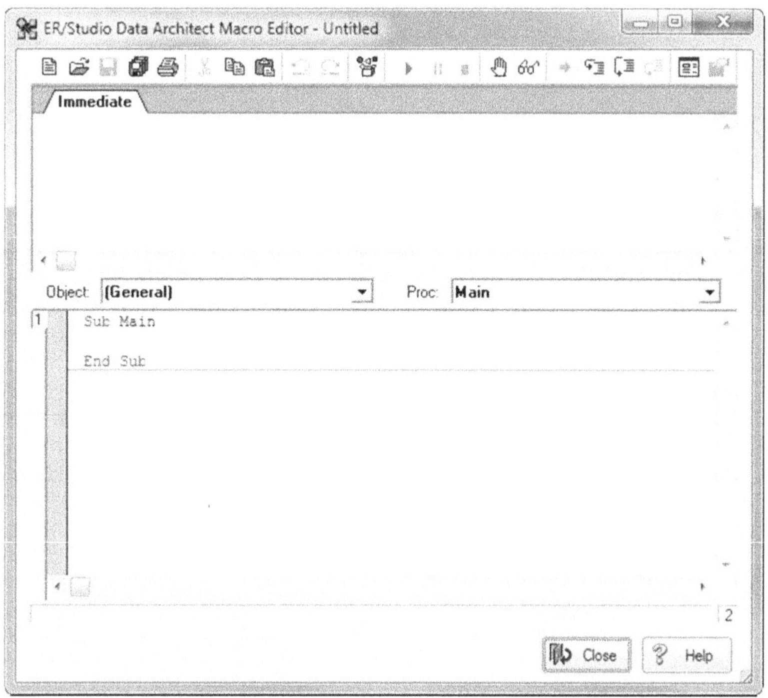

Figure 16.2 Macro Editor

ER/Studio is equipped with a well-documented automation interface driven by the Sax Basic language (a derivative of the Visual Basic for Applications language). There are two main reasons to use the automation interface:

- **Automate Routine Tasks**. Automate tedious, routine modeling tasks or customize ER/Studio to enforce modeling practices in your organization. For example, you can write a macro that will automatically colorize child tables containing propagated foreign keys. Or you can write a macro to automatically insert a specific name and primary key into new entities as they are created.

- **Collaborate with Other Applications**. ER/Studio models contain valuable metadata you can access from applications such as Microsoft Excel, Access, and Outlook. Using ER/Studio's automation interface, you can collaborate with any external application that has an exposed API or its own automation interface.

EDITING MACROS

In *Explorer*, click on the *Macros* tab on the bottom of the window. You can edit a macro using one of these commands:

Menu	Toolbar	Explorer	Shortcut Key	Shortcut Menu
n/a	Application toolbar:	Right-click on macro, `Edit Macro...`	Right-click on macro, then <E> or <ALT + T>, then <B>	n/a

Viewing the source code for an existing macro is a great way to pick up tips on working with the Sax Basic language.

DELETING MACROS

In *Explorer*, click on the *Macros* tab on the bottom of the window. You can delete a macro using one of these commands:

Menu	Toolbar	Explorer	Shortcut Key	Shortcut Menu
n/a	n/a	Right-click on macro, `Delete Macro`	Right-click on macro, then <D>	n/a

RENAMING MACROS

In *Explorer*, click on the *Macros* tab on the bottom of the window. You can rename a macro using one of these commands:

Menu	Toolbar	Explorer	Shortcut Key	Shortcut Menu
n/a	n/a	Right-click on macro, `Rename Macro`	Right-click on macro, then <N>	n/a

EXERCISE 16.1: CREATING AND RUNNING MACROS

Open your publishing data model and practice running some of the macros, especially my "Top 5" favorites. If you are feeling adventurous, you can edit some of these macros and see what happens. You can also try creating your own. Live on the edge!

REUSABLE PROCEDURE LOGIC

Reusable procedure logic is code that is created once yet can be used many times. Under the Data Dictionary tab, you can create three types of reusable procedure logic, which are organized by database platform:

- Reusable Triggers
- Reusable Procedures
- Libraries

REUSABLE TRIGGERS

A database trigger (*trigger* for short) is procedural code that is automatically executed in response to certain events on a particular table or view in a database. A trigger executes when data modification operations such as INSERT, UPDATE, or DELETE occur. Because triggers are customizable and fire automatically, they are often used to maintain referential integrity in a database.

In ER/Studio you can write the code for the trigger and then reference this code many times. Click on the table on the physical data model that the trigger will impact. Then under the Data Dictionary tab by expanding *Reusable Procedural Logic* and then *Reusable Triggers*.

Menu	Toolbar	Explorer	Shortcut Key	Shortcut Menu
n/a	n/a	Right-click on the database (e.g. Oracle) and select `New Trigger…`	n/a	n/a
Become an ER/Studio Hotshot: Once the trigger is created, you can edit it by double-clicking its name under the Data Dictionary tab.				

You can enter your code in BASIC as well as import or export existing BASIC code files (.bas files).

REUSABLE PROCEDURES

A procedure is a compartmentalized set of code that performs one or more operations. For example, if there is a set of logic that needs to be applied to determine whether a customer order is eligible for a discount, a procedure can apply this logic. Similar to the trigger, you can create a procedure under the Data Dictionary tab by expanding *Reusable Procedural Logic* and then *Reusable Procedures*.

Menu	Toolbar	Explorer	Shortcut Key	Shortcut Menu
n/a	n/a	Right-click on the database (e.g., Oracle) and select `New Procedure…`	n/a	n/a
Become an ER/Studio Hotshot: Once the procedure is created, you can edit it by double-clicking its name under the Data Dictionary tab.				

You can enter your code in BASIC as well as import or export existing BASIC code files (.bas files).

LIBRARIES

A library contains blocks of code used to generate SQL for Reusable Triggers and Reusable Procedures. This lets you reuse blocks of code. Reusable triggers or procedure code can call library functions. The editor that launches when creating new procedural logic is the Sax Basic editor, which is compatible with Microsoft Visual Basic. Similar to how to create triggers and reusable procedures, you can create a library under the Data Dictionary tab by expanding *Reusable Procedural Logic*.

Menu	Toolbar	Explorer	Shortcut Key	Shortcut Menu
n/a	n/a	Right-click on `Libraries` and select `New Library...`	n/a	n/a
Become an ER/Studio Hotshot: Once the library is created, you can edit it by double-clicking its name under the Data Dictionary tab.				

CHANGE MANAGEMENT

Change Management is a feature of the Repository and not directly available in ER/Studio Data Architect. However, it is an important feature of agile development, and therefore we will briefly discuss it here.

Change Management is a model check-in/check-out feature so that multiple modelers can work within the same model at different times. This feature also records every change made to the model and who made the change for audit purposes. It also allows assigning tasks to data model changes which can connect agile user stories with subsets of the model.

To invoke `Change Management`:

Menu	Toolbar	Explorer	Shortcut Key	Shortcut Menu
`Repository > Change Management Center`	Repository toolbar	n/a	<ALT + R>, then <H>	n/a

When the Change Management Center is opened, there are two tabs as shown in Figure 16.3: The first is for entry/display of tasks and the second shows the change records. The tasks can also be expanded to show change records indented beneath them.

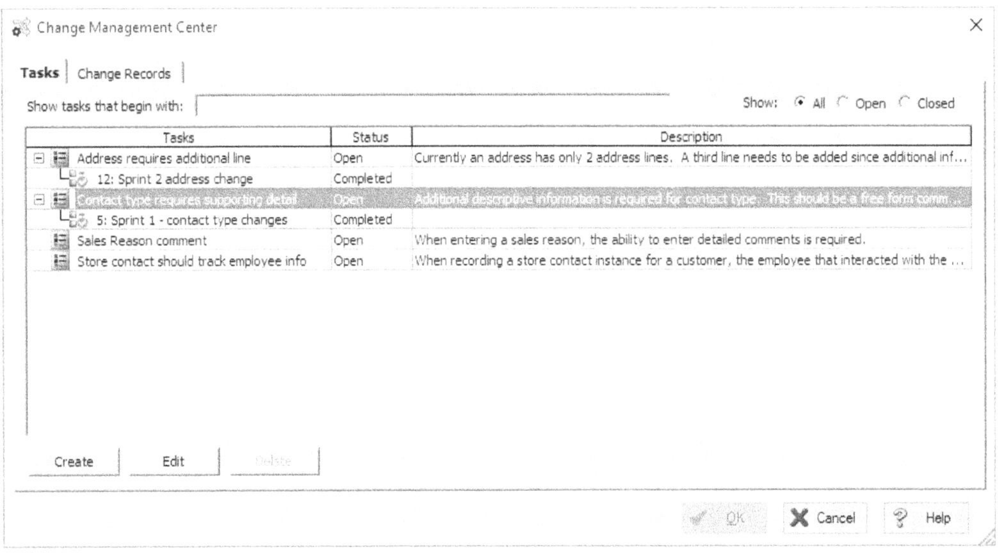

Figure 16.3 Change Management Center

The change management capability is also flexible to fit different work practices by allowing tasks to be associated to changes at check-in or check-out. The change record view is shown in Figure 16.4.

A change record can be selected, which then allows the<Details> button to be clicked, as shown in Figure 16.5.

The change details are indicated by the yellow delta symbols. In this example, a column was inserted before another. Dependent views that were impacted by the change are also indicated.

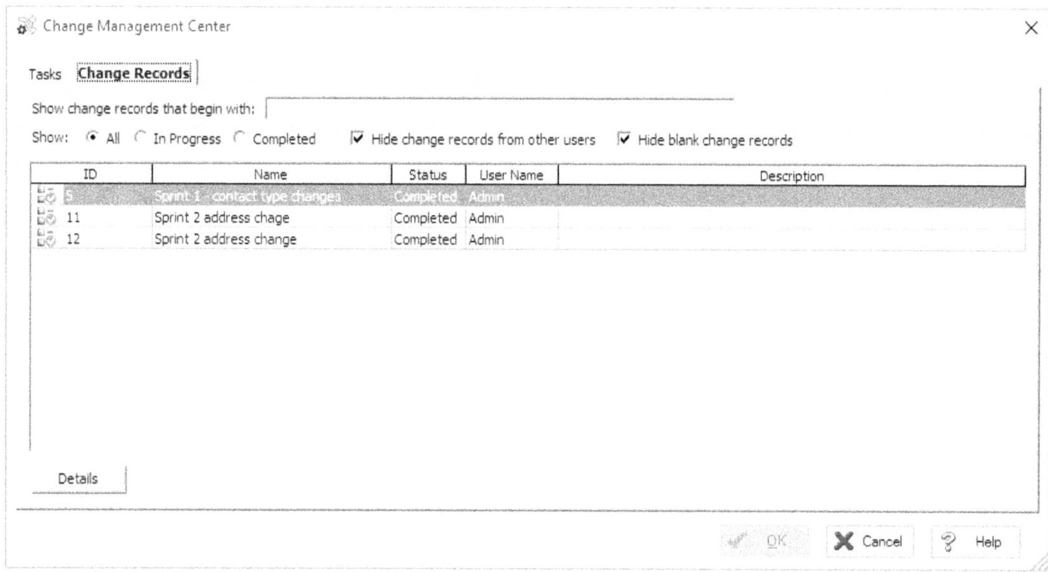

Figure 16.4 Change Records

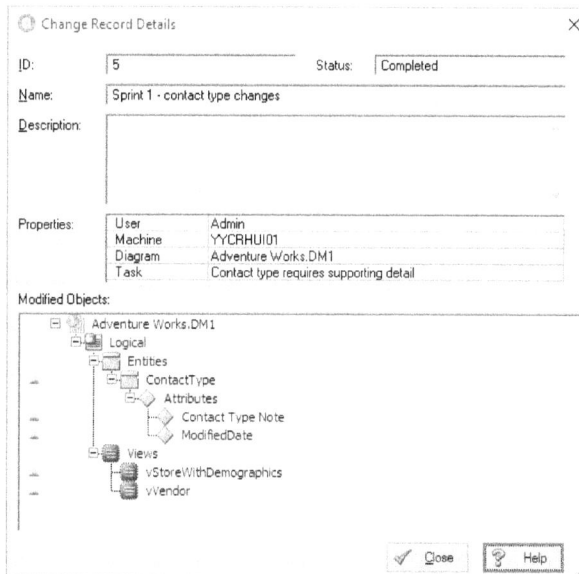

Change Record Details

ID: 5 Status: Completed

Name: Sprint 1 - contact type changes

Description:

Properties:

User	Admin
Machine	YYCRHUI01
Diagram	Adventure Works.DM1
Task	Contact type requires supporting detail

Modified Objects:

- Adventure Works.DM1
  - Logical
    - Entities
      - ContactType
        - Attributes
          - Contact Type Note
          - ModifiedDate
    - Views
      - vStoreWithDemographics
      - vVendor

Close Help

Figure 16.5 Change Record Details

NAMED RELEASES

Named Releases are read-only archived snapshots of diagrams managed within the Repository. These snapshots are useful for viewing the state of a data model at a particular point in time, such as at the end of an agile sprint. You can view a named release, but, in general, you cannot modify it. A special repository operation, *Rollback Diagram*, lets you check in a named release as the latest version of a diagram. Once the Rollback operation is completed, you can check out the diagram (or a portion of it) to modify it. Under `Repository > Releases`, you will find operations to create, retrieve, and delete named releases.

MODEL VALIDATION

Model Validation contains over 50 checks to improve the quality of your logical or physical data model such as catching missing object definitions, unused domains, identical unique indexes, and circular relationships. You can choose which validation options to use and sort the report results found by the wizard to highlight higher priority items that need to be addressed.

To invoke the *Model Validation* wizard:

Menu	Toolbar	Explorer	Shortcut Key	Shortcut Menu
`Model > Validate Model…`	Application toolbar: ☑	Right-click on model, `Validate Logical [or Physical] Data Model…`	<ALT + M>, then <V>	`Model > Validate Model…`

The *Model Validation* appears as shown in Figure 16.6. On the *Validation Options* tab, you can choose the rules you would like checked for each model component. On the *Object Selection* tab, you can choose which parts of the model to check. Click <Select All> to check the entire data model. Click <Run Validation>. Now the Output tab contains the results of the check. Click <Export Results> to export the checks in a comma delimited file.

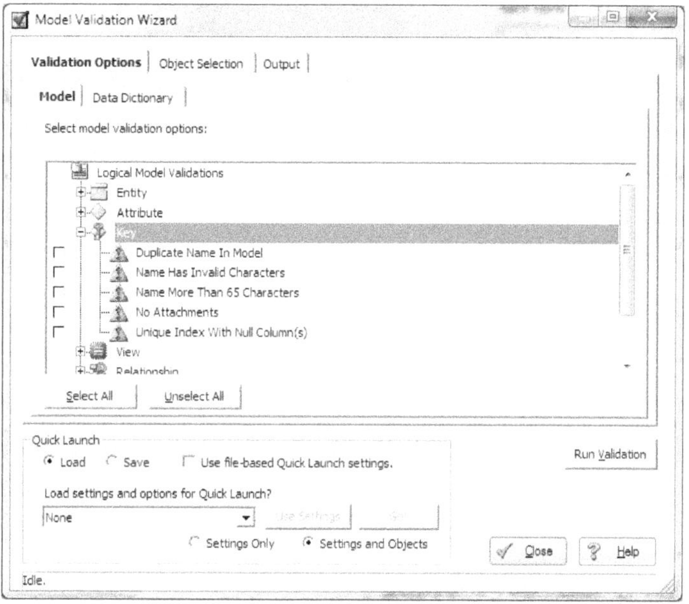

Figure 16.6 Model Validation Wizard

Key Points

- A macro is a function that is not part of the standard set of ER/Studio functionality, which automates or simplifies complex or repetitive tasks.
- ER/Studio comes shipped with over 70 existing macros and also provides you with the functionality to edit these existing macros as well as to create your own.
- Reusable procedure logic is code that is created once yet can be used many times, which includes triggers, procedures, and libraries.
- Change Management is a model check-in/check-out feature that provides detailed traceability of changes implemented and associated with tasks.
- Named Releases are read-only archived snapshots of diagrams managed within the Repository.
- Model Validation contains over 50 checks to improve the quality of your logical or physical data model such as catching missing object definitions, unused domains, identical unique indexes, and circular relationships.

APPENDIX A
References

Burns, Larry. Building the Agile Database: How to Build a Successful Application Using Agile Without Sacrificing Data Management. Technics Publications, LLC, 2011. ISBN 9781935504153.

DAMA International. The DAMA Dictionary of Data Management, 2nd Edition: Over 2,000 Terms Defined for IT and Business Professionals. Technics Publications, LLC, 2011. ISBN 9781935504122.

DAMA International. The DAMA Guide to the Data Management Body of Knowledge. Technics Publications, LLC, 2009. ISBN 9780977140084.

Hay, David C. Enterprise Model Patterns: Describing the World (UML Version). Technics Publications, LLC, 2011. ISBN 9781935504054.

Hoberman, Steve. Data Modeling Master Class Training Manual 6th Edition. Technics Publications, LLC, 2015. ISBN 9781634620901.

Hoberman, Steve. The Data Modeler's Workbench. Tools and Techniques for Analysis and Design. John Wiley & Sons, 2001. ISBN 0471111759.

Hoberman, Steve, and Burbank, Donna and Bradley, Chris. Data Modeling For the Business: A Handbook for Aligning the Business with IT using High-Level Data Models. Technics Publications, LLC, 2009. ISBN 9780977140077.

Hoberman, Steve. Data Modeling Made Simple 2nd Edition: A Practical Guide for Business & Information Technology Professionals. Technics Publications, LLC, 2009. ISBN 9780977140060.

Kent, William. Data and Reality: A Timeless Perspective on Perceiving and Managing Information in Our Imprecise World. 3rd Edition, Technics Publications, LLC, 2012. ISBN 9781935504214.

Reingruber, Michael. C. and William W. Gregory. The Data Modeling Handbook: A Best-Practice Approach to Building Quality Data Models. John Wiley & Sons, 1994. ISBN 0471052906.

Silverston, Len. The Data Model Resource Book, Volume 1: A Library of Universal Data Models for All Enterprises, 2nd Edition, John Wiley & Sons, 2001. ISBN 0471380237.

Silverston, Len. The Data Model Resource Book, Volume 2: A Library of Data Models for Specific Industries, 2nd Edition. John Wiley & Sons, 2001. ISBN 0471353485.

Silverston, Len. The Data Model Resource Book, Volume 3: Universal Patterns for Data Modeling. John Wiley & Sons, 2009. ISBN 9780470178454.

Simsion, Graeme C. and Graham C. Witt. Data Modeling Essentials, 3rd Edition. Morgan Kaufmann, 2005. ISBN 0126445516.

Simsion, Graeme C. Data Modeling Theory and Practice. Technics Publications, LLC, 2007. ISBN 9780977140015.

APPENDIX B
Answers to Exercises

This section contains my responses to a number of the exercises.

EXERCISE 1.1: EDUCATING YOUR NEIGHBOR

I find the analogy that I use most frequently is comparing the data model to a blueprint. Most non-technical friends, family, and neighbors understand this analogy. "Just like you need a blueprint to ensure a sound building structure, you need a data model to ensure a sound application." Sometimes I also explain to people that a data model is nothing more than a fancy spreadsheet that contains not just the spreadsheet columns, but also the business rules binding these columns. If both the blueprint and spreadsheet analogies fail, I quickly change the subject to the other person and ask what they do (and hope that they never ask me again!).

EXERCISE 5.1: CHANGING SETTINGS IN SUBMODELS

Setting	Applied to only submodel	Applied to entire model
Changing submodel's background color	x	
Changing an entity's name		x
Changing an entity's background color	Will only be applied to submodel unless `Apply to all submodels` is checked	
Resizing an entity	x	
Creating an entity		x
Deleting an entity	Will only be applied to submodel unless `Delete from Model` is checked	
Rearranging entities	x	

EXERCISE 6.2: CLARIFYING CUSTOMER ID

There are three terms within this definition that require an explanation: *unique, identifier,* and *Customer.*

DOCUMENT UNIQUENESS PROPERTIES

The term *unique* is ambiguous and could easily be interpreted differently by readers of this definition. To maintain clarity and correctness, these questions should be answered within the definition:

> Are identifier values ever reused?
> What is the scope of uniqueness?
> How is the identifier validated?

DOCUMENT THE CHARACTERISTICS OF THE IDENTIFIER

We can describe the actual identifier in more detail by addressing these areas:

- **Purpose.** For example, perhaps the identifier is needed because there are multiple source systems for customer data, each with their own Id. To enable a common set of data to be held about them, this identifier needed to be created to facilitate integration and guarantee uniqueness across all customers.

- **Business or surrogate key.** Document whether the identifier is meaningful to the business (i.e., the business or natural key) or whether it is a meaningless integer counter (i.e., the surrogate key).

- **Assignment.** Document how a new customer identifier is assigned. The party that is responsible for creating new identifiers should also be mentioned.

DEFINE THE CUSTOMER

A great way to define the customer in the definition for **Customer ID** is to have a hyperlink back to the entity or concept definition of customer, such as in a Wiki.

EXERCISE 7.1: READING A MODEL

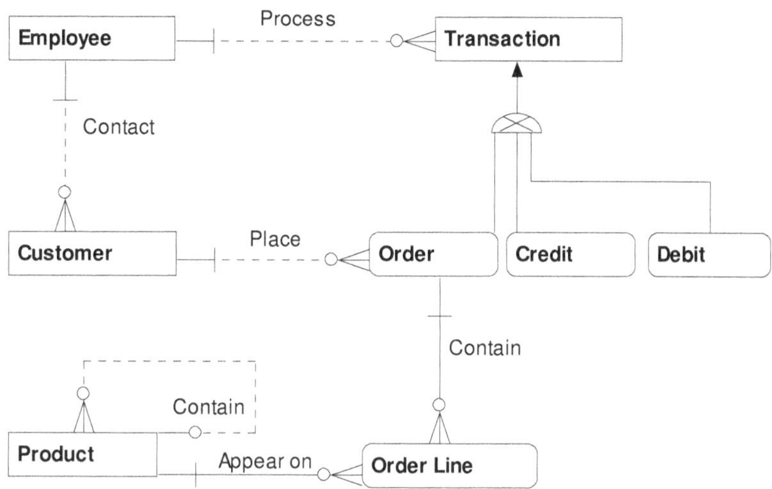

The following statements can be made about the business rules, based on the role names specified in the relationships in ER/Studio. The role names are shown *in italics*.

Each Employee may *process* one or many Transactions.
Each Transaction must *be processed by* one Employee.
Each Transaction must *be either an* Order, a Credit, or a Debit.
Each Order *is a* Transaction.
Each Credit *is a* Transaction.
Each Debit *is a* Transaction.
Each Employee may *contact* one or many Customers.
Each Customer must *be contacted by* one Employee.
Each Customer may *place* one or many Orders.
Each Order must *be placed by* one Customer.
Each Order may *contain* one or many Order Lines.
Each Order Line must *belong to* one Order.
Each Product may *appear on* one or many Order Lines.
Each Order Line must *reference* one Product.
Each Product may *contain* one or many Products.
Each Product may *belong to* at most one other Product.

EXERCISE 8.1: CREATING A CONCEPTUAL DATA MODEL

Here is my solution using IE notation:

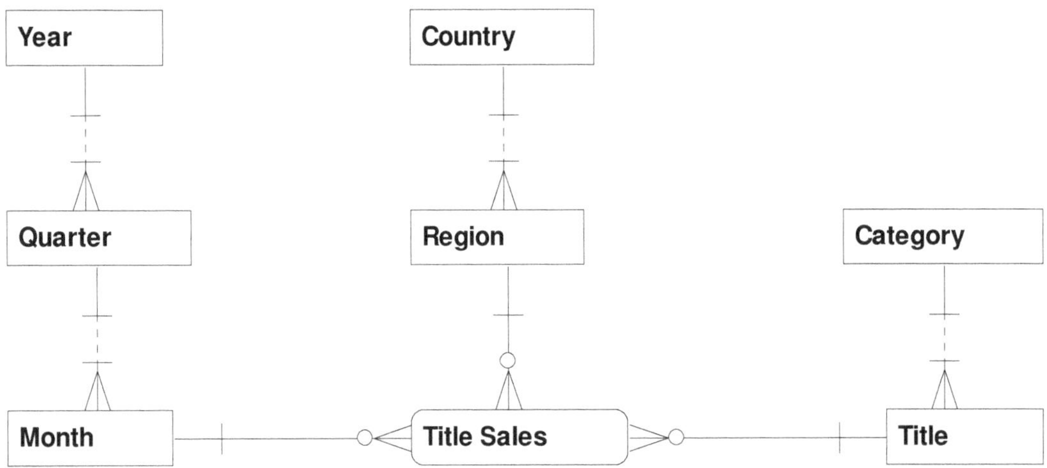

And my solution using dimensional notation:

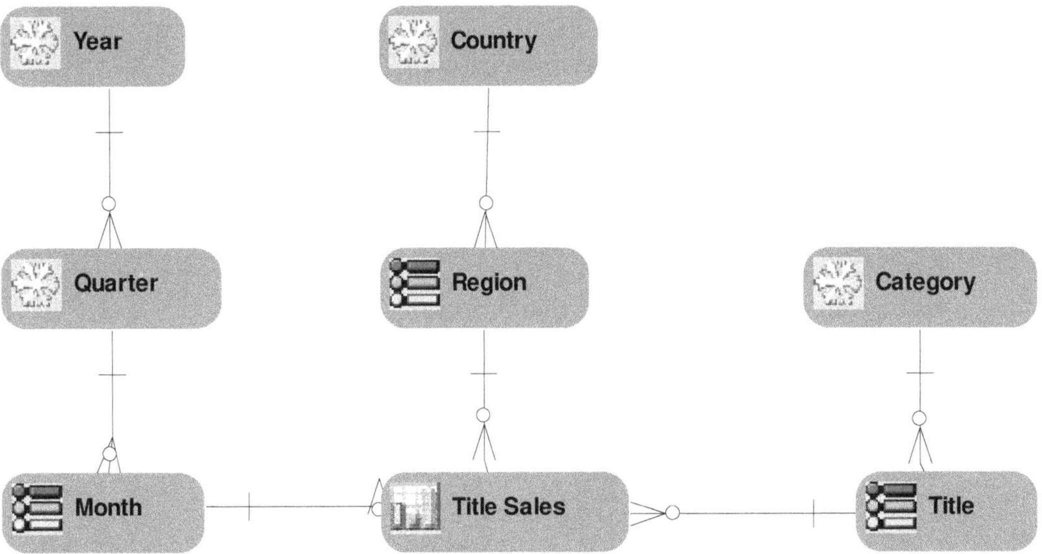

EXERCISE 8.2: Adding Definitions to a Data Model

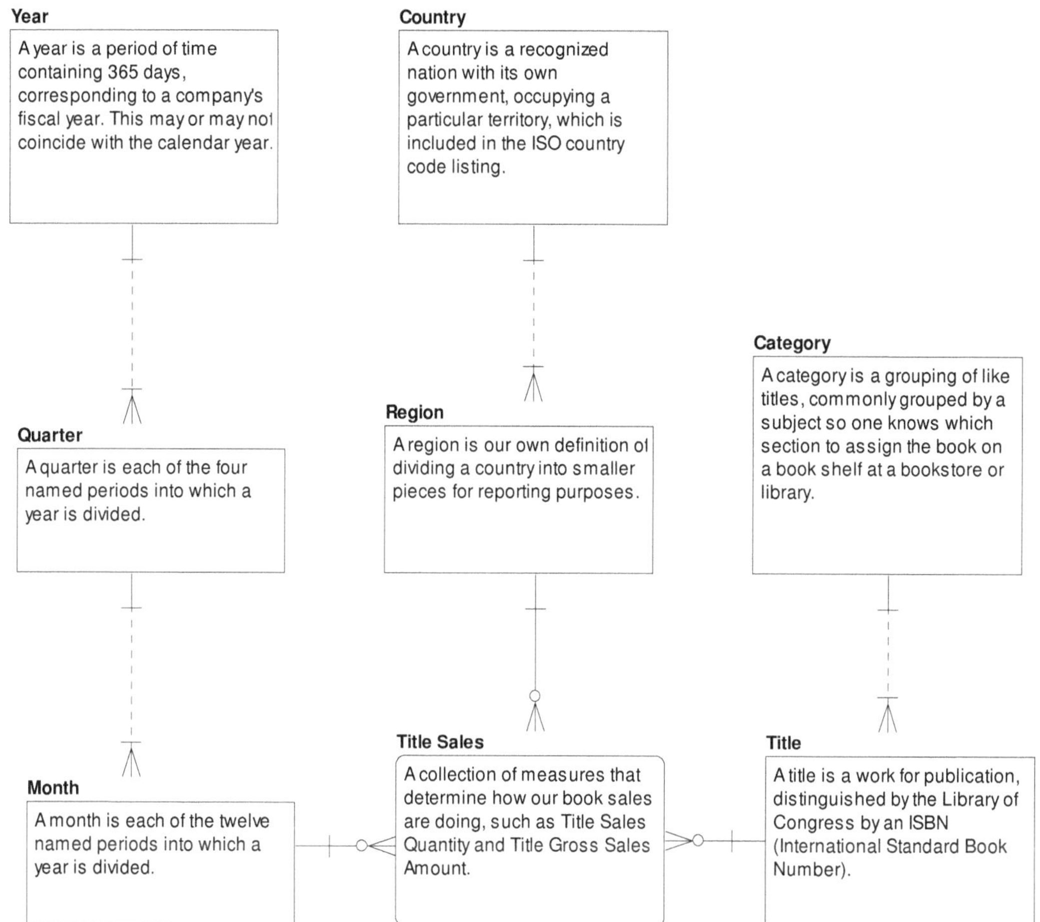
Year
A year is a period of time containing 365 days, corresponding to a company's fiscal year. This may or may not coincide with the calendar year.
Country
A country is a recognized nation with its own government, occupying a particular territory, which is included in the ISO country code listing.
Category
A category is a grouping of like titles, commonly grouped by a subject so one knows which section to assign the book on a book shelf at a bookstore or library.
Quarter
A quarter is each of the four named periods into which a year is divided.
Region
A region is our own definition of dividing a country into smaller pieces for reporting purposes.
Month
A month is each of the twelve named periods into which a year is divided.
Title Sales
A collection of measures that determine how our book sales are doing, such as Title Sales Quantity and Title Gross Sales Amount.
Title
A title is a work for publication, distinguished by the Library of Congress by an ISBN (International Standard Book Number).

APPENDIX C
Glossary

Abstraction. Brings flexibility to your data models by redefining and combining some of the attributes, entities, and relationships within the model into more generic terms. For example, we may abstract **Employee** and **Consumer** into the more generic concept of **Person**. A **Person** can play many **Roles**, two of which are **Employee** and **Consumer**.

Aggregate. A table that contains the resolution of a one-to-one relationship.

Alternate key. The one or more attributes that uniquely identify a value in an entity and that is not chosen to be *the* unique identifier.

Associative entity. An associative entity is an entity that resolves a many-to-many relationship.

Attribute. Also known as a "data element," an attribute is a property of importance to the business. Its values contribute to identifying, describing, or measuring instances of an entity. The attribute **Claim Number** identifies each claim. The attribute **Student Last Name** describes the last name of each student. The attribute **Gross Sales Amount** measures the monetary value of a transaction.

Bridge table. A table that resolves a many-to-many relationship from the dimension to the meter. In other words, a given meter instance may need to refer to more than one dimension instance. Bridge tables can be shown as the typical resolution of a many-to-many on a logical but may need a different physical structure depending on reporting tools.

Candidate key. The one or many attributes that uniquely identify an entity instance. Candidate keys are either primary or alternate keys.

Cardinality. Defines the number of instances of each entity that can participate in a relationship. It is represented by the symbols that appear on both ends of a relationship line.

Class word. The last term in an attribute name such as **Amount**, **Code**, and **Name**. Class words allow for the assignment of common domains.

Concept. A key idea that is both *basic* and *critical* to your audience. "Basic" means this term is probably mentioned many times a day in conversations with the people who are the audience for the model, which includes the people who need to validate the model as well as the people who need to use the model. "Critical" means the business would be very different or non-existent without this concept.

Conceptual Data Model (CDM). A set of symbols and text representing the key concepts and rules binding these key concepts for a specific business or application scope. The CDM represents the business need.

Conformed dimension. Built with the organization in mind, instead of just a particular application, to support drill across queries and enterprise consistency. Conformed dimensions do not need to be identical with each other; they just need to be from the same superset. Conformed dimensions allow the navigator the ability to ask questions that cross multiple marts.

Data model. A set of symbols and text that precisely explains a business information landscape. A box with the word "Customer" within it represents the concept of a real **Customer**, such as *Bob*, *IBM*, or *Walmart*, on a data model. A line represents a relationship between two concepts such as capturing that a **Customer** may own one or many **Accounts**.

Data modeler. A data modeler is one who confirms and documents data requirements. This role performs the data modeling process.

Data modeling. The process of learning about the data; regardless of technology, this process must be performed for a successful application.

Degenerate dimension. A dimension whose attribute(s) have been moved to the fact table. A degenerate dimension is most common when the original dimension contained only a single attribute such as a transaction identifier.

Denormalization. The process of selectively violating normalization rules and reintroducing redundancy into the model. This extra redundancy can reduce data retrieval time and produce a more user-friendly model.

Dependent entity. Also known as a weak entity, a dependent entity is an object of interest to the business that depends on one or many other entities for its existence. The entities that a dependent entity depends on can be independent entities or other dependent entities. A dependent entity is depicted as a rectangle with rounded edges.

Dimension. A subject area whose purpose is to add meaning to the measures. All of the different ways of filtering, sorting, and summing measures make use of dimensions. Dimensions are often, but not exclusively, hierarchies.

Domain. The complete set of all possible values that an attribute can be assigned.

Entity. A collection of information about something that the business deems important and worthy of capture. A noun or noun phrase identifies a specific entity. It fits into one of several categories: who, what, when, where, why, or how.

Entity instance. The occurrences or values of a particular entity. The entity **Customer** may have multiple customer instances with names *Bob*, *Joe*, *Jane*, and so forth. The entity **Account** can have instances of *Bob's checking account*, *Bob's savings account*, *Joe's brokerage account*, and so on.

Fact. *See measure.*

Factless fact. A fact table that does not contain any facts. Factless facts count events by summing relationship occurrences between the dimensions.

Field. The concept of a physical attribute (also called a column).

Foreign key. An attribute that provides a link to another entity. A foreign key allows a database management system to navigate from one entity to another.

Forward engineer. The process of building a new application by starting from the conceptual data model and ending with a database.

Grain. The lowest level of detail available in the meter on a dimensional data model.

Grain Matrix. A spreadsheet, which captures the levels of reporting for each fact or measurement. It is the spreadsheet view of an initial design, which could result in a star schema.

Hierarchy. An arrangement of items (objects, names, values, categories, etc.) in which the items are represented as being "above," "below," or "at the same level as" one another.

Independent entity. Also known as a kernel entity, an independent entity is an object of interest to the business that does not depend on any other entity for its identification. Each occurrence of an independent entity can be identified without referring to any other entity on the model. An independent entity is depicted as a rectangle.

Index. A pointer to something that needs to be retrieved. The index points directly to the place on the disk where the data is stored, thus reducing retrieval time. Indexes work best on attributes whose values are requested frequently but rarely updated.

Inversion Entry (IE). A non-unique index (also known as a secondary key).

Junk dimension. A dimension containing all the possible combinations of a small and somewhat related set of indicators and codes.

Key-value. A NoSQL database that allows the application to store its data in only two columns ("key" and "value") with more complex information sometimes stored within the "value" columns.

Logical Data Model (LDM). The detailed business solution to a business problem. It is how the modeler captures the business requirements without complicating the model with implementation concerns such as software and hardware.

Measure. An attribute in a dimensional data model's meter that helps answer one or more business questions.

Metadata. Text, voice, or image that describes what the audience wants or needs to see or experience. The audience could be a person, group, or software program.

Meter. An entity containing a related set of measures. It is a bucket of common measures. As a group, common measures address a business process such as Profitability, Employee Satisfaction, or Sales.

Model. A set of symbols and text used to make a complex concept easier to grasp.

Natural key. Also known as a business key, a natural key is what the business sees as the unique identifier for an entity.

Network. A many-to-many relationship between entities (or between entity instances).

Normalization. The process of applying a set of rules with the goal of organizing something. With respect to attributes, normalization ensures that every attribute is single valued and provides a fact completely and only about its primary key.

NoSQL. NoSQL is a name for the category of databases built on non-relational technology. NoSQL is not a good name for what it represents as it is less about how to query the database (which is where SQL comes in) and more about how the data is stored (which is where relational structures comes in).

Partition. A structure that divides or separates. Specific to the physical design, partitioning is used to break a table into rows, columns, or both. There are two types of partitioning: vertical and horizontal. Vertical partitioning means separating the columns (the attributes) into separate tables. Horizontal means separating rows (the entity instances) into separate tables.

Physical Data Model (PDM). Represents the detailed technical solution. The PDM is the logical data model modified for a specific set of software or hardware. The PDM often gives up perfection for practicality, factoring in real concerns such as speed, space, and security.

Primary key. The one or more attributes that uniquely identify a value in an entity and that is chosen to be *the* unique identifier.

Program. A large, centrally organized initiative that contains multiple projects. It has a start date and, if successful, no end date. Programs can be very complex and require long-term modeling assignments. Examples include a data warehouse or a customer relationship management system.

Project. A complete software development effort, often defined by a set of deliverables with due dates. Examples include a sales data mart, broker trading application, reservations system, or an enhancement to an existing application.

Recursive relationship. A relationship between instances of the same entity. For instance, one organization can report to another organization.

Relational Database Management System. Represents the traditional relational database invented by E. F. Codd at IBM in 1970 and first commercially available in 1979 (which was Oracle) [Wikipedia].

Relational model. Captures how the business works and contains business rules such as "A **Customer** must have at least one **Account**" or "A **Product** must have a **Product Short Name**."

Relationship. Rules are captured on our data model through relationships. A relationship is displayed as a line connecting two entities.

Reverse engineer. The process of understanding an existing application by starting with its database and working up through the modeling levels until a conceptual data model is built.

Secondary key. One or more attributes (if more than one attribute, it is called a composite secondary key) that are accessed frequently and need to be retrieved quickly. A secondary key does not have to be unique, or stable, or always contain a value.

Snapshot measure. Monitor the impact of events created from a business process such as **Account Balance Amount**, **Ozone Layer Thickness**, and **Average Survey Question Score**.

Slowly Changing Dimension (SCD). A term for any reference entity where we need to consider how to handle data changes. There are four basic ways to manage history. An SCD of Type 0 means we are only interested in the original state, an SCD of Type 1 means only the most current state, an SCD of

Type 2 means the most current along with all history, and an SCD of Type 3 means the most current and some history will be stored.

Snowflake. A physical dimensional modeling structure where each set of tables is implemented separately; very similar in structure to the logical dimensional model.

Spreadsheet. A representation of a paper worksheet containing a grid defined by rows and columns where each cell in the grid can contain text or numbers. The columns often contain different types of information.

Stakeholder. A person who has an interest in the successful completion of a project.

Star schema. The most common physical dimensional data model structure. A star schema results when each set of structures that make up a dimension is flattened into a single structure. The fact table is in the center of the model, and each of the dimensions relate to the fact table at the lowest level of detail.

Subtyping. Grouping together the common properties of entities while retaining what is unique within each entity.

Summarization. A table that contains information at a higher level of granularity than exists in the business.

Surrogate key. A primary key that substitutes for a natural key, which is what the business sees as the unique identifier for an entity. It has no embedded intelligence and is used by IT (and not the business) for integration or performance reasons.

View. A virtual table. It is a dynamic "view" or window into one or more tables (or other views) where the actual data is stored.

APPENDIX D
ER/Studio Commands Quick Reference

MOST FREQUENTLY USED COMMANDS

Here are the most common keyboard commands:

- Page Up: Scrolls up the *Data Model Window.*
- Page Down: Scrolls down the *Data Model Window.*
- Up Arrow: Scrolls up one line.
- Down Arrow: Scrolls down one line.
- Right Arrow: Scrolls over one position to the right.
- Left Arrow: Scrolls over one position to the left.
- <->: Decreases zoom level by one step (first need to click on model white space).
- <SHIFT + F8>: Allows you to freeze the Zoom window so that you can pan around the diagram and still maintain focus on a specific diagram object. The same command unfreezes the Zoom window.
- <CTRL + Home>: Scrolls to the upper left hand page of the model.

Here are the function keys:

- <F1>: Opens the online *Help.*
- <F4>: Opens the *Find Entity/View* dialog.
- <F7>: Activates or deactivates shadowing.
- <F8>: Opens or closes a zoom window.
- <F9>: Opens or closes the overview window.

Here are the most common shortcuts:

- Double-click: Allows you to edit the object you double-clicked on
- <CTRL + A>: Selects all entities in the *Data Model Window*.
- <CTRL + C>: Copies the selected structures.
- <CTRL + V>: Pastes what has been copied into the active window.
- <CTRL + Z>: Restores your model to the last stage of edit (the invaluable "undo" command).
- <CTRL + Y>: Redoes the last undo command (the "redo" command).
- <Delete>: Removes what is highlighted from the data model.

Model Level Commands

	Menu	Toolbar	Explorer	Shortcut Key
Model options	Tools > Options…	n/a	n/a	<ALT + T>, then <P>
Create model	File > New	Application toolbar:	n/a	<CTRL + N> or <ALT + F>, then <N>
Save model	File > Save or File > Save As	Application toolbar:	n/a	<CTRL + S> or for Save: <ALT + F>, then <S> or for Save As: <ALT + F>, then <A>
Close model	File > Close	n/a	n/a	<ALT + F>, then <C>
Open model	File > Open	Application toolbar:	n/a	<CTRL + O> or <ALT + F>, then <O>

	Menu	Toolbar	Explorer	Shortcut Key
Generate PDM	Model > Generate Physical Data Model...	Application toolbar:	Right-click on model, Generate Physical Data Model...	<ALT + M>, then <G>
Change database platform	Database > Change Database Platform...	Application toolbar:	Right-click on physical data model, Change Database Platform...	<ALT + B>, then <C>
Generate database	Database > Generate Database...		Right-click on physical data model, Generate Database...	<ALT + B>, then <G>
Create title block	Insert > Title Block	Drawing Shapes toolbar:	n/a	<ALT + I>, then <B>
Edit title block	Edit > Edit Title Block...	n/a	n/a	<ALT + E>, then <E>
Delete title block	Edit > Delete Title Block	n/a	n/a	<DELETE> or <ALT + E>, then <D>
Import data dictionary	File > Import Data Dictionary	n/a	n/a	<ALT + F>, then <Y>
Create attachment	n/a	n/a	Right-click the Attachments folder and then select New Attachment Type...	n/a
Create new source (repository)	n/a	n/a	Right-click on Other Sources and then select New Source...	n/a

	Menu	Toolbar	Explorer	Shortcut Key
Create new source	n/a	n/a	Right-click on Other Sources and then select Import New Source…	n/a
Create data movement rule	n/a	n/a	Right-click the Data Movement Rules node and then New Data Movement Rule	n/a
Create data flow	n/a	n/a	Right-click the Data Flows node and then select Create Data Flow	n/a
Create transformation	Insert > Transformation	Modeling toolbar:	Right-click on data flow, Create Transformation	<ALT + I>, then <T>
Create data stream	Insert > Data Stream	Modeling toolbar:	n/a	<ALT + I>, then <D>
Import data model	File > New…, then Import Model From or File > Import File	Application toolbar:	n/a	<ALT + F>, then <N> or <ALT + F>, then <M>
Export data model	File > Export File	n/a	n/a	<ALT + F>, then <F>
Export image	File > Export Image	n/a	n/a	<ALT + F>, then <E>

	Menu	Toolbar	Explorer	Shortcut Key
Print model	File > Print…	Application toolbar:	Right-click on model or submodel folder, Print Model…	<ALT + F>, then <T> or <CTRL + P>
Generate report	Tools > Generate Reports…	Application toolbar:	Right-click on model, Generate Reports…	<ALT + T>, then <R>
Create naming standard template	Tools > Naming Standards Template Editor…	n/a	Right-click on Naming Standards Template, then New Naming Standards Template…	n/a
Invoke *Naming Standards Utility*	Model > Naming Standards Utility…	Application toolbar:	Right-click on model name, Naming Standards Utility…	<ALT + M>, then <T>
Invoke *Compare and Merge Utility*	Model > Compare and Merge Utility…	Application toolbar:	Right-click on source model (or submodel), Compare and Merge Utility…	<ALT + M>, then <M>
Invoke *Model Validation*	Model > Validate Model…	Application toolbar:	Right-click on model, Validate Logical [or Physical] Data Model…	<ALT + M>, then <V>

	Menu	Toolbar	Explorer	Shortcut Key
Display *Welcome Page*	View, followed by the toolbar name	n/a	n/a	<ALT + V>, followed by the letter for the appropriate toolbar name
Display toolbar	View, followed by the toolbar name	n/a	n/a	<ALT + V>, followed by the letter for the appropriate toolbar name
Change color	Format > Colors & Fonts…	Diagram toolbar:	n/a	<ALT + O>, then <C>
Create trigger	n/a	n/a	Right-click on the database (e.g. Oracle) and select New Trigger…	n/a
Create reusable procedure	n/a	n/a	Right-click on the database (e.g. Oracle) and select New Procedure…	n/a
Create Library	n/a	n/a	Right-click on Libraries and select New Library…	n/a

ENTITY AND TABLE LEVEL COMMANDS

	Menu	Toolbar	Explorer	Shortcut Key
Create entity	Insert > Entity	Modeling toolbar:	Right-click on Entities, New Entity…	<ALT + I>, then <E>

	Menu	Toolbar	Explorer	Shortcut Key
Edit entity	Edit > Edit Entity…	n/a	Right-click on entity, Entities, Edit Entity… Or Double-click on the entity	<ALT + E>, then <E>
Change entity name	Edit > Edit Entity (in the upper left corner you can rename the entity)	n/a	Modify Name	<ALT + E>, then <E> (in the upper left corner you can rename the entity)
Delete entity	Edit > Delete Entity	Diagram toolbar:	Right-click on entity, Delete Entity	<DELETE> or <ALT + E>, then <D>
Resize entity	Format > Resize Entity/View	n/a	n/a	<ALT + O>, then <R>
Copy entity	Edit > Copy, then Edit > Paste	Diagram toolbar: (copy), then (paste)	Drag entities to the *Data Model Window*	<CTRL + C> then <CTRL + V> or <ALT + E>, then <C> for copy, <ALT + E>, then <P> for paste
Find entity	Edit > Find Entity/View…	Application toolbar:	n/a	<F4> or <ALT + E>, then <F>
Find and replace entity	Tools > Universal Naming Utility	Application toolbar:	n/a	<CTRL + F>

	Menu	Toolbar	Explorer	Shortcut Key
Edit table	Click on table, Edit > Edit Table…	n/a	Right-click on table, Edit Table…	Click on table, <ALT + E>, then <E>
Rollup or rolldown	Model > Denormalization Mapping > Rollups or Rolldowns	Modeling toolbar:	n/a	<ALT + M>, then <Z>, then either <R> for Rollups or <O> for Rolldowns
Create view	Insert > View	Modeling toolbar:	Right-click on Views, New View…	<ALT + I>, then <V>
Change view	Click on view, Edit > Edit Database View…	n/a	Right-click on view, Edit > Edit Database View…	Click on view, <ALT + E>, then <E>
Create horizontal partition	Model > Denormalization Mapping > Horizontal Splits…	Modeling toolbar:	Right-click on table, Denormalization Mapping > Horizontal Splits…	<ALT + M>, then <Z>, then <H>
Create vertical partition	Click on table, Model > Denormalization Mapping > Vertical Splits…	Modeling toolbar:	Right-click on table, Denormalization Mapping > Vertical Splits…	Click on table, <ALT + M>, then <Z>, then <V>
Change color	Format > Entity Color and Font Settings	n/a	Right-click on entity, Entity Color and Font Settings	<ALT + O>, click on Entity Color and Font Settings

SUBLEVEL COMMANDS

	Menu	Toolbar	Explorer	Shortcut Key
Create submodel	Model > Create Submodel...		Right-click where submodel should be added, Create Submodel...	<ALT + M>, then <C>
Edit submodel	Model > Edit Submodel...	n/a	Right-click on submodel, Edit Submodel...	<ALT + M>, then <E>
Delete submodel	Model > Delete Submodel...	n/a	Right-click on submodel to delete and choose Delete Submodel	<ALT + M>, then <D>

ATTRIBUTE AND KEY COMMANDS

	Menu	Toolbar	Explorer	Shortcut Key
Create attribute	Edit > Edit Entity...	n/a	Right-click on entity, New Attribute Or Double-click on the entity	<ALT + E>, then <E>
Edit attribute	Edit > Edit Entity...	n/a	Right-click on entity, Edit Entity... Or Double-click on the entity	<ALT + E>, then <E>
Delete attribute	Edit > Delete Attribute	Diagram toolbar:	Right-click on attribute, Delete Attribute	<DELETE> or <ALT + E>, then <D>

	Menu	Toolbar	Explorer	Shortcut Key
Copy attribute	Edit > Copy, then Edit > Paste	Diagram toolbar: (copy), then (paste)	Drag attributes to the desired entity in the *Data Model Window*	<CTRL + C> then <CTRL + V> or <ALT + E>, then <C> for copy, <ALT + E>, then <P> for paste
Find attribute	Tools > Universal Naming Utility	Application toolbar:	n/a	<CTRL + F>
Change datatypes	Tools > Datatype Mapping Editor	n/a	n/a	<ALT + T>, then choose Datatype Mapping Editor
Create domain	n/a	n/a	Right-click on Domains (or on a domain folder) then choose New Domain	n/a
Create user-defined datatype	n/a	n/a	Right-click the User Datatypes node and then select New User Datatype…	n/a
Create reference value	n/a	n/a	Right-click the Reference Values node and then select New Reference Value…	n/a

	Menu	Toolbar	Explorer	Shortcut Key
Create index	Click on table, Edit > Edit Table…	n/a	Right-click on table, Edit Table…	Click on table, <ALT + E>, then <E>
Change color	Format > Entity Color and Font Settings	n/a	Right-click on entity, Entity Color and Font Settings	<ALT + O>, click on Entity Color and Font Settings
Create key	Edit > Edit Entity…	n/a	Right-click on entity, Edit Entity… Or Double-click on the entity	<ALT + E>, then <E>
Edit key	Edit > Edit Entity…	n/a	Right-click on entity, Edit Entity… Or Double-click on the entity	<ALT + E>, then <E>

RELATIONSHIP COMMANDS

	Menu	Toolbar	Explorer	Shortcut Key
Create relationship	Insert > Relationship	Modeling toolbar:	Right-click on Relationships, New Relationship…	<ALT + I>, then <R>
Create subtype	Insert > Subtype Cluster > Complete or Incomplete	Modeling toolbar:	n/a	n/a
Create view relationship	Insert > Relationship > View Relationship	Modeling toolbar:	n/a	<ALT + I>, then <R>, then <V>

	Menu	Toolbar	Explorer	Shortcut Key
Create containment relationship	Insert > Containment relationship	Modeling toolbar:	n/a	n/a
Delete relationship	Edit > Delete Relationship	n/a	Right-click on relationship, Delete Relationship	<DELETE> or <ALT + E>, then <D>
Display relationship description	View > Cursor Popup Help Options > Display Relationship Help	n/a	n/a	n/a
Find relationship	Insert > Relationship Navigation	Diagram toolbar:	n/a	<ALT + I>, then <G>
Change color	n/a	n/a	Right-click on relationship, Relationship Color	n/a

MACRO COMMANDS

	Menu	Toolbar	Explorer	Shortcut Key
Run macro	n/a	n/a	Right-click on macro, Run Macro	Right-click on macro, then <U>
Create macro	Tools > Basic Macro Editor	n/a	Right-click on macro or macro folder, Add Macro…	Right-click on macro or macro folder, then <A> or <ALT + T>, then <B>

	Menu	Toolbar	Explorer	Shortcut Key
Edit macro	n/a	Application toolbar:	Right-click on macro, Edit Macro…	Right-click on macro, then <E> or <ALT + T>, then <B>
Delete macro	n/a	n/a	Right-click on macro, Delete Macro	Right-click on macro, then <D>
Rename macro	n/a	n/a	Right-click on macro, Rename Macro	Right-click on macro, then <N>

Bold page numbers indicate where term is defined

www.ingramcontent.com/pod-product-compliance
Lightning Source LLC
Chambersburg PA
CBHW080917220326
41598CB00034B/5594

* 9 7 8 1 6 3 4 6 2 0 9 2 5 *